FOR PAT, DOUG, MAUREEN, AND CATHRINE

THE DRAGON'S WINGS

THE
CHINA NATIONAL AVIATION CORPORATION
AND THE DEVELOPMENT OF
COMMERCIAL AVIATION
IN CHINA

WILLIAM M. LEARY, JR.

THE UNIVERSITY OF GEORGIA PRESS
ATHENS

Paperback edition, 2016
© 1976 by the University of Georgia Press
Athens, Georgia 30602
www.ugapress.org
All rights reserved
Set in 10 on 13 pt. Primer type

Most University of Georgia Press titles are
available from popular e-book vendors.

Printed digitally

The Library of Congress has cataloged the
hardcover edition of this book as follows:
Leary, William M. (William Matthew), 1934–
The dragon's wings : the China National Aviation Corporation and
the development of commercial aviation in China / William M. Leary, Jr.
xiii, 279 p., [8] leaves of plates : ill. ; 24 cm.
ISBN 0-8203-0366-6
Bibliography: p. [263]–271.
Includes index.
1. China National Aviation Corporation.
2. Pan American Airways Corporation.
I. Title.

HE9870.C5 L4
387.7'0951   74-15205
Paperback ISBN 978-0-8203-3256-7

CONTENTS

List of Illustrations ix
Preface xi
Chapter 1: From Peking to Shanghai, 1919–1930 1
Chapter 2: Along the Yangtze, 1930–1933 32
Chapter 3: Pan American and Prosperity, 1933–1937 70
Chapter 4: China's Lifeline, 1937–1941 109
Chapter 5: Over the Hump, 1941–1945 143
Chapter 6: Revolution, Inflation, and Collapse,
   1945–1949 193
Conclusion 224
Appendices
  A. Chronology of Commercial Aviation in China 227
  B. CNAC Traffic Statistics, 1929–1941 230
  C. CNAC Contract Operations, India-China 1942–1945 230
  D. Major Accidents and Losses, April 1942–September 1945 233
Notes 236
Bibliography 263
Index 272

LIST OF ILLUSTRATIONS

CNAC's first operations office, Shanghai, 1929 *facing page*	16
Loening amphibian, 1930	16
Stinson Detroiter, 1932	17
Sikorsky S-38 refueling at Shanghai, 1933	17
E. M. Allison after unsuccessful search for missing S-38, 1934	49
CNAC's first permanent hangar, Shanghai, 1934	49
Ki Chun, director of CNAC, and Harold M. Bixby beside Ford trimotor, 1935	80
Ford trimotor over the Temple of Heaven, Peking, 1935	81
How cargo was brought from the Gobi desert: Peking, 1935	112
Douglas Dolphin, 1936	112
CNAC's main passenger terminal, Shanghai, 1937	144
CNAC's fleet of DC-2s, Shanghai, 1937	145
DC-2 over downtown Shanghai, 1937	145
DC-2 and Curtiss Condor, Hong Kong, 1941	152
After the first flight over the Hump: plane #47 at Liang, Nov. 23, 1941	152
After Japanese attack: DC-3 at Suifu, 1941	153
CNAC's "DC-2½"	153
CNAC's operations office, Calcutta, 1943	184
CNAC's operations office, Dinjan, 1943	184
C-46, 1945	185
C. L. Sharp, "steady as a rock," 1944	216
Quentin Roosevelt, vice-president and director when killed in 1948	217

MAPS

Air lines existing and proposed, 1933 *facing page*	48
Air routes, 1937	113

PREFACE

THE DEVELOPMENT of commercial aviation in China is essentially the story of the China National Aviation Corporation. There were earlier attempts to bring China into the Air Age. The first came after World War I, at a time when the British sought a market for surplus aeronautical equipment. Inadequate financing and the political turbulence that followed the collapse of the Manchu Dynasty doomed this initial effort to establish air service in the Middle Kingdom.

Domestic upheaval continued in China during the 1920s as regional warlords competed for power. It was not until late in the decade, when Chiang Kai-shek and his Nationalist followers brought a modicum of stability to the troubled land, that China again attracted attention as a promising field for aeronautical development.

American business enterprise took the lead in advancing a program to inaugurate commercial air service in China. Curtiss-Wright, the leading aeronautical corporation in the United States at the time, founded the China National Aviation Corporation (CNAC) in partnership with the Chinese government in 1929. Subsequently taken over by Pan American Airways in 1933, CNAC pioneered commercial air service throughout the Middle Kingdom until the airline's demise in 1949. The technical and economic problems faced by the company during these years were monumental. But CNAC endured. Its operation in the face of war, revolution, and all manner of difficulties is one of the epic stories in the early history of commercial aviation.

CNAC is viewed from the perspective of the American partner. The Chinese side of the story has not been related in comparable detail due to limitations of language and records. Also, the impact of the enterprise on the economic and political development of China is noted only in passing and can more properly be left to experts in those fields. I hope that this work will assist them in their task.

My scholarly and personal debts to others have grown through the years. Dr. Arthur S. Link, Edwards Professor of American History and Editor of the Papers of Woodrow Wilson at Princeton University, first introduced me to the world of the professional historian; his later advice, encouragement, and friendship are deeply appreciated. Mr. Alexander P. Clark and his staff at the Firestone Library, Princeton University, eased the task of research. Archivists at the Hoover Institution, Stanford University, and at the National Archives, Washington, D.C., were efficient, cooperative, and patient. Officials of Pan American Airways permitted access to various company records, and I am grateful to them.

Many individuals formerly associated with CNAC have contributed to this work, directly and indirectly. Their contribution is obvious from the footnotes, but special mention should be made of Mr. William L. Bond, who gave the author the benefit of his unique knowledge about CNAC, and Dr. Arthur N. Young, who permitted access to his invaluable collection of personal papers, reviewed the manuscript in detail, and displayed unfailing courtesy and kindness.

Dr. Richard K. Smith freely volunteered his services as editor, critic, and friend. *The Dragon's Wings* owes much to his suggestions about format and style. Moreover, his encouragement and enthusiasm sustained me during a difficult period.

Earlier versions of some material in this work appeared in *Aerospace Historian, Pacific Historical Review, Modern Asian Studies,* and *China Quarterly*. They have been reprinted with permission. For permission to reproduce the photographs in this book, grateful acknowledgement is made to E. M. Allison, Fabian Bachrach, Mrs. Harold M. Bixby, J. R. McCleskey, William C. McDonald, Pan American World Airways, R. W. Pottschmidt, C. L. Sharp, and Arthur N. Young.

Last, but certainly not least, needed funds to continue my research at various times were generously supplied by Princeton University, the University of Victoria, and the Canada Council.

WILLIAM M. LEARY, JR.

Athens, Georgia

THE DRAGON'S WINGS

CHAPTER ONE
FROM PEKING TO SHANGHAI
1919-1930

— I —

AVIATION in China had a spectacular if rather unpromising beginning. In 1909, six years after the first powered heavier-than-air flight near Kitty Hawk, a French aviator by the name of Vallon welcomed the Middle Kingdom to the new Air Age with a number of exhibition flights in the Shanghai area. Chinese coolies gazed aloft in awe. Westerners were equally impressed but somewhat more subdued. Awe turned to horror, however, when the intrepid Frenchman crashed his Sommer biplane in the middle of the Shanghai race course during a race meeting and was killed. "The incident struck fear into those present," reported one British observer, "and a general doubt regarding the safety of flying was entertained."[1]

There were a number of more successful flights during the next decade, but political turbulence prevented any concerted effort to develop aviation in China. These difficult years marked the final collapse of the Manchu regime and the abortive beginnings of the Republic under Yuan Shih-kai. Yuan's death in 1916 would be followed by years of chronic instability, a time when "China," indeed, was only a geographical expression. However, a modicum of centralized authority—at least in North China—did exist for several years after 1916. During this brief time of relative quiet the first plan for commercial air service in China was born.[2]

The government in Peking recognized the economic and political benefits of air transportation, not to mention the prestige attached to initiating such service, and in 1918 established a Bureau for the Planning of Aeronautical Affairs under the Ministry of Communications. Headed by the energetic General Ting Shih-yuan, the bureau drew up ambitious plans for air service to connect Peking with the southern commercial centers of Hankow and Shanghai. The government approved the scheme and authorized General Ting to seek aircraft and technical assistance from the West.[3]

Heightened Chinese interest in aviation coincided with the end of World War I. Inquiries from Peking therefore found a receptive audience in Europe as the former Allies were anxious to dispose of their large stocks of surplus aircraft. The British were particularly active in the field, and agents from the two leading wartime manufacturers, Handley Page and Vickers, were soon in hot pursuit of the Chinese contract.[4]

Handley Page emerged victorious, at least initially. On February 24, 1919, General Ting signed a contract with T. A. Barson of Peking Syndicate, Handley Page's representative in China, for the purchase for six large 0/400 aircraft at a reported price of £10,540 each.[5] No sooner had the ink dried on the contract when a powerful dissident faction began political maneuvers for a share in what appeared to be a lucrative enterprise. As the central government represented a delicate balance of competing interests, it reluctantly authorized the dissidents to establish their own aviation agency, the Aeronautics Department, which reported directly to the Cabinet. The Aeronautics Department, under General Tinn King, lost no time in signing an even larger contract with the Vickers company for the purchase of 95 aircraft.[6]

In order to bring some order to the growing chaos, the Peking government asked the British authorities to recommend an adviser to render assistance on all matters pertaining to the development of aviation. Sir John Jordan, the British ambassador, warmly supported the proposal. "If a suitable man is chosen for post," Sir John advised Whitehall, "he may have considerable influence over the future policy of the Chinese, and it is highly desirable that we should encourage in every possible way the productive use of the machines now destined for China."[7] London agreed. The selection of Colonel F. V. Holt for the position indicated the importance that British authorites attached to the aviation project. Commander of 18 Wing during the war and the driving force behind the development of effective home air defenses, Holt was regarded as an outstanding thinker on aviation matters and one of the most promising officers in the Royal Air Force.[8]

The first crated Handley Page machine arrived in Peking after the long sea voyage from England in early November 1919. It took nearly a month to assemble the aircraft. On December 6 a successful test flight took place. Two days later, the 14,000-pound machine, powered by two Rolls-Royce 350-hp engines, carried Chinese officials on a half-hour tour of the Peking area.[9]

Preparations went forward during the early months of 1920 looking toward the inauguration of China's first commercial air service. A trial flight between Peking and Tientsin, 80 miles to the southeast, was flown on April 24, followed by a second flight on May 8. On the return portion of the latter trip, mail and cargo were carried by air for the first time in Chinese history.[10]

Full-scale air service appeared imminent, and prospects for success were high. Then the bubble burst. A festering internal struggle in North China broke out into open warfare in the summer of 1920. General Ting immediately commandeered all aircraft for military use. The British government had no desire to be drawn into a Chinese civil war, and British subjects were withdrawn from the Peking aerodrome. This action forestalled, at least temporarily, the military use of the aircraft as the Chinese had no pilots capable of operating the machines. But General Ting did not give up hope. He offered a bribe to anyone willing to undertake military missions. The only response came from a Swiss mechanic in the employ of Handley Page. This individual, with little or no flying experience (and intoxicated, according to one report) managed to fly one bombing mission. The bombs did little damage. The mechanic collected his bribe of 60,000 francs and promptly fled the country.[11]

The situation in North China quieted by November, and Colonel Holt took charge of the effort to bring some order to the chaos of Chinese aviation. Certainly, if anyone could accomplish this difficult task, Holt seemed to be the man. The young officer, Air Chief Marshal Joubert later recalled, "possessed a clear brain and considerable imagination. Impatient of people mentally less-equipped than himself he was not very popular, but he produced results."[12]

Holt established a school for the training of Chinese commercial aviators at Nanyuan, near Peking. He soon encountered problems. Students, he found, were sent to the school on the basis of political considerations rather than suitability for flying training. Language difficulties produced more headaches. General Chiao Bo-cheng, later prominent in the Nationalist Air Force, once told of some of the consequences of the language barrier. Chiao, during his training at Nanyuan, advanced through primary instruction to the point of soloing without hazard except for his tendency to land with the tail of his aircraft too high. His British instructor, through an interpreter, sought to impress upon Chiao the necessity to land with the nose high. Finally, he turned the fledgling aviator loose for the first solo flight with the parting advice, duly translated, "Keep your nose up." Chiao followed these instructions to the letter. On his first landing, he tilted his head backward and pointed his nose toward the sky. Strangely enough, this somewhat unorthodox technique worked: Chiao made a perfect three-point landing. He failed, however, to see the plane that taxied into his path. The resultant crash wiped out two aircraft and broke Chiao's jaw.[13]

Meanwhile, Holt proceeded with his scheme for a commercial air service, flown initially by British pilots, to link Peking with Shanghai via Tientsin, Tsinan, Hsuchow, and Nanking. He planned to use 40 large Vickers Vimy Commercials on the route. The schedule called for departure from Peking at 5:30 A.M. Sunday, Wednesday, and Friday mornings, reaching Shanghai, 750 miles distant, at 6 P.M. the same day. The return trip would leave Shanghai on Tuesday, Thursday, and Saturday mornings. "This line," Colonel Holt told the press, "is a big experiment. It is about one of the longest airlines in the world, and its success or failure depends a great deal upon business men in the cities along the route."[14]

Holt soon learned that the fate of the line depended upon more than the patronage of businessmen. His first rude awakening came when authorities in South China, fearing that the air service was a step toward political domination by the Peking regime, refused to lease or sell land for the construction of aerodromes. Holt had to scale down his elaborate plans. Service began between Peking and Tsinan on July 1, 1921, with the remaining 500 miles of the trip to Shanghai completed by train. The airline suspended operations on July 10, resumed on July 18, and suspended again on August 15. The problem was mainly economic. Each round trip cost approximately Mex.$1,000 to operate; revenue from mail carried on each trip averaged Mex.$10. The Aeronautical Department quickly ran out of money, and the Vickers company, which had subsidized the line, refused to make available additional funds.[15]

Colonel Holt did not give up. Several flights operated during August and September between Peking and Peitaiho, a popular summer resort on the Gulf of Chihli some 225 miles east of the capital. Holt planned to resume the Peking-Shanghai service in 1922, but, once again, the summer months saw civil war break out in North China. This time the fighting expanded southward, and soon the entire country was in flames. Discouraged at last, Holt failed to renew his contract. The British mission left China, it was reported, "much disillusioned by their experience in the Orient."[16]

The British effort to introduce commercial air service thus ended in failure. The plans had been far too ambitious. The Chinese government was not capable of providing the necessary financial support for the operation, nor were the British willing to commit large funds to the enterprise beyond the initial investment. Above all, the chaotic political situation in China ruled out the possibility of a successful airline. Political stability and centralization of authority were essential prerequisites for the development of aviation, or, for that matter, any large-scale economic enterprise in China.

— II —

The 1920s saw constant civil war, as regional warlords struggled for power. Not until late in the decade did Chiang Kai-shek and the Nationalists bring a semblance of order to China. Following a series of succesful military campaigns, Chiang established the nationalist government at Nanking in southern China during April 1927. The new regime purported to speak for the entire country; actually, the Nationalists firmly controlled only the lower Yangtze Valley. It would take nearly another ten years of fighting and political intrigue before Chiang could truly claim to speak for "China." The Nationalists, nevertheless, were clearly the most powerful single element in the country by the end of the 1920s. They ruled the economic heart of China and brought to the Middle Kingdom a greater measure of centralized authority than it had seen for a generation.[17]

Renewed interest in the development of aviation followed in the wake of Nationalist victory. Chiang realized that efficient internal communication was necessary for the economic and political unification of China. Roads and railways took years to build and demanded tremendous financial commitments. Air service, on the other hand, could be instituted in a short time and with comparatively small expenditures. Consequently, the Nationalist ministries of Communications and Railways were soon at work developing schemes for commercial airlines.

As it happened, renewed Chinese interest in aeronautics occurred at the height of the aviation boom in the United States. The Army Air Corps Act, 1926, and the Navy's Five-Year-Program Act of the same year resulted in a large-scale procurement program. Then, in 1927, Charles Lindbergh flew alone across the Atlantic to Paris. Investors had displayed little interest in aviation securities prior to Lindbergh's flight. "Suddenly," reported a leading aviation journal, "the public was made to realize that there was an aviation industry and it began to want to buy aeronautical stocks so as to make the same profits that were gained by those who got in on the ground floor of the radio and automobile business." Sale of aviation securities reached phenomenal proportions. Between March 1928 and December 1929, eager investors snapped up $300 million worth of aviation securities, mostly common stock. During the golden summer of 1929 that preceded the Great Crash, aviation stocks rocketed to a market value of $1 billion. This was at a time when the aviation industry had a gross output of $90 million, and ranked 144th among manufacturing industries, just below the corset industry.[18]

By the late 1920s, the outstanding feature of the burgeoning aviation inudustry was a move toward consolidation. Most of the large, established companies passed out of the hands of aviation pioneers and were taken over by investment bankers, men who possessed the necessary facilities and knowledge to raise the large amounts of money required for expansion. Eventually, two groups emerged to dominate the industry, United Aircraft and Curtiss-Wright.

The head of the giant Curtiss-Wright complex, which included 29 subsidiary and 18 affiliated companies, and the man destined to father commercial aviation in China, was Clement M. Keys. A naturalized American citizen born in Chatsworth, Ontario, in 1877, Keys graduated from the University of Toronto in 1897, then taught classics in Ridley College, St. Catherine's, Ontario, for two years. Apparently the life of an impoverished scholar held little appeal for the young man. He left the academic world in 1899 and took a job as reporter for the *Wall Street Journal*. Keys spent seven years with the newspaper, rising to railroad editor, before joining the magazine *World's Work* in 1906 as financial editor. In 1911, his apprenticeship in the world of business and finance completed, the former teacher of classics founded C. M. Keys and Company, an investment service. The company prospered, and within a few years expanded into an investment banking house. Keys's first contact with the aviation industry came in 1916, when he accepted a non-salaried vice-presidency with the Glenn Curtiss Company. The Curtiss firm prospered during the war years, producing 3,240 aircraft in 1918, but the postwar depression nearly ruined the company. Curtiss manufactured only 147 aircraft in 1919 and was $3.5 million in debt. Keys purchased the near bankrupt company in 1920 for $650,000.

Keys nursed Curtiss through the lean years of the Jazz Age. He cut wages and laid off personnel. But, Keys later noted, "Never was the engineering budget reduced as much as a nickel. Those of us who could get along without them drew no salaries; but as rapidly as we could we increased the research budget." This philosophy paid dividends. Curtiss aircraft repeatedly broke speed records during the 1920s, and the company became the main supplier of military aircraft to the Air Corps. Later in the decade, Keys joined with the Pennsylvania Railroad to establish Transcontinental Air Transport. Passengers could now travel coast-to-coast in 48 hours, by airplane during the day and by train through the night. An established figure in aviation before the boom, and an experienced investment banker, Keys was able to put together the first great American aviation empire.

Noted for his pragmatic and business-like approach to aviation, Keys never seemed caught up in the glamor and excitement of flight. His favorite expression revealed a good deal about his attitude. "Ten per cent of aviation is in the air," Keys frequently said, "and 90 per cent on the ground." But this hard-headed businessman did have a dream. Ever since his days as railroad editor of the *Wall Street Journal,* Keys had admired James J. Hill, the railroad tycoon. And just as Hill had spanned the continent with steel rails, Keys hoped to circle the globe with aircraft. The capital that began to pour into the aircraft industry during the late 1920s provided the opportunity for Keys to realize his ambition.[19]

Keys, in partnership with investment banker Clarence Dillon, formed Intercontinental Aviation, Inc., in 1928 as the corporate vehicle for his planned expansion throughout the world. The company had available $10 million to be used to develop transportation lines and other aeronautical activities in foreign countries. A smaller subsidiary company, Aviation Exploration, Inc., was set up to carry out preliminary explorations abroad.[20]

Keys negotiated with eleven governments in South America, Europe, and Asia during 1928. These discussions led to the establishment of an aircraft factory in Turkey and an airline in Cuba. China, however, seemed to offer the most attractive prospect of all. R. O. Hayward, Keys's associate, arrived in China in December 1928 for discussions with Minister of Railways Sun Fo, son of Sun Yat-sen, founding father of the Chinese Republic. Hayward advised Sun Fo that funds might be available for the development of commercial aviation in China in return for a monopoly on all mail and passenger service. Minister Sun thought that such an arrangement might be possible. Negotiations, they agreed, should continue. The Chinese government promised not to contract with any other party for commercial air service before April 1, 1929.[21]

Keys prepared to send a survey party to China to investigate conditions for investment and, if warranted, conclude the necessary contract. First, however, he sought the sanction and support of the American government for the project. Colonel Paul Henderson, former Postal Department official now associated with Keys, called on President Calvin Coolidge on January 5, 1929. The president, according to Henderson, "indicated his approval." Two days later, Burdett S. Wright and William Henry White of Curtiss-Wright discussed the project with officers of the State Department's Far Eastern Division. The two men outlined progress to date and asked if the department would object to an agreement with the Chinese government. Stanley K. Hornbeck, chief of the Far Eastern Division, would not commit himself, but he did point out that the department would not favor any monopolistic contract in violation of existing treaties.[22]

Keys elaborated upon his intentions in a letter to Secretary of State Frank B. Kellogg on January 8. The proposed agreement with the Chinese, wrote Keys, would involve the establishment of commercial air service between certain important cities, organization of a flying school to train Chinese pilots, and formation of a trading company to deal with air cargo. "Our group," he stressed, "is not seeking to obtain a subsidy from the Chinese Government or a monopoly on all aviation in China, but in order to justify any considerable investment it will be necessary to require that certain of the mail and other contracts will be exclusive to the company to be formed by our group for a period of years, under arrangements similar to those which have been made by our own government for the carriage of its mail to foreign countries."[23]

The position finally adopted by the State Department fell far short of the support hoped for by Keys. The business of America might indeed be business, as President Coolidge was fond of saying, but the State Department's attitude gave no cause for great cheer. After due consideration, the department stated that it had no objection in principle, but that it would reserve judgment until learning the final terms of the contract. Furthermore, the department made clear, the American government could not in any way lend itself to the negotiations with the Chinese. If a non-objectionable contract was signed, State said, the government would extend to Keys "the same type of support it gives any other American enterprise legitimately entered into and carried on abroad."[24]

Keys learned the limits of governmental support when he tried to obtain the services of military aviators for the survey party. "It is felt in this Division," Stanley Hornbeck noted when the request reached his desk, "that the proposal to employ Navy and Army flyers in connection with this enterprise should be discouraged." Hornbeck suspected that Keys hoped to give the appearance of governmental support by this maneuver. "It has already become apparent," Hornbeck continued, "that the promoters hope to gain for this enterprise special 'countenance' from the Department. If Army and Navy officers appear among the employees of the company, unfortunate impressions will be created in the Far East; it will be assumed that the American Government is actively behind the enterprise." Hornbeck's recommendation to deny permission to employ military personnel received the full approval of his superiors.[25]

Meanwhile, preparation went forward for the expedition to China. Keys selected Major William B. Robertson, pioneer aircraft manufacturer and airline operator whose company had been acquired by Curtiss-Wright, to head the survey mission. Roland R. Riggs, a lawyer, and James Wilson, a former missionary who spoke Chinese, would assist Robertson. Two veteran pilots, E. L. Sloniger and A. L. Caperton, two mechanics, and Mrs. Robertson and her sister completed the party. Several small aircraft were shipped to China for demonstration and survey purposes.

Prior to the expedition's departure, Keys prepared a detailed letter of instructions for Robertson, setting forth the purposes and intentions of the airline project. Wrote Keys:

The policy of my group and of myself in dealing with foreign enterprises may be defined rather easily. I have no desire to dominate with American capital the transportation enterprises of any country. If in any country there are responsible business groups able and willing to participate in aviation enterprises in that country or to supply the majority of the capital required, my interests will be glad to co-operate with these gentlemen for the carrying on of any enterprise that seems to us to be promising. This may be particularly true in China, and if so you are instructed to carry on negotiations looking toward co-operation with these groups.

In China you will look very carefully into the general subject of air transportation and decide whether or not conditions justify the expectation that air transportation will be profitable in that country. Under direct contract with the government, you will investigate the possibilities of air mail contracts, contracts for the transportation of government officials, etc., and the transportation of government goods. In strictly commercial aviation, you will investigate the possibility of a combination of trading and transport on specified routes, having in mind purchasing, transport and sale of high grade commodities, especially in cases where distance between places where such commodities are produced and places where they find their final market, are very great and the routes are dangerous for other forms of transportation. . . .

Specifically, please, keep one fact in mind: It would be perfectly ridiculous, I think, under the present conditions in China, to start out to establish a large number of aviation lines. It seems to me that it is necessary to start out with one or two important lines involving a capital expenditure that might not in the first instance be over $500,000, and which should be started quickly. This would mean probably that the stops on such a route or routes would all be places where oil and gasoline can be obtained and which are established centers of trade population. We could throw such a line into operation within a comparatively short time and we could obtain from the operation of this line certain definite experience as to the advisability of the expansion of lines in China. Again, if we should determine upon such a line to be established in the immediate future, we could begin from that line to build up on paper a system to suit the needs of the Chinese people and the needs of the Chinese government.

If it is possible, we should start using Chinese personnel in the beginning; if it is not possible, we should start with a definite policy that we will use Chinese personnel just as soon as such personnel is available. . . .

There is no limit to what we shall do in China if the Chinese government really wants us to co-operate and the Chinese commercial interests welcome us into China. You may say definitely to the Chinese government that we are prepared to follow up the present expedition on a much more comprehensive scale. If, for instance, after consultation with them it seems to you reasonable to expect that big ships could be put into profitable operation quickly, we shall ship as quickly as possible a Sikorsky and a Ford tri-motored all metal plane. The Ford Motor Company desires to co-operate with us and will furnish its equipment to us together with personnel."[26]

Armed with these instructions, which seem prudent and sensible, Robertson sailed from Seattle on the *President Pierce* on January 26, 1929, reaching Shanghai in mid-February. Demonstration and survey flights took place during March and April, while Robertson negotiated with Sun Fo. In accordance with his instructions, Robertson proposed that a corporation be organized under the China Trade Act with an authorized capital stock of $10 million. American investors would take 60 percent of the issue with the remainder to be acquired by private Chinese interests. The company would receive from the Chinese government exclusive mail and passenger rights on three routes. One route would follow the Yangtze Valley to the commercial city of Hankow, thence to the Nationalist capital of Nanking. A second route would go from Shanghai to Hankow, then follow the coast to the port of Canton. The final route would connect Nanking with the Imperial city of Peking in the north, with an intermediate stop at either Tsinan or Tientsin. Sun Fo agreed to the routes but expressed doubt that either private investors or the government would be able to raise $4 million. He suggested an alternative arrangement whereby the government would subsidize the carriage of mail on the airline during the developmental period. The subsidy would be paid in government bonds at interest.[27]

R. O. Hayward opposed Sun's proposal when it was referred back to New York. He pointed out that American investors would supply aircraft, personnel, and operating funds, while the Chinese government would only pledge their credit. Furthermore, given the past financial record of Chinese governments, the bonds would likely prove worthless. James Wilson, the Old China Hand, also expressed reservations to Keys about the proposed arrangements. Wilson had secured statistics from the postal commissioner in Shanghai that indicated only a small volume of mail passed daily from Shanghai to Hankow and Peking. The prospects for an air mail service, therefore, did not appear promising.[28]

When Robertson seemed to hestitate, Sun Fo adroitly applied pressure by entering into discussions with other American companies that were interested in providing air service for China. Also, Sun let it be known that German aviation interests would like to enter the field. Robertson and Riggs, with the expiration of their April 1 option drawing near, recommended acceptance of the Chinese proposal with certain modifications. Keys ordered the men to proceed.[29]

The Chinese government on April 12, 1929, created the China National Aviation Corporation, a government-controlled organization, to manage aviation affairs. Through this device, the government hoped to blunt the expected criticism from the more nationalistic elements in the country. "From the Chinese point of view," a representative of Keys commented, "it was a blind to conceal the fact that a foreign corporation, not subject to Chinese jurisdiction, was to operate air transport routes in China." Eight days later, Sun Fo, acting as president of the new company, signed contracts with Robertson for the development of aviation in China.[30]

The American company, Aviation Exploration, received exclusive air mail rights for ten years on the three routes originally requested by Robertson. The Americans agreed to operate "up-to-date first-class and efficient equipment," conduct one round trip daily along the routes, and fly a minimum of 3,000 miles each day. The Chinese would establish adequate airports at the cities to be served and construct intermediate landing fields along the routes. In response to American objections regarding the possibility of limited quantities of mail, the Chinese agreed to compensate the airline for miles flown instead of pounds carried. Payments would range from $1.50 per mile for aircraft with a carrying capacity of less than 700 pounds to $4.50 to aircraft with a capacity of more than 2,800 pounds. The Chinese company would pay to the operator on the 15th of each month in cash the total postal receipts for the preceding month. The difference between these receipts and the compensation due for miles flown would be paid in promissory notes, maturing in not more than eight years and bearing interest at the rate of 8 percent, payable semiannually. The contract specified that the notes were "unconditionally guaranteed" by the Chinese government. A second contract granted options to the Americans for establishment of flying schools and aircraft factories in China.[31]

Obviously, the agreements provided advantages for both parties. The Chinese would secure commercial air service without having to put up any cash. The Americans stood to profit handsomely. The rate of $1.50 was more than double the estimated operating costs of the aircraft (an estimate that would prove much too low). In fact, the figure of $1.50 had been advanced for bargaining purposes, and Robertson would have settled for much less. He had been surprised and delighted when Sun Fo agreed to the initial figure without comment. It all sounded very good, but with mail receipts expected to be minimal, profits would depend upon the value of the promissory notes. American diplomatic and consular officials in China were not optimistic on this point. Frank S. Williams, trade commissioner in Shanghai, commented that the Americans "are taking a pretty long chance of collecting their money," while Consul General Edwin S. Cunningham wrote: "the scheme has the best wishes of all of us, but really it seems Utopian to some of us."[32]

Keys went into the project with his eyes open. He recognized that the financial arrangements depended upon the stability and good faith of the Nationalist government. "The risks of this adventure," he wrote to Hornbeck, "are well understood by myself and by my group of associates and . . . we enter upon them as more or less of a business adventure with full intention of financing them ourselves and meeting the gains and losses incident to them from our own resources."[33]

No sooner had the contract been signed when trouble broke out in China. The Chinese National Aeronautics Association, representing China's military aviators, protested vigorously against the agreement. General Chang Ching-yu, president of the association, commander of the Nationalist Air Force, and assistant chief of the Aviation Bureau of the Ministry of War, called upon the State Council to abolish the China National Aviation Corporation and repudiate the contract with the Americans. The project, Chang argued, encroached upon China's sovereignty.

Although he spoke in patriotic terms, Chang actually wanted to keep control of all aviation in the hands of the military.[34]

The Ministry of War naturally sided with Chang. The airfields to be used by the airline for commercial operations were controlled by the ministry, and these were now denied to the China National Aviation Corporation. Sun Fo, his position and prestige threatened but reluctant to provoke a confrontation with the powerful Ministry of War, turned for assistance to the Americans. As the military fields could not be used, he suggested that Aviation Exploration construct its own airfields. But this cost money, and Sun Fo did not have any. While the Americans were reluctant to commit further sums to China, they realized that lack of airports doomed the project before it could even begin. They finally agreed, reluctantly, to loan $1 million to the China National Aviation Corporation for construction of airports.[35]

The difficulty with the Ministry of War brought home the limitations of centralized control in Nationalist China. Chiang Kai-shek, no less than the rulers of China following World War I, headed a coalition of interests. Various powerful factions developed their own spheres of influence within the government and competed for power. Chiang had to assert his authority with caution lest the coalition break down. Although the Generalissimo would respond to challenges to his own power, he normally would permit contending groups to battle without interference in relatively minor matters, such as the dispute over control of aviation. China's standing in the international community might be damaged by this kind of bureaucratic struggle, but the issue was not considered sufficiently important to warrant Chiang's intervention.[36]

The problem with the Ministry of War was merely the opening skirmish in the battle for control of aviation in China. Two main factions vied for power. Sun Fo headed one group, while Minister of Communications Wang Po-chun, in partnership with the Ministry of War, led the other. The State Council, a body with more prestige than power, sought to mediate the dispute by appointing Wang vice president of the China National Aviation Corporation. But this conciliatory gesture failed. The minister of communications wanted nothing less than complete control over aviation. As the first step to achieve this goal, he established a competing airline.

In May 1929, less than a month after conclusion of the contract with Aviation Exploration, the Ministry of Communications signed an agreement with the Stinson company for operation of mail services between Shanghai and Nanking. This agreement clearly violated the terms of the contract with Aviation Exploration, but the central government took no action. Four Stinson Detroiter aircraft, single-engine, high-wing monoplanes that could carry four passengers, were shipped to China with two pilots and a mechanic. Service to Nanking by the Shanghai-Chengtu Air Mail Line began on July 8, and was to continue sporadically for several months thereafter. Although the company was soon to be plagued by equipment shortages and personnel problems, the beginning was auspicious. Dr. Liu Shu-fan, director general of posts, showed up for the opening ceremonies and pledged the full cooperation of his department. This was hardly surprising: the Postal Department fell under the jurisdiction of the Ministry of Communications.[37]

Wang Po-chun clearly had the upper hand in the bureaucratic struggle against Sun Fo. In late June, the Central Executive Committee of the Kuomintang, the most powerful political body in China, adopted a resolution to place all civil aviation under the Ministry of Communications. Sun Fo immediately issued a statement that this decision would not affect the contract with Aviation Exploration, a rather doubtful view.[38]

The problem in China was noted by the American press. The *New York Times*, for example, printed an editorial about the situation on June 23. It began with an account of the problems that had been connected with establishment of railroads in China. "The organizations now trying to install the latest types of communication," the *Times* continued, "are facing the same kind of obstacles as did those who sought to create a railroad system for China. In the interest of the Chinese people it is to be hoped that they will not be discouraged by the vexing delays."

Keys, for one, showed no signs of discouragement. In a letter

C N A C's first operations office, Shanghai, 1929

Loening amphibian, 1930

Stinson Detroiter, 1932

Sikorsky S-38 refueling at Shanghai, 1933

to the editor of the *Times*, he stated that Aviation Exploration had received the fullest cooperation from Chinese officials. Everything was going smoothly. Equipment and personnel would sail for China within two weeks. "I do not think," he concluded, "it is fair to government officials who are, so far as our experience goes, definitely trying to eliminate the abuses of the past, to imply that these abuses still exist."[39]

Obviously, Keys had adopted an attitude of determined optimism. He had no time for "knockers." E. L. Sloniger, one of the survey pilots, had remained in China after the Robertson party sailed for home in order to investigate further the projected routes. During his stay, he heard nothing but pessimistic opinions from American businessmen and diplomats. He visited Keys upon return to New York and passed along what he had learned. "When I told him what they all said," Sloniger recalled, "he kind of looked at me coldly and said, 'If I want to invest a million dollars that is my business.' I sort of dropped the subject."[40]

Keys could afford to be unconcerned about trouble in China. During June 1929, the *Times* average of industrial stocks shot up 52 points, with aviation securities leading the advance. Industrials were to gain another 25 points in July and 33 in August, equalling the total gain in 1928. By late August 1929, Curtiss-Wright stock had a market value of $171.6 million. Keys, understandably, did not blanch at the prospect of losing a million dollars in China, should that prove to be the case.[41]

— III —

Aviation Exploration had until October 17, 1929, to begin service on the Shanghai-Hankow route under the terms of its contract with the China National Aviation Corporation. Obviously, the success or failure of the enterprise depended to a large extent upon the ability of the operations manager of the airline, the man responsible for selecting the operating personnel and equipment and for organizing and conducting flight operations in China. In early June, Keys picked Harry G. Smith for this important post.[42]

Smith appeared well-qualified for the demanding task. Graduating from Simpson College, Indianola, Iowa, in 1917, Smith went on to study engineering at the University of Nebraska. He joined the Air Corps in 1918, took flight training, then became an instructor at Kelly Field, Texas. Later, Smith headed the inspection department in the aircraft procurement program. He took a job with the Post Office after the war and flew the mail with Charles Lindbergh in the western part of the United States. He also became an expert in aerial photography and was known for his extraordinary pictures of cloud formations. He was chief engineer for Aero Engineering and Advisory Service of Plainfield, New Jersey, at the time he agreed to go to China.[43]

Smith made his first important decision in mid-June 1929, when it became clear that Sun Fo would not be able to secure the necessary aerodromes to begin service in October. As the route from Shanghai to Hankow followed the Yangtze River, Smith suggested the use of amphibious aircraft. This would give the airline a choice of land or water operations, or a combination of the two. His recommendation accepted, Smith chose the Loening Air Yacht over competing types of aircraft. Developed by Grover Loening and Leroy Grumman in 1927, the Air Yacht amphibian could carry a payload of 1,000 pounds at a cruising speed of 100 miles per hour. There was room for six passengers in an enclosed cabin. The pilot and copilot sat side-by-side in an open cockpit above the cabin. Driven by a single 525-hp Pratt & Whitney Hornet engine, the Loening was underpowered, a common failing of aircraft at this stage of technological development. The squarish biplane was not pretty, but it was a rugged machine that had proved its durability during tests by the American Air Corps in South America during the late 1920s. And it was fairly economical to operate. Pilots and executives of the airline later agreed that Smith had made the right decision.[44]

Smith took equal care in assembling his operating staff. Three experienced air mail pilots, men who had flown with Smith in the early 1920s, would command the Loenings. Ernest M. Allison, the senior pilot, had 8,000 flying hours to his credit. S. T. Kaufman and Birger Johnsen had 4,200 and 4,900 hours, respectively. Oscar C. Wilke headed a group of five mechanics. A. P. St. Louis, radio engineer, and four radio operators completed the party that sailed from Seattle on July 27, 1929.[45]

August brought two important developments: the airline acquired a name and a president. On the 26th of the month, China Airways, a wholly owned subsidiary of Intercontinent Aviation, the parent company of Aviation Exploration, was incorporated under provisions of the China Trade Act of 1922. Ernest B. Price became the first president of China Airways the following week. Price's responsibility for the success of the venture in China would be great. The operations manager had the safe and efficient use of the aircraft to worry about; the president had to handle relations with the Chinese. If Keys's dictum held true—that 90 percent of aviation was on the ground—then Price had his work cut out for him.[46]

Price, like Smith, appeared ideally suited for his job. Born of American parents in Burma in 1890, Price graduated from the University of Rochester in 1913. He studied international law for one year at Columbia University before joining the Foreign Service. Price went to the Legation in Peking in 1914 as a student interpreter. Following two years of language training, he was posted to Tientsin as vice consul. He later served in Foochow (1920), Canton (1921), Foochow again (as consul, 1921-1928), Tsinan (1928), and finally, Nanking (1929).[47]

Price decided to leave the Foreign Service for personal reasons in 1929. Major Robertson had offered Price a position with the projected airline during the negotiations with the Chinese government in April. Aware that the success of the airline depended upon the cooperation and goodwill of the Chinese, Robertson had been impressed with Price's close relationship with Sun Fo. Price had met Sun in 1921, when the American was consul in Canton and Sun was mayor of the city, and they had become good friends. In fact, Sun probably recommended Price for the job with the airline. But Price had declined Robertson's offer because he hoped to join the Institute for Current World Affairs in New York. When Price failed to receive an acceptable offer from the institute, however, he went to see Keys about the position in China. Impressed with the former diplomat, Keys offered Price the presidency of China Airways at a salary of $10,000 a year. Price accepted. "It is a distinct relief," he wrote to a friend, "to be freed from the horror of genteel poverty."[48]

During his discussions in New York, Price drew up for Keys a lengthy memorandum, designed to give "some further idea of what I may be able to accomplish for you. . . . " Price reviewed in detail the requirements for successful operations in China and the course he planned to follow. Price was unconcerned about the technical aspect of the project. He assumed that this could be handled without undue difficulty, and he planned to leave the details of flight operations in the hands of qualified individuals, exerting only general supervision. The attitude of the Chinese would be the crucial factor in the success or failure of the airline. Price went on to argue that Sun Fo was the key to the entire operation. "The Chinese Corporation and the enterprise of Aviation Exploration, Incorporated," he predicted, "will stand or fall, succeed or fail, largely as Sun Fo stands or falls, succeeds or fails, as a factor in the Chinese Government."

Price considered Sun's future prospects reasonably good. His prestige as the only son of Sun Yat-sen, the Chinese Republic's George Washington, was a strong element in his favor. Also, as leader of the "Canton faction," that is, the group in the government that controlled the important province of Kwangtung, Sun Fo had a strong political base. Only the "Soong Dynasty"— T. V. Soong, minister of finance, and his three sisters, Mesdames Chiang Kai-shek, H. H. Kung, and Sun Yat-sen—could claim more strength and influence. Finally, Sun was a capable man, favorably disposed toward the West in general and the United States in particular.

The main threat to Sun, and the aviation contract, came from the minister of communications, Wang Po-chun. Sun would need all the help he could get in this precarious situation. While the president of the airline, Price wrote, should "refrain from getting involved either in Chinese politics or in personal controversies," it would be necessary to assist the Chinese corporation "to neutralize opposition, as well as keeping Government officials friendly toward and well-informed concerning the enterprise." Price did not explain how he could aid Sun in neutralizing the opposition and at the same time remain aloof from Chinese politics.[49]

In any event, Price was in high spirits on the eve of his departure for China. It felt good to be part of a "coordinated team." The high esprit de corps of the Keys organization contrasted favorably with the depressing attitude found in the Foreign Service. "I do not under-estimate the difficulties of the task before us," he reflected, "but the job appears to present a unique opportunity for a piece of constructive work of eventual benefit to China as well as our group of companies, and American trade as a whole."[50]

Progress in China following Harry Smith's arrival in mid-August 1929 scarcely justified much optimism. The China National Aviation Corporation failed to meet its obligation "to furnish, equip, police, maintain and have ready for operation adequate airports." China Airways received only a small piece of land on the muddy banks of the Whangpoo River, just large enough for two bamboo hangars and a combination tool-shed repair-shop operations-office, built out of aircraft shipping crates. To the amusement of all, someone painted "Empire State" on the front of the makeshift structure, an uncomplimentary reference to the world's tallest building then under construction in New York City. The Army garrison at Lungwha had to be crossed to reach these facilities. The military prohibited access to the post after 6 P.M., and personnel of China Airways could not obtain passes. The situation along the projected route was not much better. When the Ministry of War refused permission to use the military airport at Nanking, China Airways had to settle for a mooring buoy in the middle of the river. Fortunately, there was a lake that could be used for water landings at Kiukiang, an intermediate stop on the line. The military authorities did allow use of their field at Hankow, but they would not let China Airways erect a hangar.[51]

Smith made do as best he could. He had the five Loenings

uncrated and assembled, established radio stations and other ground facilities along the route, and prepared for operations. The first trial flight took place on October 12–13, 1929. Edgar Snow, then Far Eastern correspondent for the *Chicago Tribune* and later to gain fame for his books on China, went along. "We roared," reported Snow in one of his less memorable pieces of writing. "We sped through the clouds as casually as any red-blooded demon skimming across the dominion over which he ruled in a properly devastating fashion." Carried away with enthusiasm, Snow hailed the air service as the start of "a new era in the history of China." Air transport, safe and swift, would quicken understanding between hitherto isolated communities. He envisioned the day when the warring factions in China at critical moments would "meet in hurried common council and face to face, settle their difficulties by pacific means."[52]

Price notified the China National Aviation Corporation that China Airways would begin regular service on October 17. At the same time, he sought confirmation of the airline's exclusive right to carry air mail along the route. Price of course knew that the Postal Department, under orders from the minister of communications, dispatched all air mail via the Stinsons of the Shanghai-Chengtu Line that had been operating intermittent service to Nanking since July. Sun Fo could appeal to the State Council to settle the matter, but he refused to press the issue. Instead, he urged Price to commence operations without confirmation of air mail rights, indicating that he would take the matter before the Council at a later date. Price said no. "We clearly stated," he explained to New York, "failure to give us exclusive air mail rights from date of commencement would constitute breach of contract on their part." Sun finally agreed to raise the matter at the Council's meeting of October 18. Meanwhile, start of service would be postponed. The State Council at its 52nd Regular Meeting issued instructions to the minister of communications to conform with the contract between the China National Aviation Corporation and China Airways. Sun Fo had won, or so it seemed.[53]

Scheduled service between Shanghai and the river port of

Hankow, 525 miles distant along the serpentine Yangtze, began on October 21, 1929. Birger Johnsen, in goggles and helmet, lifted his Loening off the waters of the Whangpoo shortly after 8 A.M. The inaugural flight carried one pound of mail and two passengers—Mr. and Mrs. Sun Fo. The plane covered the 165 miles to Nanking in two hours, then proceeded to Hankow via Kiukiang. Meanwhile the first east-bound flight, commanded by Ernest Allison, completed the trip from Hankow to Shanghai without incident. Price and Smith had prevailed in the face of great difficulty, at least temporarily. The great enterprise had been launched. "I am rather proud of what we have thus far accomplished," wrote Price.[54]

Three days after service started in China, "Black Thursday" rocked the New York Stock Exchange. Market conditions had been unsettled during September. Prices had begun to fall in October. Panic hit the market on the 24th, when nearly 13 million shares were traded. Friday brought a brief recovery, but the following week produced a flood of "sell" orders. The Great Crash was at hand.

Aircraft securities led the downward spiral. The market value of all aviation stocks stood at $567,112,000 on August 23, 1929. Three months later, the stocks were worth $227,900,000. Curtiss-Wright suffered less than most other companies. Still, stock in Keys's enterprise fell from a value of $171.6 million to $106 million during this period.[55]

Shock waves from the market crash reached China Airways within a week. With the first route well started, Sun Fo began to press for service on the two other routes, Shanghai to Canton and Peking, specified in the contract. Price telegraphed New York for instructions. "Situation here badly disturbed," read the reply. "Directors unwilling to proceed with additional large capital investment without definite information on revenue and operating conditions present line and further assurance of government support. Advise urging slowness starting additional routes." C. M. Keys no longer had a million dollars to invest as he saw fit. China Airways would have to start paying its way.[56]

Price arranged a six-month delay without difficulty. He

merely pointed out to Sun Fo that the promised facilities for the Shanghai-Hankow service had not been provided and that nothing had been done to acquire land for the necessary airports on the other routes. He agreed to continue surveys while awaiting action by the Chinese company.[57]

China Airways operated the daily (except Sunday) round-trip service from Shanghai to Hankow without default during the last ten days of October. On November 15 the company tried to collect the cash receipts and promissory notes due under the mileage agreement, a total of $15,480. The minister of communications ignored instructions from the State Council and refused to release the postal receipts. The China National Aviation Corporation asked Price to wait until December 15 for the money. At the same time, they wanted a different method used to compute cash payments, and they asked the Americans to accept a great proportion of promissory notes. This would result in a 43 percent reduction in cash receipts and a 33 percent drop in total compensation. Price refused to consider such a modification of the contract and informed New York of the situation. Two days later New York instructed: "Suggest entire contract be indefinitely suspended or cancelled if Chinese Government wishes. Believe this will be best course at present time."[58]

Price flew to Nanking on November 20 to meet with Sun Fo. Sun informed Price that he had taken the matter before the State Council, and the Council again had ordered the minister of communications to pay the money. He urged Price to continue service until December 15, at which time China Airways would receive all the money owed to them. Price agreed.[59]

The difficulties in China were paralleled by the continuing financial crisis in the United States. C. M. Keys, in the midst of graver problems, turned his attention in early December to the situation in the Far East. "It is necessary," Keys wrote to Price, "to impress upon you the need of extreme conservatism and extreme economy." The market crash had made it "utterly impossible" to raise additional funds. Keys would accept any reasonable modification of the contract with the Chinese. On the other hand, he did not find the rate of $1.50 per mile excessive in view of operating costs of $1.25 per mile. "I do not see," he noted, "how it is possible to make money even though the full rate were received in gold each day." Keys concluded on an encouraging note: "So far I have been satisfied with the administration of the enterprise and hope for good news after the fifteenth of December."[60]

But there would be no good news from China. The minister of communications still refused to remit the postal receipts. Sun Fo threatened to resign the presidency of the China National Aviation Corporation unless the Council forced the minister to comply with its order. The Council, however, was impotent. It could only set the legal seal of approval on decisions made elsewhere by powerful factions in the government, not take coercive action on its own. When the Council failed to take further action against the minister of communications, Sun Fo made good his threat to resign. As expected, the Council thereupon confirmed Minister Wang Po-chun's victory in the struggle for control over aviation by naming him to replace Sun as president of the China National Aviation Corporation.[61]

Price decided to make the best of a bad situation and called upon the new president two days before the December 15 payment fell due. He urged Wang to fulfill the terms of the contract. Wang was "polite but evasive." The minister did not know if payment could be made. Furthermore, Wang went on, he had never approved the contract in the first place. This hardly came as news to Price.[62]

Up to this point, Price had carefully refrained from interfering in Chinese internal political matters. Now, he turned for assistance to the influential minister of finance, whose sister was married to Chiang Kai-shek, T. V. Soong. Although Soong promised to do what he could to straighten out the matter, December 15 came and went and there was no payment. Price claimed violation of contract and suspended service. Within hours of his announcement, the long-awaited cash receipts appeared in the offices of China Airways. Flights began operating again on December 17.[63]

Wang had backed down, no doubt because of the intervention

of Soong, a person with much more political clout than Sun Fo. But the minister of communications was in no way reconciled to the continued existence of China Airways. A few days later, Wang attacked the Americans in a statement released to the Chinese press, a statement designed to undercut Soong by mobilizing public opinion. Wang termed the air mail contract completely unreasonable, The ministry was losing $10,000 a month on the air service. "How," he asked, "can the Ministry bear such a heavy burden?" He had no choice, he said, but to cancel the contract.[64]

Price could also play this kind of game. If Wang was going to use the Chinese press to whip up public sentiment in his favor, Price could employ the Western press to bring pressure on a government that was looking to the West for all manner of technical and economic assistance to modernize the economy. Price pointed out in his statement to the newspapers that the rate of $1.50 a mile received by China Airways compared favorably with the $2.00 per mile paid to Pan American Airways by the American government. Figured another way, China Airways received $2.40 a pound for air mail, whereas compensation to American domestic air carriers ranged from $2.40 to $3.00 a pound. Any way you look at it, "the cost of our service is very reasonable." Furthermore, the service could even turn a profit for the Chinese. China Airways charged $1,584 for each round trip between Shanghai and Hankow. This sum could be realized by carrying an average load of 240 pounds of mail and four passengers each way each day. The aircraft still would have an unused capacity of 100 pounds. Thus, any additional payload would mean money in the pockets of the Chinese.[65]

While Price fought in China to save the airline, the ground was being cut from under him in New York. Minard Hamilton had been sent to the Orient in August 1929 as the personal representative of C. M. Keys. Although carried on the books of China Airways as a vice president and nominally under Price's authority, Hamilton received his salary from the parent company (Intercontinent Aviation) and reported directly to New York. Upon his return to the United States in mid-December,

Hamilton submitted an utterly damning and largely unfair report to Keys on the enterprise in China.

He began his tale of woe with the Robertson mission. "Robertson," wrote Hamilton, "was the wrong man for leader, Riggs was the wrong man for legal adviser, and Wilson was exactly the wrong man for guide. . . . The whole junket was run like a joy ride. The ideas to buy champaign [sic] for everybody in Shanghai and make big whoopie." Robertson had bungled the job. He had misjudged the stability of the Nationalist government. The government, according to Hamilton, was run by "an ex-concubine-dealer called Chiang Kai-shek" and would not endure. Robertson should have called off the negotiation. Instead, he went on to conclude an agreement with the wrong man. Sun Fo— "the Cantonese call him a 'fat head' "—had only his father's name and lacked ability and influence. The course of the project since its disastrous inception had been all downhill. "Of course," Hamilton went on, "all this sounds pretty pessimistic. I don't want to paint the picture any blacker than it is, but it really *is* pretty black." The airline, he concluded, had the potential to at least pay operating expenses, it had some publicity value, and it might lead to the sale of military aircraft to the Chinese. For these reasons the line might be allowed to continue operating. But, he emphasized, no further investment should be made in the project.[66]

A shift in New York's attitude toward the China venture—from gloom to despair—could be detected in early January 1930. "We will not consider any further capital expenditure," New York cabled on the 10th, "or even continue operations route one [Shanghai-Hankow] unless contract revision definitely settled." New York would accept $1.25 per mile *in cash* or payment *in cash* of $0.80 a pound for carrying all first class mail with a guarantee of at least 1,800 pounds daily. The message ended: "If neither basis possible endeavor to negotiate sale entire investment."[67]

Price hurried to Nanking to discuss revision of the contract, but Minister Wang refused to see him. Price then took up the matter with other high government officials. He came away with the impression that the government "on the whole" was not opposed to the contract. In fact, he was so encouraged that he wired Keys: "Considering all the circumstances . . . still believe we can eventually suceed if we are patient."[68]

The State Council met to consider Wang's petition for cancellation of the contract on January 31, 1930. On the eve of the meeting, Price wrote to all members of the Council, setting forth a detailed history of the controversy. He listed five specific breaches of contract and noted the constant harrassment by the minister of communications. Despite all this, China Airways stood willing to negotiate an amicable revision of the contract. He could not believe, Price concluded, that the Chinese government would disregard its contractual obligations and cancel a valid agreement.[69]

Price's efforts proved unavailing. The State Council voided the contract. Although it did not immediately announce the decision, Minister Wang gleefully leaked the news to the press, together with a garbled version of Price's letter. Price then released the full text of the letter.[70]

The foreign press in China were quick to condemn the Council's action. The comments of the conservative and respected Shanghai journal, *Finance & Commerce*, were typical. While not prepared to pass on the merits of the dispute, the journal voiced its concern about the reliability of contracts signed by the government. The government, warned the journal, "must stand by the pledges given if it attaches any importance to its credit and good name in international affairs."[71]

The criticism appearing in the press no doubt had an impact on important government officials, like T. V. Soong, who were concerned with China's reputation as a safe, profitable area for Western investment. Should Soong have missed the point, Dr. Arthur N. Young, financial adviser to the government, drew his attention to the matter. The result of unilaterally cancelling the contract, Young wrote in a confidential letter to the minister, "would be injurious to the credit and prestige of the Government, and would tend to discourage further investment of capital in the country."[72]

The results of the power struggle going on within the government became known on February 7 when the State Council voted to cancel the cancellation order. At the same time, it instructed the minister of communications to negotiate a revision of the contract with China Airways.⁷³

Price—and Soong—had scored an impressive victory but the personal cost proved high to the president of China Airways. Wang remained a powerful factor in the government despite the damage to his prestige. He might have to negotiate contract revision with China Airways, but not with Ernest Price. The axe fell the following month. "Stockholders feel that expenses must be curtailed to the extent of possible," cabled New York. "Regret to advise you that on account of continued uncertainty do not feel continued expense your services warranted." Price suspected, and he was probably right, that Wang had requested his dismissal. New York's objective was a more profitable—or at least less expensive—financial arrangement with the Chinese. Wang may have indicated that such an agreement might be possible should a new representative be appointed. If so, Price's services could be dispensed with.⁷⁴

Disappointed and embittered at his dismissal, Price found himself unemployed and without future prospects at age forty. "One thing is certain," he wrote to a friend before leaving Shanghai, "and that is I do not wish to return to China." Price toyed with the idea of farming a small fruit ranch in California but he abandoned the idea in favor of a more practical career as a scholar. He received his doctorate in international affairs from Johns Hopkins University in 1933. The Walter Hines Page School of International Relations published his dissertation, *Russo-Japanese Treaties of 1907-1916*, the same year. Price lectured at the University of Chicago for a time, then joined the Institute of Pacific Relations. He never returned to China.⁷⁵

— IV —

The first decade of commercial aviation in China had proved disappointing to all concerned. Internal dissension, chronic political instability, and lack of adequate funds had thwarted the British attempt to develop aeronautical enterprises after World War I. The American effort that had followed in the late 1920s had fared little better. Clement Keys and his associates had gone to the Far East with high hopes of tapping the wealth of the great China market. By the spring of 1930, however, the venture appeared on the verge of collapse. Like the British, the Americans had run afoul of the treacherous cross-currents of Chinese politics. The financial disaster in the United States seemed merely to hasten the inevitable.

The Chinese wanted and needed air service. "It is obvious," one observer noted in the 1920s, "that commercial aviation could be of more value to China than to almost any other country in the world."[76] Yet the government proved unwilling or incapable of supplying the necessary financial support and political cooperation. Air routes have to be carefully nurtured during their early stages. Service between the large commercial centers of Shanghai and Hankow could certainly be profitable once people became convinced that air transportation was convenient, reliable, and safe. But this takes time—and money. China Airways' average operating expenses during the first three months of 1930 came to less than $20,000 a month. Revenue from mail and passenger traffic amounted to a little over $7,000 a month. The airline required a subsidy of $150,000 to $200,000 a year to stay in business.[77]

Was the air transportation project worth the cost to China, and, if so, could China afford to pay the price? Many other nations in the world at that time considered the economic and political value of air transportation sufficiently important to warrant subsidies. The later history of commercial aviation in China suggests that the nation benefited from the service. In fact, by the late 1930s air transportation had become a vital element in the continued survival of an independent China. There were of course severe financial restrictions on the government, and the Chinese surely would have been hard-pressed to find even the $150,000 to $200,000 a year to support commercial aviation. But, in the long run, it would prove worth the effort.[78]

FROM PEKING TO SHANGHAI   31

One thing seemed clear during the winter of 1929–1930: Clement Keys did not intend to commit any more American money to the project without a new contract that held greater promise of financial return. Whether it would be possible to obtain such an agreement remained to be seen.

CHAPTER TWO
ALONG THE YANGTZE
1930–1933

— I —

MAX S. POLIN was the man picked by Keys to renegotiate the airline contract and thereby determine the fate of the enterprise in China. Polin, like Price, was an Old China Hand, although the new American representative had acquired his expertise during business dealing with the Chinese rather than through diplomacy. Polin had been representing the Oil Export Company in Shanghai when Cyril McNear, a personal friend with connections to the Keys organization, asked him to assist Major Robertson in 1929. Polin had recommended the negotiations be conducted with the minister of communications because of Wang Po-chun's authority over the Postal Department. When Robertson rejected this advice and signed a contract with Sun Fo, Polin had written to New York and predicted the failure of the venture. Because events had proved him right and because he was on good terms with Minister Wang, Polin seemed the logical choice to work out a viable understanding with the Chinese.¹

While Polin undertook the month-long journey from New York, where he had been on a visit, to Shanghai, Price continued informal discussions with government officials. He learned that the Chinese wanted a new operating company, incorporated under Chinese law and under Chinese jurisdiction. The Ministry of Communications would have a two-thirds controlling interest in the new company. The Americans would have the remaining third and would advance the Chinese share as a loan. The new company would obtain exclusive domestic air mail rights on specified routes for ten years. Compensation would be $1.50 per pound of mail carried, with a guaranteed minimum of 550 pounds a day. The difference between cash receipts and the guaranteed minimum, if any, would be paid to the company by the government in promissory notes. "Naturally," Price reported to Keys, "I took care to express no opinion, whatever, on these ideas, but to you I will record my belief that the proposition is wholly untenable."[2]

Polin thus had his work cut out for him when he reached Shanghai in mid-March 1930. It was the same old story, only worse. The Chinese not only wanted the Americans to supply all the cash, they also sought control of the airline. New York, on the other hand, did not intend to put any more money into the enterprise without a reasonable expectation of profit. The agreement that finally emerged after four months of bargaining proved a compromise, acceptable, if not completely satisfactory, to both parties.

The new Sino-American contract, signed on July 8, 1930, by Polin and Minister Wang, involved the amalgamation of China Airways, the China National Aviation Corporation, and the moribund Shanghai-Chengtu Line of the Ministry of Communications into a single organization. The new company would be called the China National Aviation Corporation (CNAC), an entirely different and distinct entity despite the fact that it carried the same name as the old government-controlled company. CNAC was a limited liability share company, incorporated under the laws of China, with an authorized capital of $3.3 million. The Ministry of Communications would acquire 55 percent of the stock and the American partner, 45 percent. The contract provided for paid-in capital of $1.3 million, $715,000 by the Chinese and $585,000 by the Americans. The Chinese received a credit of $240,000 for their investment in the old China National Aviation Corporation and the Shanghai-Chengtu Line. This was a generous figure, as neither company had much in the way of facilities or equipment except for the five Stinsons of the Shanghai-Chengtu Line. The Chinese would pay the balance of $675,000 in four equal installments: upon ratification of the contract by the State Council, December 1, 1930, and June 1 and December 1, 1931. As the Americans were credited with $585,000 for their investment in China Airways, CNAC would begin operations with cash assets of $185,000 (included was cash turned over to the new company by the old China National Aviation Corporation) and the promise of an additional $558,000 during the first eighteen months of service.

CNAC would be managed by a board of directors, four members to be appointed by the Chinese and three by the Americans (the total number of directors might change from time to time, but the ratio would remain constant). The board would elect a president from among its own members who would also serve as managing director of the airline, and two vice presidents. The Chinese would nominate the president and one vice president; the Americans could select the other vice president. The company would have three operating divisions, Business, Finance, and Operations. Business and Finance would be headed by Chinese with American assistants, while an American with a Chinese assistant would be in charge of Operations.

The contract authorized CNAC to operate three routes: (1) Shanghai to Chengtu via Nanking, Kiukiang, Hankow, Ichang, Wanhsieu, and Chungking; (2) Shanghai/Nanking to Peking via Hsuchow, Tsinan, and Tientsin; and (3) Shanghai to Canton via Ningpo, Wenchow, Foochow, Amoy, and Swatow. CNAC had exclusive air mail rights on these routes. Operations were to begin immediately on the first route and within three years on the other routes under penalty of forfeit.

Revenue from mail, passengers, and freight would accrue to the company. In what was to prove the most optimistic part of the agreement, the contract provided for the payment of dividends, after deductions for operating expenses, repayment of loans, provisions for a sinking fund, and so forth. There was no provision in the contract for subsidy by either partner to cover losses.

Other important features of the agreement involved preference for Curtiss-Wright products and the cancellation of outstanding notes held by China Airways ($221,275) and previous contracts. The agreement specified that it would be the "definite policy" of CNAC to use qualified Chinese pilots, mechanics, and other personnel as soon as they were available. The American partner was to provide training for Chinese pilots, mechanics, and radio operators.

The contract would remain in force for ten years and, if neither party signified its intent to terminate the agreement at that time, for an additional five years. The Chinese obtained the right to purchase all property of the company "at a reasonable valuation" upon expiration of the contract.[3]

This pathbreaking agreement marked the beginning of a new era in China's commercial relations with the West. There had been prior partnership agreements on a 50-50 basis, but never before had the Chinese secured a majority interest. "This is one of the great achievements accomplished under the Nationalist regime," commented the *China Weekly Review*, "the first [agreement] that is really 'compatible' with Chinese sovereignty." The CNAC contract established a precedent. The agreement concluded with German aviation interests the following month, as we shall see, provided for two-thirds Chinese ownership, and, shortly thereafter, the Nationalists changed the law governing foreign participation in mining activities in China to require 51 percent Chinese interest.[4]

Polin had had little choice but to defer to the force of Chinese nationalism, especially in light of New York's insistence that further cash would have to come from the Chinese. The Americans were more concerned with salvaging their investment than with the traditions of Western business relations with China. The value of the five Loenings owned by China Airways did not amount to much, given the depressed market in the United States, and the protection offered by treaties was not worth a nickel. Chinese jurisdiction might afford little security, but it did not appear that things could get much worse. And, they *might* get better. In any event, the contract contained a number of protective devices. For example, 80 percent of the stockholders had to approve all important fiscal decisions, such as an increase of paid-in capital, borrowing, purchase of new equipment, and so forth. Disbursements would be by check, signed by representatives of both sides. Above all, Americans controlled operations, the heart of the airline.

An organizational meeting of the new company took place at the Ministry of Communications in Nanking on July 10, 1930. The participants decided that a five-member instead of a seven-member board of directors would be appointed, at least for the present. Wang Po-chun became the first president of the company. Liu Shu-fan, director general of posts, and Wei I-fu, vice minister of communications, joined him on the board. The American partner selected Max Polin and Minard Hamilton, the Cassandra of China Airways. One week later, on July 17, the State Council ratified the contract.[5]

The future seemed to augur well. Polin had hammered out a good agreement. Chinese and Americans would work together, and the Chinese would be putting up the cash. But nothing was that simple in China. CNAC would soon face difficulties in expanding its routes. Also, the threat of competition loomed on the horizon.

Less than a month after the State Council placed its seal of approval on the Sino-American agreement, the Chinese government signed a contract with Lufthansa, the German national airline. The Germans had an ambitious scheme for an air mail service between Berlin and Shanghai via the Soviet Union. The Sino-German contract established the Eurasia Aviation Corporation, capitalized at $1 million. The Chinese would purchase two-thirds of the stock, and the Germans would take the balance. There would be a board of directors of six Chinese and three Germans. Unlike the agreement with the Americans, the Sino-German contract specified that the Chinese and Germans would share administration and operation of the company on a two-thirds/one-third basis.[6]

Eurasia inaugurated the Shanghai-Berlin service on May 30, 1931. After one flight, however, the Soviet government withdrew permission for operations over its territory, probably out of belated fear that the flights could be used for military reconnaissance. As this came at a time of supposed Soviet-German friendship, the Russians offered an alternative. Eurasia would deliver mail and passengers to Manchuli, a town some 650 miles north of Peking on the Soviet border. The trip would then continue to Irkutsk by train, then by Soviet aircraft to Berlin.

The line to Manchuli proved ill-fated. Service of three round trips weekly in single-engine Junkers all-metal monoplanes began in June 1931. Lack of traffic soon caused reduction in service to twice weekly. The airline ran into more severe problems in early July when Mongolian bandits shot down one of its aircraft that was en route from Linsi in Jehol province to Manchuli. The pilot and copilot were taken captive and not released for several weeks.

Eurasia put aside plans for an international air service following this incident. During the next ten years, until the Germans withdrew from China in 1941, the company concentrated on domestic routes. Eurasia developed two main services. One connected Shanghai to Lanchow, 1,050 miles to the west in Kansu province, via Nanking, Loyang, and Sian. The other route extended from Peking southward to Canton, 1,100 miles distant, via Taiyuan, Loyang, Hankow, and Changsha. During 1935 Eurasia acquired a fleet of four tri-motored Junkers Ju 52 aircraft, one of the finest machines of its time. As it worked out in the end, Eurasia provided little competition for CNAC, as the routes of the two airlines were largely complementary.[7]

While Eurasia struggled to develop its routes in the early 1930s, CNAC attempted to push the Yangtze line further into the interior of China. The first major effort came during the late summer and fall of 1930 and involved extension of service from Hankow to Ichang, Wanhsien, and Chungking. The Board of Directors approved the purchase of a sixth Loening, optimistically christened *Chungking*, and preparations began for the expected inaugural date for service of October 10, the new Chinese national holiday. On paper, at least, the route extension did not seem difficult. There were a number of technical problems to be solved, especially of the Ichang-Chungking segment that followed the Yangtze Gorges, although certainly nothing beyond the competence of the flight personnel. But the route beyond Ichang would take the airline for the first time into a region not under the direct control of a central government.[8]

Chiang Kai-shek and the Nationalists had fared well in 1930. The year had gotten off to a bad start when several powerful warlords had rebelled against the central government. The dissidents had scored a few initial victories, but the tide had turned during the summer when Chang Hseuh-liang of Manchuria, the "Young Marshal," had intervened on the side of the Nationalists. These developments, predicted Arnold Toynbee in his survey of the year's events, "would bring China a greater measure of internal political stability than she had ever yet enjoyed since the beginning of the revolution some twenty years earlier."[9]

Despite the brightening prospects for political centralization under the Nationalists, numerous regions remained beyond Nanking's authority, including the upper Yangtze Valley. Marshal Liu Hsiang controlled Szechwan province, an area four-fifths the size of Texas with a population of over 50 million. Liu did not want to provoke a quarrel with the Nationalists, especially in light of their growing power; nor did Chiang Kai-shek desire any trouble with the marshal. Each side treated the other with politeness and care.[10]

Minard Hamilton, who was now in command of the enterprise he had once so heartily condemned, was either unaware or, more likely, insensitive to the delicate situation. He handled the survey of the route between Hankow and Chungking as if the line to be opened were between Cleveland and Buffalo. Hamilton and Harry Smith left Hankow for Ichang on September 12, 1930, intending to proceed on to Wanhsien and Chungking. Hamilton did not even bother to consult Marshal Liu or his subordinate at Wanhsien, General Wang Fun-jao, before departure. General Wang heard about the proposed flight from the local Socony Oil agent shortly before the plane was to leave Ichang, while Marshal Liu received the information from a "hostile" source. Liu responded to what he considered an affront to his dignity by threatening to shoot at the aircraft if it proceeded up river. Hamilton decided that discretion was the better part of valor and retreated to Hankow.[11]

Although the initial attempt to extend service to Chungking misfired, the fall of 1930 did bring some good news for the company in the form of a marked increase in mail and passenger traffic between Shanghai and Hankow. Revenue increased 20 percent in terms of Chinese dollars. Unfortunately, as CNAC's revenue went up, the price of silver went down. Before the economic disaster of 1929, one Chinese dollar, based on the silver standard, was worth 42 cents in American currency, based on the gold standard. The value of the Chinese dollar in relation to American funds declined an average of 33 cents in March 1930 and 28 cents in September. As a major part of CNAC's operating expenses consisted of salaries and charges for equipment payable in American dollars, the airline's monthly deficit remained constant despite increased revenue.[12]

As deficits continued and the prospects for financial return remained dim despite the new contract, the Keys group once again sought to reassess its position toward the venture in China. In early December 1930, Keys sent George Conrad Westervelt across the Pacific to decide whether or not the American partner should continue to participate in CNAC.

Westervelt is one of the more significant figures in the early development of aviation, although his career has been little noted by historians. A native of Corpus Christi, Texas, Westervelt graduated from the United States Naval Academy in 1901, ranking tenth in a class of sixty that included the future Fleet Admiral Ernest J. King. Three years of sea duty followed; then the young officer studied naval architecture at the Massachusetts Institute of Technology. Westervelt became interested in aviation at MIT, especially the design and construction of seaplanes. In 1915 Westervelt and another graduate of MIT, a young Chinese named Wong Tsu, joined William Boeing in the construction of the first in what was to prove a long line of Boeing aircraft. The B & W (Boeing and Westervelt) float seaplane proved a technical if not a commercial triumph. According to one student of commercial aviation, the success of the B & W floatplane led Boeing to devote his full attention to the construction of aircraft.[13] Westervelt and Boeing planned a partnership, but American entry into World War I diverted Westervelt into naval aviation. Westervelt supervised the construction of all naval aircraft during the war. He traveled twice to Europe as a member of commissions whose recommendations defined American naval activity in European waters. After the war, Westervelt joined with Jerome C. Hunsaker in the design and construction of the famous "N.C." flying boats. One of these aircraft made the first successful east-to-west crossing of the Atlantic Ocean in May 1919. They were the largest flying boats in the world for a decade and held the record for most people carried aloft at one time (51). Captain Westervelt commanded the Naval Aircraft Factory at Philadelphia between 1920 and 1927, the largest governmental aircraft facility in the world at that time. He retired in 1927 and joined the Curtiss-Wright enterprises as an expert in the design, construction, and operation of aircraft factories. He supervised construction of an aircraft factory in Turkey and the Curtiss-Caproni plant in Baltimore, among other projects.[14]

"There was never any lukewarm attitude toward Captain Westervelt," his wife later recalled. "He was either not liked at all, or very much liked and respected." Ralph S. Barnaby, then a young ensign and later a close friend, remembered his first encounter with Westervelt in 1918: "He was a short plump man with a very stern demeanor. While his face was round, his slightly aggressive chin and protruding lower lip gave him a rather forbidding aspect. It was easy to understand why he had acquired the nickname of 'Scrappy' at the Naval Academy. He just looked belligerent!" Later, when Westervelt and Barnaby came to know one another better, the captain explained (perhaps with tongue in cheek; one never knew with Westervelt): "'Barnaby, people as short as you and I are, have to act tough or people will walk all over us!'" Barnaby also recalled words of advice that Westervelt once offered and that Barnaby, some forty years later, considered "the most important piece of advice I was ever to receive,—one which shaped my whole career." Westervelt had said that one should never expect higher authority to solve problems encountered in the field. The person higher up is not on the spot and is not aware of all the necessary details. Instead, said Westervelt, tell him the problem, let him know what you propose to do about it, wait a reasonable length of time for objections, then act. Westervelt was to follow his own advice in China.[15]

George Conrad Westervelt had a gentler side. He possessed a

droll sense of humor. He wrote seventeen plays, four of which were produced on Broadway, and several unpublished novels. He authored a book of children's stories, based on tales he used to tell his two daughters. He loved the land and was an active conservationist. He designed farm machinery, conducted agricultural experiments, and bred cattle. He saved the Sandhill cranes from extinction in Highland County, Florida. But it was the Westervelt to whom people feared to say "Good morning" lest they be expected to prove it, who was sent to China in 1930.[16]

The situation in China may have been unpromising when Westervelt sailed from the West Coast in early December; while he was en route to the Orient it very nearly became disastrous. The airline had flown nearly 400,000 miles and carried 3,000 passengers without injury since the beginning of operations in October 1929. The credit for this excellent safety record belonged to the airline's flight and ground personnel and to the operations manager, Harry Smith. By December 1930, however, Smith had become disillusioned about the prospects for commercial aviation in China, and he communicated this discontent to the pilots. In addition, Smith and his senior pilot, Ernest Allison, were quarreling over the competence of several replacement pilots who had been sent out from the United States. Paul F. Baer was one of the new arrivals. Baer had come to China with a distinguished record. He had flown with the Lafayette Escadrille prior to America's entry into World War I, then with the 103rd Pursuit Squadron. Credited with nine victories, Baer ended the war as the tenth-ranking American ace. On the other hand, Baer had not had much commercial flying experience. Allison "absolutely refused" to pass Baer as ready to command a Loening. Smith overruled him and placed Baer on the regular service to Hankow.[17]

On the morning of December 9, 1930, Baer, his Chinese copilot-student K. F. Pan, and four passengers boarded a Loening for the scheduled trip to Hankow. Baer taxied into the center of the Whangpoo River, then began his take-off run downstream (south to north), just abeam CNAC's hangars at Lunghwa. The green-painted aircraft (green was the traditional color of the

Chinese Postal service) lifted off the water and began to climb straight ahead. A crosswind caused the aircraft to drift to the left. Because of the cowling of the engine on the Loening, the pilot, who sat in the left seat, had little vision to the right and ahead. It is not known whether Baer's copilot ever saw the obstacle. In any event, the lower right wing of the aircraft, close to the fuselage, struck the top of the main mast of a large Chinese junk laying at anchor near the bank of the river. The plane flipped over on its back and plunged into the marshy river bank, upside down, at an angle of approximately 60 degrees. Baer, his copilot, and two passengers perished. The remaining two passengers, including the garrison commander of the Shanghai-Woosung district who was making his first flight, were seriously injured.[18]

Another incident took place two weeks later, one less serious in terms of death and injury, but nearly fatal to the airline. An aide to Chiang Kai-shek called CNAC's local agent at Hankow in the late afternoon of December 24 and reserved all six seats on the next morning's plane to take the Generalissimo and his party to Nanking. Although the flight was due to leave at 8 A.M., the aide asked that the plane be held until 9 A.M. The young Chinese agent notified the American field manager, Ray Ott, of the situation in the morning. Ott could not have cared less. The schedule called for 8 A.M., and the plane would leave at 8 A.M. It did. Chiang and his party showed up a half-hour later. The Generalissimo turned purple when he found that the plane had left without him. He jailed the agent and the field manager. CNAC's head office had learned of the situation by this time and had ordered the plane to return to Hankow. When it arrived, Chiang refused to use the aircraft, threw the pilot into jail, and proceeded to Nanking via a Chinese gunboat.[19]

Westervelt landed in Shanghai the day after this fiasco. In one of his first acts with CNAC he fired Ott and the hapless Chinese agent. He grounded the pilot, C. S. Vaughn, who had not known that Chiang had reserved the plane. Westervelt did not want to dismiss Vaughn, whom he characterized as "an especially valuable pilot [who] has given excellent service," and after a decent interval Vaughn returned to flying status. The young Loening pilot later became assistant vice president for operations with Pan American Airways, in charge of the North Atlantic route.

The Christmas episode seemed to Westervelt symptomatic of the major problem of American employees of CNAC. The incident, he wrote to Keys a few days later, "has grown out of a lack of appreciation by the American personnel of the relation of their activities to the Republic itself." The Americans had an "insular" point of view with respect to the Chinese. They treated the natives haughtily and brusquely, instead of with consideration, courtesy, and respect. He blamed the foreign atmosphere of Shanghai for the ideas that had developed among the Americans in CNAC. The enterprise could only work in partnership with the Chinese. In the future, Westervelt warned, "employees who cannot bring themselves into a proper relation with the facts, can be dispensed with."[20]

There were other problems. Hamilton was "in a state of great perturbation" and wanted to be relieved of his duties. "He is of a temperamental nature," Westervelt explained, "and finds it exceedingly difficult to meet disappointing and discouraging occurances . . . without rather powerful emotional reactions." Traffic along the Yangtze had increased, but the decline in silver prices meant a constant deficit in terms of gold. He predicted that this situation would get worse before it would get better, and CNAC must be prepared for a period of monthly losses. There were sufficient funds to operate for a time but not indefinitely. Progress in extending the river route and preparing for operation on the other routes authorized by the contract had been poor. "It is my opinion," he wrote, "that we must proceed on the establishment of the lines, or abandon them to other operators, an abandonment which would be almost equivalent to an admission by ourselves that we are only half-hearted in our Chinese endeavor."

The picture was not all black. The extent of Nationalist control over the country impressed Westervelt. He had the "definite feeling" that the present government "is working in the interests of the people of China, and in the attempt to build a great unified nation with pride in its own existence and in its nationality." If these initial impressions were correct, Westervelt concluded, then "the opportunities which exist in China are probably beyond those which exist in any other portion of the world at the present time."[21]

Westervelt spent five months in China on this first visit. Besides insuring that the American personnel were indoctrinated with respect to proper behavior toward the Chinese, he directed his main efforts to route expansion and the repair of operating equipment.

Westervelt believed that with only the Shanghai-Hankow route there would "never be any chance of breaking even with the type of operation to which we are now committed." Much of the operating budget represented fixed costs; therefore, the added revenue from expanded service would likely be much greater than the additional operating costs. The Yangtze route beyond Hankow seemed to offer the best prospects for expansion. It took nearly nine days by steamer to travel the 540 miles through the rapids of the Upper Yangtze to Chungking from Hankow. An exchange of letters between Shanghai and Chungking, allowing one day for reply, consumed nearly a month. Air service could reduce this to one week or less.[22]

The first scheduled flight to Ichang left Hankow the afternoon of March 31, 1931. Westervelt rode as passenger, planning to continue up river by steamer and survey the projected expansion to Wanhsien and Chungking. He arrived at Ichang at 5:50 P.M., then boarded a French vessel for the trip to Chungking. The trip up river convinced Westervelt that the route, while difficult, presented no serious operational problem. Traveling through the Yangtze Gorges, he noted that the peaks rose to 3,500 feet and were partially covered by clouds. There were no emergency landing sites; however, the river could be used for emergency landings except in one or two places. Fog often enveloped the valley, but it did not lie on the swift-moving water. An expert pilot in a small 'plane could safely follow the river, flying between the Gorges and underneath the fog.

Westervelt sought an interview with Marshal Liu Hsiang upon reaching Chungking. He found the warlord occupied with "a small war in the interior." Liu's deputy stated that the marshal regretted the previous misunderstanding and would welcome air service. Westervelt then called on the local postal commissioner, from whom he received disappointing news regarding the volume of first-class mail handled at Chungking.

Westervelt stopped at Wanhsien on the return trip from Chungking and visited with General Wang Fun-jao, commander of the local area under Marshal Liu. The general, he noted, was "an exceedingly alert and interesting man of about 45." He had received his military training in Japan, and he did not speak English. "The General has a moustache which is rather pronounced for a Chinese growth of this nature, and wears very heavy dark glasses, which are so heavily colored that his eyes can be seen only very indistinctly through them." Wang apologized for the trouble the previous September. He, too, desired mail service. Contacting the local postal commissioner, Westervelt learned that the bulk of mail to and from Chengtu, the largest city of Szechwan province, passed through Wanhsien. Adding together the figures from Wanhsien and Chungking, Westervelt predicted that the route extension would bring $2,700 a month in air mail revenue alone. "There is a most excellent chance," Westervelt reported, "that this River extension would become almost immediately self supporting, and might even produce some profit."

Westervelt returned to Shanghai on April 14, 1931, two weeks after his departure. "The trip," he wrote, "has served to dispel most of the uncertainty which has existed regarding the up-river conditions, and the practicality of an extension of the air line. We can, now, go ahead with confidence in planning this extension, and, in our belief, it will be successful from a physical as well as financial standpoint."[23]

CNAC completed the initial extension without incident in late April and, as Westervelt had predicted, it turned out to be immediately profitable. Allison made a survey flight further up river on October 11, and regular twice-weekly service to Chungking via Wanhsien commenced on October 31. A preliminary analysis of receipts and expenses, Westervelt noted upon his return to China in November, "indicates that it is already on more than a self-supporting basis."[24]

The second route authorized under the contract extended from Shanghai/Nanking to Peking. Westervelt preferred to push ahead on the third route, along the coast to Canton, because the Peking line would have to compete with excellent rail service; but the new managing director, Ho Chi-wei, pressed him to begin the Peking service with the five Stinsons and Chinese pilots obtained from the old Shanghai-Chengtu Line. The added costs of the operation did not appear to be great. The Chinese pilots only made $85 to $200 per month. While this was high compared with salaries of Chinese military pilots ($30 to $85), it did not amount to much in terms of American wages. Also, the equipment had been stored in warehouses since the merger and might as well be put to productive use. Captain Allison, however, did not consider the Chinese aviators, who had been flying as copilots on the Loenings, qualified to handle the operation with safety. In addition, Westervelt learned that the single-engine Stinson monoplanes were powered by Wright 300-hp engines of the "unfortunate" 1929 series. "They are inherently of bad design," Westervelt noted, "due to insufficient cooling surfaces on the cylinders." Westervelt had a problem. He did not intend to inform the Chinese of the deficiencies of Curtiss-Wright products; also, he sympathized with their desire to participate more fully in the flight operations of the company. He finally decided to go ahead with the Peking line. He ordered modifications on the engines. He pointed out to Allison that the terrain between Shanghai and Nanking was flat with abundant emergency landing areas. The Chinese pilots could navigate by following the railroad tracks. Westervelt and Allison agreed on a six-month trial period during which no passengers would be carried.[25]

Service to Peking began on April 15. Operations during the first week were erratic, with few trips completed even close to schedule. The amount of mail carried, Westervelt observed, had been "of ridiculously small poundage." Engine failures during May threatened to end the service. Westervelt found out to his disgust that the engines had been only partly overhauled because the maintenance staff had not been aware of more recent engineering bulletins. The old engines had to be replaced. Although this would be a serious financial blow to CNAC, as new engines would cost $14,000 to $16,000, Westervelt decided to go ahead. He suspended service on the Peking route on June 8 and awaited the arrival of the new power plants.[26]

Progress lagged on the coastal route to Canton. Due to a severe shortage of equipment, a survey flight could not be scheduled until May. When an aircraft did become available, the formation of an anti-Nationalist government in Canton precluded the flight. Westervelt recommended to the managing director that service be delayed until March 1932. The managing director agreed.[27]

Westervelt's efforts to extend CNAC's routes produced mixed results, but his attempt to solve the airline's equipment problems proved more successful. Only three of CNAC's six Loenings were in operating condition when Westervelt arrived in December 1930. Baer's ill-fated aircraft would require major reconstruction if it were ever to fly again, and two other planes were in various states of disrepair. To add to CNAC's troubles, another aircraft suffered extensive damage in February 1931 when a pilot landed gear-down in the water. Westervelt located Wong Tsu, the MIT graduate who had earlier worked on the B & W seaplane and who had returned to China after the war and established a pioneering aircraft factory at Foochow, and offered him a contract to rehabilitate the damaged aircraft. Wong accepted. He set up shop at Lunghwa and undertook an extensive maintenance and repair program, involving the complete rebuilding of severely damaged aircraft. The rebuilt planes, Captain Allison recalled, "were of excellent quality—in fact in some regards they were better than the originals." Wong also embarked on a weight-saving project, in which the Loenings were converted into flying boats. He removed the landing gear, had the wheel wells skinned over, bilge lines inserted, water rudder installed, and so forth. This greatly improved the performance of the underpowered Loenings. Westervelt could report in May that Wong "is doing a remarkably effective job, and at an astonishing low price." Loening pilot C. S. Vaughn, recalling his experiences with CNAC, believes that Wong's activities "more than any one influence kept CNAC afloat."[28]

Operations had been poor during January 1931, with only 75 percent of scheduled trips completed, mainly due to extensive fog. The weather remained unfavorable in February. March brought sunny skies and increased revenue. "Our Chinese investment," Westervelt reported at the end of the month, "is not only not a wash-out but will eventually fully justify itself." Successful service to Ichang in April and increased traffic on the other stations along the Yangtze route produced the highest receipts for any month since the airline began operations. As Westervelt prepared to return to the United States in May, he wrote to New York that "about as much will have been accomplished by then as can be accomplished." He concluded: "The possibilities of securing enough business to cover all out-of-pocket expenditures, does not appear in any way unpromising."[29]

Westervelt had wrought many needed changes during his five months in China. Unsuitable personnel had been weeded out of the organization, beginnings of a better relationship between Chinese and American employees could be seen, the extension of the Yangtze route to Chungking had been well started, and the equipment problems were on the way being solved. In terms of the long-range future of CNAC, however, Westervelt took his most significant action when he selected a new American representative to replace the ineffectual Minard Hamilton.

— II —

William Langhorne Bond, Westervelt's choice to take charge of the American interests in China, would prove a man of rare talent and temperament in the difficult years to come. Striking parallels can be drawn between Bond and Didier Daurat, the great managing director of the Lignes Aérienne Latécoère and model for Revière in Saint-Exupéry's *Vol de Nuit*. The Latécoère line pioneered air mail service from France to South America by way of Africa during the 1920s. "The success of the venture," Marcel Migeo has written of Daurat, "was largely due to his faith in it, his will to succeed, and the will to succeed with which he managed to inspire his men." A modest, serious, determined and dedicated

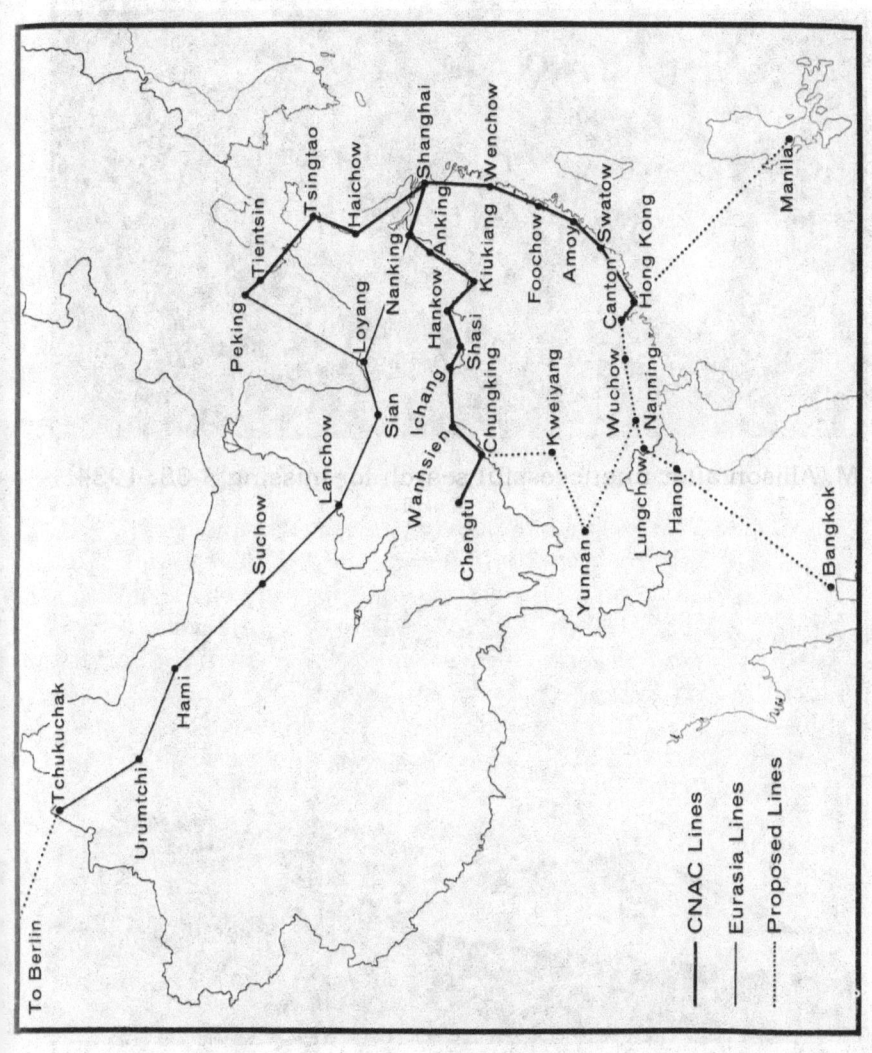

Air lines existing and proposed, 1933

E. M. Allison after unsuccessful search for missing S-38, 1934

C N A C's first permanent hangar, Shanghai, 1934

individual, Daurat was known for his ruthlessness and his intolerance of failure and mistakes. He loved his pilots, but he masked his deepest feelings behind a taciturn demeanor. He possessed great strength and great weakness. But, as Migeo has pointed out, "Had Monsieur Daurat not been what he was ... the line would not have endured." The same could be said of W. L. Bond.[30]

Bond shared many of Daurat's characteristics. From the time Bond left New York for China in February 1931 until he left Hong Kong at the end of 1949, he recalled, "I was never faced with any situation except that of survival." CNAC stood on the brink of failure countless times during these years. It survived in large part because Bond stubbornly refused to admit defeat. When pressed on the motives for his actions, this shy, reticent man could only reply: "I seem to be a stubborn man with a one track mind and little imagination." But management of the airline was more than just a job. It became Bond's passion and gave meaning to his existence. This kind of devotion cannot be explained as a "lack of imagination."[31]

Bond ran a gravel plant for the Miami Gravel Company of Miamitown, Ohio, at the time Charles Lindbergh flew the Atlantic in 1927. This epic flight prompted Bond to take his first airplane ride with a barnstorming pilot. It was a case of love at first flight. Westervelt, who had married Bond's first cousin, Rieta Langhorne, found a job for the new air enthusiast at the Curtiss-Caproni factory in Baltimore. Westervelt was then general manager of the company that would produce aircraft designed by Gianni Caproni. The market crash came just as the factory neared completion. The plant was stripped of machinery, and Bond stayed on "more or less as a glorified watchman." Meanwhile, he took the courses in aviation at Johns Hopkins University offered by Curtiss-Wright Flying Service, and he secured his private pilot's license.[32]

Dissatisfied with Hamilton and Smith, Westervelt asked that Bond be sent to China. Bond did not hesitate. "I had had one pay cut [at Curtiss-Caproni]," he explained, "everyone did, but I knew that the next cut would mean amputation from the payroll for me so I was happy to go to China for the same pay as the chief mechanic [$500 a month], who had a pre-crash contract." Bond called at the Curtiss-Wright offices in New York before leaving for the Far East. He found Keys unwell. Keys had little to say about the project and did not seem interested in China. Bond's longest interview was with Thomas Morgan, who headed the Sperry Gyroscope Division in the Curtiss-Wright complex. They talked mainly about bridge construction. Morgan admitted that he knew little about airline operations and less about China. He believed, however, that the main problem came down to the lack of common sense by the people who had been sent to China. Bond, he said at the close of the interview, appeared to have common sense and would likely do well.[33]

Bond reached Shanghai on March 17, 1931. His first night produced a fair taste of what was to come. He went to see Westervelt. Bond later recalled the scene:

"Bond," Westervelt said, "this situation is as bad as it can be. If you burn down the hangar and blow up the planes you would not make it any worse."

"Well," Bond replied, "that is encouraging anyway."

"What in hell do you mean by that?" Westervelt shot back.

Bond answered: "I can't fail. It has already been done for us and you know it. But that doesn't mean I can't succeed."

Westervelt undoubtedly exaggerated the situation with CNAC, at least in part, for dramatic effect. Bond also exaggerated a bit. "I never thought I could succeed," he later wrote, "but I never admitted it even to myself. When your back is against the wall you don't look back."[34]

Bond first turned to the festering morale problem in CNAC. He found a widespread sense of defeat among the American personnel. Harry Smith told newly arrived pilots not to buy any furniture because they would not be around long enough to use it. This defeatism showed up in the increasing number of accidents and generally lax operating procedures. Also, the attitude of the Americans toward the Chinese, as Westervelt had observed, left much to be desired. Bond believed with Westervelt that there would be no problem with the Chinese if only common sense and common courtesy were used. "The idea of most of the

Americans of common sense and courtesy," Bond commented, "was to be superior and patronizing as hell." Bond called the American personnel together for a little lecture. If aviation could not succeed in China, he told them, there had to be one of two things wrong: either there was no future in aviation or they were not the right people for the job. He called upon the pilots to improve the "image" of the company. You cannot be boisterous in the club, he said, and expect people to want to fly with you. You have to live aviation all the time so that people will have faith in you and want to fly.[35]

Bond's words did not sit too well with some of the older pilots. Daurat had commanded a squadron during World War I, and his men had accepted him as a full-fledged member of the close-knit fraternity of professional pilots. But Bond had only a private pilot's license and no experience in running an airline. Bond's philosophy in dealing with the pilots was "to treat them like men and like gentlemen." The question, said Bond, was not of his getting along with them, but of their getting along with him. Most of the pilots accepted Bond's authority, if somewhat reluctantly. Harry Smith, however, considered himself a member of the "Old School." Neither a retired naval captain nor an ex-gravel-contractor could tell him how to run an airline. Smith exited the scene in late August.[36]

Bond carried through on the groundwork that had been laid by Westervelt in the months that followed. Radio stations, manned by Chinese operators, were installed on the route beyond Ichang. Wong's men continued with the repair and renovation of the airline's fleet. The Stinsons for the Peking service received new engines. Bond reduced the operating budget under instructions from Westervelt by returning three American radio operators to the United States and allowing the contracts of four mechanics to expire. He replaced only two men. Also, Bond assumed the duties of both Hamilton and Smith after their departure. All this resulted in a net savings of $32,000 a year. While operating costs went down, mileage flown increased 130 percent.[37]

As had happened in the past, and would happen again in the

future with frustrating regularity, just as the airline's prospects brightened, conditions in China took a turn for the worse. The summer of 1931 brought the most severe floods in the nation's history, disrupting service along the Yangtze. At the same time, civil war once again threatened to plunge the country into chaos, as the left wing of the ruling Kuomintang party split with the right-wing faction led by Chiang Kai-shek. The dissidents gathered at Canton and proclaimed their independence on May 28. War between Canton and Nanking failed to break out only because a common enemy loomed on the horizon. Fighting flared up in Manchuria in September between the Japanese Kwantung army and the forces of Chang Hsueh-liang. Chiang Kai-shek realized that his army was no match for the Japanese and could only appeal to the League of Nations. The conflict in Manchuria prompted an outburst of nationalistic sentiment and a boycott of Japanese goods. Accusing the government of adopting a dilatory attitude, students stormed the Ministry of Foreign Affairs in late September and injured the minister.[38]

Westervelt returned to China in November 1931. He seemed pleased with the airline's progress. Revenue had taken a turn for the better after the decline in late summer due to the floods. In fact, November promised to show the smallest loss since the organization of CNAC. Operating expenses were down, and the price of silver had been advancing for several months. The Stinsons, equipped with new engines, had been performing satisfactorily on Peking line since resumption of operations on September 12. Passengers were now being carried (since October 15), and, while traffic remained light, improvements could be expected as the service gained a reputation for reliability.

On the other hand, there were problems on the Hankow-Chungking route for which Westervelt had only himself to blame. Over the strenuous objections of the airline's pilots, Westervelt had insisted on ordering several Wright Cyclone replacement engines for the Loenings. Westervelt had recognized the superiority of the Pratt & Whitney Hornet engines, which had hitherto given excellent service. In fact, he had written: "If CNAC were my own personal possession, I would stick to Hornets." But CNAC was supposed to be a showcase for Curtiss-Wright products, so Westervelt had ordered the Cyclones. This had resulted in a series of engine failures on the dangerous Hankow-Chungking service. No one had been injured, but there had been some bad moments for both passengers and crew.

The incident of the replacement engines pointed out the problems that arise when an aircraft manufacturer operates an airline. It also revealed a rather unpleasant side of Sino-American relations in CNAC. "This has been a most costly and unpleasant incident for our interests," Westervelt wrote to New York. "Not only has it cost Curtiss-Wright some thousands of dollars, but has cost CNAC many thousands of dollars. So far as Curtiss-Wright prestige is concerned: The American personnel here . . . have done everything they could to cover up the details. Altho our discussions with New York has [sic] been very frank, our discussions with our Chinese associates have not been along similar lines at all."[39]

Overall, however, Westervelt concluded that the situation in China appeared encouraging. "The improvement," he reported to New York, "is a great and gratifying one. We have the ground work of an organization which is already giving excellent service, and which will steadily improve in this regard. It can be expanded indefinitely, and is built on the proper basis of eventual Chinese ownership and operation. Bond has done a good job, and in a very great degree has justified my confidence in him."[40]

Westervelt wrote in the eye of a typhoon. The Peking line ran into severe problems at the end of the year. The inexperienced Chinese pilots on this route proved unable to cope with the miserable weather of late November and December. A Stinson crashed into the side of Taishan Mountain on November 18, killing the pilot, copilot and two passengers. Several weeks later, two aircraft went down on the same day due to fog in the Peking area. There were no fatalities but the planes suffered extensive damage. CNAC suspended service on the Peking line indefinitely on the day after Christmas as Wong Tsu's workshop filled up with crippled Stinsons. This was no great financial loss to the company. The Peking service during its period of sporadic operations in 1931 had carried a total of only 27 passengers, most of whom had traveled under passes issued by Ministry of Communications, and 37,708 pounds of mail.[41]

Political conditions also worsened. The fall of Manchuria to the Japanese caused criticism of the government by students and others. Also, government income plummeted, due both to loss of funds from Manchuria and a general slump in economic activity. The Canton dissidents had been clamoring for a chance to run the government, and Chiang Kai-shek decided to let them try, believing that they were bound to fail. The Canton group took power in late December for what was to prove a brief and unsuccessful tenure of office.[42]

While the political situation in China proceeded from crisis to crisis, the cash assets of CNAC neared depletion. The last of four cash payments by the Chinese under terms of the contract of July 1930 came on December 1. As the airline had not yet reached a break-even point, additional funds were needed to cover losses. Westervelt had returned to China to make arrangements with the government for additional money to continue the operation of the airline. "There have been few worse times than the present to negotiate a business arrangement with a Chinese Minister," Westervelt wrote to his wife in early December. "The whole structure is liable to collapse on a day's notice. I don't know what to recommend to my directors."[43]

The Chinese directors of CNAC wanted to vote a capital increase of $222,000 for 1932. The Americans would pay their share of $100,000 on January 1, 1932. The Chinese would contribute $122,000 on July 1, to be loaned by the American partner. In short, Curtiss-Wright would put up all the cash. When Westervelt refused to consider this arrangement, the Chinese asked if the Americans would be willing to loan $35,000 to the company, to be repaid out of first profits. This sum would cover operating deficits in American funds for approximately six months. Westervelt recommended acceptance of this proposal "most strongly" to New York. The money represented only a 5 percent increase in Curtiss-Wright's capital investment in China. Westervelt said that the airline would cease operations and everything would be lost without these funds. He expressed his continued belief that Curtiss-Wright stood a reasonable chance of recovering its entire investment, and even making a profit, provided the political situation remained reasonably stable.[44]

New York, understandably, proved reluctant to sink more capital into the venture in light of political conditions in China. Despite grave reservations, Curtiss-Wright finally agreed to cover deficits in American funds up to $13,000, which would give CNAC a "breathing space" of two or three months. New York advised Westervelt to use this offer, and the promise of a further loan (with adequate security) for new equipment to operate the Canton route, as bargaining counters to obtain a subsidy from the Chinese government for the operation of air services.[45]

Negotiations proceeded in the midst of increasingly chaotic conditions. A powerful Japanese naval squadron lay at anchor on Shanghai's doorstep. An active Chinese boycott was crippling Japanese trade, and Japan demanded that it end. Serious clashes between Chinese and Japanese residents of Shanghai occurred on January 18 and 20, 1932, prompting a threat of retaliation by the Japanese naval commander. Managing Director General Ho "[and I] are seriously discussing the question of how to make CNAC financially stable," Westervelt reported on January 26. "At least, he is serious, therefore, I see no reason why I shouldn't be. This is hardly correct; I can see various reasons why it seems more or less absured at the instant to be serious, but since the General is serious it seems the courteous thing to be serious." The present situation, he continued, should not cause discouragement. "It is too absurd for that. One's attitude should be of wonder, and of hopefulness—slightly tinctured by prayer. Since China is polytheist, he should play safe and pray to every God he can think of."[46]

Considerable anger lurked behind Westervelt's outward flippancy. He had worked long and hard on the China project, and everything seemed about to collapse. He kept up a good front when he wrote to his superiors in New York, but his letters to his wife occasionally reflected the depths of his frustration. He now castigated the Nationalist government he had once praised. "The Chinese are paying in national humiliation for their own shortcomings," he wrote on January 28. "With few exceptions their politicans are thieves and grafters of the most cold blooded, selfish and unpatriotic type, and the day when they may attain to the status of a real nation seems distant."[47]

On the night of January 28/29, 1932, as Westervelt poured out his feelings to his wife, Japanese troops attacked Shanghai. Warships and aircraft bombarded the city the next day. Bond went to Nanking on the morning flight on January 29. Westervelt ordered him to remain there and suspended operations. Bond wired back: "CONSIDER IT IMPERATIVE WE KEEP THIS LINE RUNNING STOP ITS FUTURE DEPENDS ON IT STOP AM NOT BEING INSUBORDINATE BUT BELIEVE YOUR DECISION WAS MERELY FOR OUR SAFETY STOP WE ARE COMING THROUGH STOP"

"The last STOP was unnecessary," Westervelt explained to his wife. "We would have stopped there automatically."[48]

That evening Westervelt received information that the Japanese planned to attack a Chinese arsenal adjacent to CNAC's facilities at Lunghwa. He ordered the station evacuated and the planes moved. When the attack failed to materialize, Westervelt considered ways by which service could be resumed with reasonable assurance of safety. He sought to arrange a temporary transfer of ownership so as to make the airline an entirely American company, thus affording it the protection of the American flag. But the Chinese, he reported, would not consider it "due to national pride—which manifests itself so often in ridiculous ways." Westervelt also thought that the time was ripe to seek temporary financial assistance from the American government, and he asked New York to discuss the matter in Washington.[49]

Cyril McNear of Curtiss-Wright called at the State Department's Division of Far Eastern Affairs on February 3. McNear asked if the department believed that the best interests of the United States in China would be served by an approach to the Post Office Department for a subsidy to resume operations on the Yangtze. The Far Eastern Division agreed that reopening the

Yangtze route would benefit American interests in the area. It seemed unlikely, however, that the Post Office would be willing to spend $25,000 a month to subsidize the line. Also, such a direct American governmental interest in a Chinese company might be misinterpreted by the Japanese. "There is a further possibility," the division observed, "that Chinese military forces might comandeer the planes . . . and thus use American-owned and American-subsidized aircraft in offensive measures against Japanese military and naval forces." In light of the above, the division concluded that "it would appear undesirable for the Department to further any attempts to secure, on behalf of the China National Aviation Corporation, a government subsidy of any sort."[50]

Despite continued fighting in China and lack of support by the American government, Westervelt deemed the situation sufficiently stable to resume operations on February 9. At the same time, he developed a plan to overcome the objections of the State Department and to serve broad American interests in Asia. Westervelt believed that recent Japanese activity in China portended a clash between the United States and Japan, a view common in American naval circles since the end of World War I. Certainly, the changed circumstances in the Far East meant that it would be futile to consider independence for the Philippines in the near future, as the Philippines would be a major American naval base in any war with Japan. "Therefore," he wrote, "the speeding of communications to these islands becomes important." He proposed operation of an air service by a wholly American-owned company from Manila to Amoy, a port city in Fukien province some 450 miles northwest of the tip of Luzon. Air mail would connect with CNAC at Amoy for distribution in China.[51]

Westervelt secured strong support for the scheme from American officials in China. Julean Arnold, commercial attaché in Shanghai, favored the plan from the standpoint of American trade, and he sent a lengthy memorandum to Clarence M. Young, assistant secretary for aeronautics in the Department of Commerce, urging governmental support for the project. "The potentialities of our trade with China," Arnold wrote, "will be greater when improved communications make it possible to tap those centers of population and resources of the Asiatic continent now out of economic communications with much of the rest of the world." Young sent the memorandum to Senator Tasker L. Odie, member of the Committee on Post Offices and a friend of commercial aviation. The senator had Arnold's memorandum read into the *Congressional Record*.[52]

Edwin S. Cunningham, consul general in Shanghai, agreed with Arnold. He told the State Department that a mail subsidy for the Manila-Amoy service would be "of inestimable value to American business." By supporting the project, he continued, "it is believed that the United States government will be taking the most important step in the promotion of American trade that has been taken in the past two decades."[53]

The American ambassador, Nelson T. Johnson, placed his considerable influence behind the project. "the scheme interests me," he wrote in a personal letter to Undersecretary of State William R. Castle, "because, during my 24 years connection with this field of activity, I have been anxious to find some way whereby we could use the Philippine Islands more effectively as a basis for operation in Asia and the Pacific. We have had this springboard now for over thirty years, but have made little or no use of it." It would be unfortunate if the German-backed Eurasia line supplanted American aviation interests in China. Support of the Manila-Amoy route would mean "that mail and the influence that goes with it will flow from the Yangtze Valley through the United States toward Europe, rather than in the opposite direction, as would be the case if the Germans win in this matter." Johnson concluded: "The scheme seems to me a feasible one; I am sure that it is an important one; and I feel that it is worthy of the serious attention of everyone concerned, especially at this time when a little effort out here of this kind will go far towards helping to restore business and other morale in this area."[54]

These entreaties failed to move the Far Eastern Division. The division considered the question from the broad perspective of the relationship between American political and commercial policy in Asia. "In other countries," the division noted, "most conspicuously Japan, France, and Great Britain, business interests and their government work hand in hand for the promotion of national trade in and with China. The governments are willing to take political risks by way of making opportunities for and, in general, promoting the commercial activities of their nationals." The American government, on the other hand, has refrained from this kind of direct involvement in commercial enterprises abroad. "If this government wishes to play a competitive game in the manner in which it is played by our competitors," the division observed, "and if it is willing to take the political risks, the present case offers an excellent opportunity. If this government is not ready to do these things, it is believed that this opportunity should be turned down. For, unquestionably, entry into this field would tend to increase our political liabilities in relation to a situation where competition is becoming more and more keen." The American government decided not to "play a competitive game," and Westervelt's scheme collapsed.[55]

Fighting in China tapered off in early March 1932. The belligerents signed an armistice on May 5, and Japan withdrew its troops from China by the end of the month. While the war had thwarted Westervelt's negotiations with the Chinese, it did produce several encouraging developments in the end. First, hostility toward Japan brought together the Canton and Nanking factions of the Kuomintang. The Canton group had demonstrated its inability to rule the country and handed back power to Chiang Kai-shek. Second, the war had interrupted steamer service along the Yangtze to the benefit of CNAC's mail and passenger traffic. Finally, the conflict had made Chinese officials forcefully aware of the importance of military aviation to the survival of the nation. This last development—China's need for a modern air force—would occupy Westervelt's time and attention in the months ahead. As the fate of the military aviation program bore a direct relationship to the continued existence of Curtiss-Wright's commercial venture in China, it merits detailed treatment.

— III —

Westervelt had been trying to interest the Chinese in Curtiss-Wright military aircraft for some time. In the wake of the Shanghai Incident, which had revealed the vulnerability of Chinese cities to aerial attack and the woeful state of the Nationalist air force, Westervelt again approached the government with proposals to develop military aviation.

"I take it for granted," Westervelt wrote to Finance Minister T. V. Soong in March 1932, "that the events of the last few weeks have sufficiently demonstrated the significance of air power as differentiated from the lack of air power." Not only could the Japanese landing at Shanghai have been prevented, but air power could have done substantial damage to Japan's naval forces. Looking to the future, Westervelt held out a glowing prospect: the day when Chinese aircraft could strike the Japanese homeland. "Due to the peculiarly inflammable nature of Japanese cities, such planes could easily carry sufficient inflammable bombs of small weight to burn down the major portion of most Japanese cities, and to cause enormous economic losses which would have direct repercussion on the military efforts of that country."

Westervelt then set forth a program to meet the "extreme minimum" of Chinese aviation requirements. First, China should secure the services of a high-ranking American army officer to act as adviser on aeronautical matters. Second, the Chinese government should make arrangements for the training of Chinese aviators and technical personnel in the United States. Third, a small aircraft factory should be built in Shanghai to serve as the nucleus for a Chinese aviation industry. Finally, commercial air service should be expanded throughout China, and a modern aerodrome constructed at Shanghai.[56]

Minister Soong responded enthusiastically to the proposal, and he placed Dr. Arthur N. Young, American-born economist and financial adviser to the Chinese government, in charge of the project. Young eventually decided to work through Major Edward P. Howard, trade commissioner in Shanghai for the Department of Commerce, rather than Westervelt in order to give the government a freer hand in choosing equipment.⁵⁷

Howard drew up the outline of a training program in early April. Initially, the plan called for twelve aircraft and eight instructors to train fifty pilots within one year. The package would cost approximately $200,000. A more elaborate proposal for an expanded training mission followed. Young, with Soong's authorization, told Howard to make the necessary arrangements.⁵⁸

Colonel John H. Jouett would head the mission to China. Jouett had excellent qualifications. A squadron commander during World War I, Jouett had been chief of personnel of the Air Corps during the 1920s. He had resigned from the service in 1930 to direct the Aviation Division of Standard Oil of New Jersey. Minister Soong formally approved the appointment on May 24. He made deposits in American banks to cover advances on salaries and travel expenses, and he arranged the necessary credits for the purchase of aircraft and spare parts.⁵⁹

The Commerce Department, which had made the necessary contacts for Howard in the United States, could not have been more pleased. Leighton W. Rogers, chief of the Aeronautics Trade Division, quickly spread the good news to American aircraft manufacturers. "There is no doubt in my mind," he wrote to an officer of United Aircraft Exports, "that these activities . . . will be of tremendous assistance to American manufacturers selling in the Chinese market."⁶⁰

The State Department showed less enthusiasm. Shortly after Jouett and his party applied for passports, the Far Eastern Division called Rogers in for a talk. It was his understanding, Rogers said, that the State Department would have no objections to a *civilian* mission. Maxwell G. Hamilton, assistant chief of the Far Eastern Division, answered that this view "did not square entirely with the Department's attitude." American policy, he said, was not to become associated *in any way* with Chinese military aviation. Rogers then went on to minimize the role played by Commerce. His department, Rogers emphasized, "had merely rendered such informal assistance as would be rendered to any American citizen going abroad and . . . the Department of

Commerce was not officially associated with this project." Rogers apparently had second thoughts on this point. Later in the day he telephoned Hamilton and explained "that this whole situation had now gone pretty far; that the Department of Commerce had transmitted messages to and from the Chinese government and the interested Americans; that the interested Americans had signed a contract; that the Chinese government had advanced money; and that the interested Americans had made the necessary arrangements to leave for China." The State Department noted its displeasure, but took no action. It was certainly in no position to interpose strong objections to a project that might result in millions of dollars of sorely needed exports during the Great Depression.[61]

Colonel Jouett, in the meantime, had been gathering his staff. He examined the records of some 200 recent graduates of Air Corps training schools, who were in the reserve, and selected nine flying instructors. As a former chief of personnel, he apparently had no trouble obtaining access to the necessary files. Jouett also secured the service of a flight surgeon, four mechanics, and a secretary. The party sailed from the West Coast on the *S.S. President Hoover* in early June. En route, training courses were laid out and textbooks were brought up to date. The program would be based "on the teachings and policies of the Army Air Corps schools."[62]

The Jouett mission reached Shanghai on July 8, 1932. Jouett called on Minister Soong and submitted three training programs. The first proposal, based on Howard's original plan, involved training 150 pilots over a three-year period and construction of as few facilities as possible. It would cost an estimated $4.2 million. The second scheme envisioned training 300 pilots and establishment of a permanent training center at a cost of $8.2 million. The third plan, similar to the second, added specialized training. Under this program, to cost $13.7 million, students would receive 70 hours of advanced training in pursuit, bombardment, or observation after 60 hours of primary and 70 hours of basic training. Minister Soong approved a slightly modified version of the third plan.[63]

Jouett proceeded to Hangchow, the site selected for training, in late August. Nestled in the mountains some 100 miles south of Shanghai and situated next to a large lake, Hangchow was one of the more attractive locales in China. Unfortunately, as Jouett discovered upon his arrival, the scenic beauty was matched only by the inadequacy of training facilities. He found a field about 8,600 square feet in area, two small hangars, a few wooden barracks dating from the Manchu period, and a handful of obsolete aircraft. During the next five months, however, the Americans made remarkable progress. "The field has been cleared of all obstructions," Major Howard reported in December, "a huge modern hangar over 300 feet long is nearing completion, school buildings have been remodeled and are in use, electricity supplied, and a deep well is being dug, a radio station erected and operating, an operations office completed, a large auditorium and numerous officers' quarters well on their way to completion, woodworking shop, engine overhaul, machine shop, airplane repair shop and dope room completed with machinery being installed."[64]

Within an equally short time, Jouett made substantial progress in modernizing the administration and command structure of the Chinese Air Force. There had been no uniform system of promotion and salary for aviators prior to Jouett's arrival. Political influence determined promotion. The Finance Department paid salaries to unit commanders for distribution. "As might be expected," one observer noted, "this system resulted in widespread abuses on the part of the unit chiefs, as for instance, aircraft squadron leaders, on more than one occasion, are said to have required subordinate officers to take leaves of absence without pay in order that funds appropriated for their salary might be used to recoup financial losses of the leaders."[65]

Jouett revamped the entire promotion and pay system. He insured that seniority and merit determined promotion, and he guaranteed adequate compensation. He also reorganized the command structure of the Air Force. A disciple of General William Mitchell, Jouett advocated an independent air force. Accordingly, he removed the service from the control of the minister of war and established a General Headquarters Air Force directly under Chiang Kai-shek. "This," Jouett commented, "gives us practically the British form of organization which I have always believed to be the soundest." Jouett's objective was operational efficiency; Chiang undoubtedly approved reorganization of the command structure because it placed him in more effective control.[66]

Flight training got underway on September 17 with a refresher course for 50 officers. Of these, 6 pilots failed the physical examination and 17 were washed out for lack of flying ability. The 27 survivors required an average of four hours and twenty minutes of instruction to solo. Jouett retained the 9 most competent pilots as instructors, but 2 of these eventually had to be relieved. In all, some 200 Chinese pilots took the refresher course and only 50 survived. Appointment to the Air Force had been based on political influence. The government came under great pressure to reinstate the failed aviators, but Chiang Kai-shek backed Jouett.[67]

The first class of 88 cadets commenced training on October 18, 1932. These young men were from the elite of China. While the military profession traditionally had been held in low esteem, aviation was different. Aviation was Western, it was technical, and it was admired. The cadets were well educated; in fact, three-quarters of the class could understand some English. And they were enthusiastic. Nearly every student showed up with a copy of Charles Lindbergh's *We*, an account of his transatlantic flight.

Jouett divided the class into 15 sections, with five or six cadets assigned to individual American and Chinese instructors. He patterned flight instruction on that offered by the American Air Corps at Randolph Field, Texas. The group average proved to be 12 hours of dual instruction before solo, and the attrition rate of 50 percent compared favorably with that found in American training schools. In addition to flight training, the Jouett mission provided instruction for engineering officers, mechanics, meteorologists, photo interpreters, and flight surgeons. "Actual accomplishments since July 8," Major Howard summed up in

December 1932, "are beyond the most sanguine expectations of anyone who had had previous experience with Chinese methods."[68]

The Central Aviation School's honeymoon ended early in 1933. Chiang Kai-shek apparently grew suspicious of Minister Soong's control over what by then promised to be the effective military force in China and, in March, the Generalissimo moved the aviation school to Loyang in Honan Province, where he could exert more control over it in the event of trouble. The school fared ill at Loyang. Dust storms interrupted operations. Also, Minister Soong stopped appropriations for gasoline and new equipment. The difficulties between Chiang and Soong were smoothed over in a few weeks, and the school returned to Hangchow. But Soong was now out of the picture. General Keh Ching-on, whom Chiang appointed chief of the Aviation Bureau, took over supervision of the school. Whereas Soong had taken an active and sympathetic interest in the project, Jouett complained that General Keh "was completely ignorant and uninformed as regards aviation matters and not at all prone to ask for advice or listen when given." Jouett did not find Keh's successor, General Hsu Pei King, much better. Employing techniques that he would use throughout his career, Chiang Kai-shek had made the new force more responsive to his will, but he paid a high price.[69]

Another, and far more serious, development was the arrival in China of an Italian aviation mission. H. H. Kung, whose political star had risen following Soong's departure, had been greatly impressed by the Italians during a visit to Europe. Mussolini seemed eager to help China—and at bargain prices. He remitted a portion of the Boxer indemnity to finance an initial shipment of aircraft, and he approved a long-term credit for purchase of additional planes. He also dispatched an official mission, headed by General Lordi, to supervise training and furnish technical assistance.[70]

This situation irked Jouett. Not only did his comprehensive plan for modernization of the Chinese Air Force seem in danger, but his pride was hurt. "I am Aviation Adviser or I am not," he wrote to Dr. Young. Furthermore, Jouett continued, he did not intend to become "a temporary football for the Chinese."[71]

Jouett flew to Nanking to see Chiang and find out where he stood. The Generalissimo told him, Jouett reported, "that the Italians would not be assigned to any duty until I had been consulted and that due to my length of service with the Chinese Government and everything else considered I was senior advisor." Somewhat mollified, Jouett went back to the business of training an air force.[72]

November 12, 1933, Sun Yat-sen's birthday, was a gala occasion for Jouett and his young students. More than 10,000 spectators gathered at Nanking on this national holiday to watch the first official review of the new air force. Loud applause greeted the aerial demonstration by one squadron of Fleet trainers, one squadron of Douglas observation planes, and two squadrons of Curtiss-Wright Hawk pursuit airplanes. The aircraft were American-made and the pilots American-trained but, as one observer noted, the show was a Chinese triumph. "Chinese officialdom had ample justification for its manifestation of pride in China's youth," he continued, "and it is easy to understand the spirit which prompted the crowd to roar its applause at the Chinese air units as they soared and cavorted overhead."[73]

Jouett's cadets had occasion for a more practical test of their ability when a rebellion broke out in Fukien province. Although the Nationalist government had a much larger army, the Fukien regime had the 19th Route Army, the unit that had fought the Japanese to a standstill outside Shanghai in early 1932. Chiang called upon his new air force. The rebellion collapsed, and most observers credited the 60 cadets from the Central Aviation School with playing a key role in the Nationalist victory.[74]

Although the effectiveness of the American-trained air force had been amply demonstrated, Jouett's position did not improve. The Italian mission simply had too many advantages. First of all, it had the full support of the Italian government. Mussolini, in fact, raised the Italian legation to the status of an embassy, thereby becoming the only government besides the Soviet Union to accord Chiang such recognition. Second, it was much less expensive for the financially hard-pressed Chinese. Finally, Japanese pressure against the American mission became intense during 1934. The Japanese had complained, both publicly and officially, about the Jouett mission ever since its arrival. In April 1934, Eiju Amau, a spokesman for the Japanese Foreign Office, reiterated in the strongest possible terms Japan's opposition to foreign military assistance for China. Although the Japanese continued to press China concerning the American mission, they said little about the Italians.[75]

The uncertainty of the mission's status caused increasing dissension among Jouett's staff. Jouett was a hard taskmaster. Since he lacked military authority, he had to rely on cooperation and high morale to get the job done. Morale now stood at low ebb. On one occasion, all the instructors except one refused to report for duty. There was little that Jouett could do.[76]

In an attempt to buttress the position of the American mission, Jouett appealed directly to President Franklin D. Roosevelt. Pointing to increasing Italian domination of Chinese aviation, Jouett suggested that the president write to Chiang Kai-shek, express his personal pleasure with the work that had been done by the Americans, and suggest a continuance of the mission. Jouett's letter was referred to the Department of State for comment.[77]

The State Department had never supported the mission, and it was even less inclined to do so in the summer of 1934, the eve of the Nye investigations of the munitions industry. Furthermore, the government had responded to the Amau announcement with a policy calculated to avoid offending the Japanese if at all possible. State recommended that the president stay clear of the situation. Roosevelt agreed.[78]

The contract of the American mission expired on June 1, 1935. Jouett, after being awarded the Order of the Commander of the Jade, returned to the United States. Although a few Americans remained in China as instructors, the Italians were now the dominant force in the field of military aviation.[79]

The results of the Jouett mission were impressive. More than 300 cadets earned their wings at the Central Aviation School between 1932 and 1935, and another 250 were in training when Jouett left China. Facilities had been constructed that would permit continuation of the program for a long time. "The American mission," one observer commented, "has succeeded in introducing a program of training, coupled with a degree of efficiency, previously unknown to China." Indeed, China had the nucleus of a modern, well-trained, and well-equipped air force at the time of Jouett's departure. But the Chinese had made a disastrous error when they turned to the Italians. As a student of Chinese military affairs later summed up: "The planes proved to be second-rate. The aircraft factory failed to produce planes, and the air mission left China when the conflict with Japan began [in 1937]."[80]

The commercial interests of the United States certainly had been well served by the Jouett mission and by other American aviation enterprises in China. Exports of American aeronautical items amounted to $9 million in value during the years 1929–1934, a considerable sum in the midst of the depression. The United States, in fact, had captured the Chinese market. Exports of America's three leading competitors—Italy, Great Britain, and France—totalled only $4.5 million during this same period.[81]

Curtiss-Wright shared handsomely in the military market. In the early stages of development, between May 1932 and May 1933, the Chinese government placed orders for military aircraft with Curtiss-Wright totalling $675,000. A contract to build an aircraft factory promised well for the future. Curtiss-Wright finally had tapped the promise of the Chinese market after a long search, and it could now afford to carry CNAC as an unwanted stepchild of its military sales enterprises in China.[82]

— IV —

The years 1930–1932 saw alternating hope and despair over the prospects of developing commercial aviation in China. The pioneering contract between Curtiss-Wright and the Chinese government of July 1930 gave the Chinese a vested interest in the success of the enterprise, and it brought Chinese money into the venture for the first time. Captain Westervelt extended the Yangtze line from Hankow to Chungking, weeded out the malcontents in the organization, promoted harmonious relations with the Chinese, saw to the renovation of the airline's fleet, and selected the capable W. L. Bond to run CNAC.

But the company failed to prosper, and additional funds were needed to continue operations. This came at a time when Japanese attacks in Manchuria and Shanghai threatened to topple the Nationalist government and throw China into political and economic chaos. Curtiss-Wright initially sought assistance from the American government, but the United States wanted to keep clear of the dangerous situation in the Far East. The conflict with Japan, however, did lead to an expansion of the Chinese air force and an increase in sales of military equipment for Curtiss-Wright and other American aircraft manufacturers.

George Conrad Westervelt, whose energy, ability, and, above all, faith in the enterprise carried CNAC through some dark days, left Curtiss-Wright at the end of 1932 and returned to his farm in Highland County, Florida. Clement M. Keys left the scene at the same time. The father of Chinese commercial aviation had lost a fortune in the market crash and in 1932 he relinquished control of Curtiss-Wright. Ernest Price had long since gone, and so had Harry Smith. Only W. L. Bond remained, in charge of an organization that Curtiss-Wright kept only because it did not wish to offend the Chinese and possibly jeopardize its military sales.

But there were soon to be dramatic changes in CNAC. A new factor was about to enter the picture: Pan American Airways.

CHAPTER THREE
PAN AMERICAN AND PROSPERITY
1933–1937

— I —

CURTISS-WRIGHT left W. L. Bond and CNAC more or less alone following Westervelt's departure from China in the late spring of 1932. New York did not send anyone to replace him, and there were no further attempts to reach an economic understanding with the Chinese. The airline continued to make measured progress throughout the year despite dwindling financial resources. The Sino-Japanese conflict had disrupted rail and steamboat transportation in the Yangtze basin, and CNAC took advantage of the situation and scheduled extra trips to accommodate the demand for air service. The airline in 1932 carried 3,153 passengers and 111,872 pounds of mail, an increase of 25 percent over 1931.[1]

The new year brought heightened Chinese interest in the political benefits of air service, as tension increased along the Manchurian border. Tokyo had recognized the "independence" of Manchuria in September 1932 and had organized the former Chinese province under a puppet government as the state of Manchukuo. The Japanese now moved to secure the borders of the new state. Shanhaikwan, guarding a strategic pass between Manchuria and North China, fell to advancing Imperial troops on January 3, 1933. There followed a demand for withdrawal of all Chinese forces from the adjacent province of Jehol. When Nanking failed to comply, the Japanese swept into the province, reached the Great Wall on March 10, and continued southward. With Peking threatened, Chiang Kai-shek sought a truce. Japan dictated the agreement signed at Tangku on May 31. While the Chinese government remained in nominal control of the northern area, it exercised sovereignty under Japanese sufferance.[2]

Nanking sought to strengthen its ties to the northern region in the face of increasing Japanese influence. One part of this program involved an unprecedented offer to subsidize CNAC's service to Peking, which had been suspended since December 1931. The Chinese government not only agreed in early January 1933 to pay $3,500 a month for three years to protect the airline against expected losses, it also permitted CNAC to use American pilots on the route, at least until Chinese aviators could be trained.[3]

Ernest Allison took off from Shanghai on January 12, 1933, to begin service. The schedule called for nine-hour service to Peking via the coastal cities of Haichow, Tsingtao, and Tientsin, operating twice weekly. J. R. McCleskey and Hewitt F. Mitchell, young army-trained pilots, were hired in the United States and sent to China to fly the Stinsons. Allison took charge of flight operations for the first few months. The only problem encountered on the route was the extreme cold in the north, and new heaters were ordered for the cabins of the Stinsons; in the meantime, pilot and passengers wore heavily padded Chinese clothing.[4]

The early months of 1933 were a time for guarded optimism about CNAC's future. Traffic along the Yangtze continued to increase, the Peking route was operating satisfactorily, and the small subsidy seemed to portend a change of attitude by the government. The fiscal year ending June 30, 1933, proved the best in the history of the airline. Revenue was up $65,268 over the previous fiscal year, while expenses decreased $58,570. CNAC's deficit, which had been averaging nearly $250,000 a year, was cut to $121,250. "By 1935," commented the *China Weekly Review*, "it is probable that the company will be paying returns on invested capital."[5]

CNAC was making progress, but many areas of China remained untouched by air transportation. The airline's Loenings and Stinsons, with their limited carrying capacity, were obsolete. CNAC needed improved equipment, modern communication systems, and new ground facilities. It would be a long time before the company's profits would permit such expenditures. Curtiss-Wright was an unlikely source of needed capital, and the Chinese government, although willing to grant a small subsidy, did not seem prepared to supply the necessary funds. CNAC had reached a deadend in the spring of 1933, or at best it was condemned to slow and painful progress. But the airline's fortunes were about to undergo a significant change: CNAC was to become an outpost in the vast aerial empire of Pan American Airways.

Under the astute direction of Juan T. Trippe, Pan American had emerged as one of the world's great airlines by the early 1930s. The company operated 20,600 miles of routes in 1933, connecting Central and South America with the United States. Gross revenue exceeded $9 million, while profits approached $1 million. A pioneer in the use of long-range flying boats in Latin America, the airline in the summer of 1932 placed orders with the Sikorsky and Martin companies for huge four-engined aircraft. Trippe intended to use these giant flying boats on a transatlantic route. When political complications over landing rights thwarted this plan, Trippe turned toward the Far East.[6]

Some preliminary work had been done, most notably a survey of the Great Circle route to Asia by Charles Lindbergh in 1931. "I conceived, organized, and financed this flight personally," Lindbergh has pointed out, "but since I was a consultant to Pan American, all the information I obtained and the conclusions I reached were available to, and made use of by, the company." Although there were numerous operating problems to be solved, Pan American manifested its serious interest in the Great Circle route when it purchased two small Alaskan air carriers in 1932. Again, political problems—this time objections from Japan and the Soviet Union—forced abandonment of the project. Intent upon putting Pan American around the world, Trippe now looked to a transpacific route via Midway Island, Wake Island, Guam, and the Philippines.[7]

International airline agreements involve provisions for reciprocal landing privileges and are negotiated between governments today. During the early 1930s, however, the United States refused to grant landing rights to other nations. This meant that Pan American had to cope with the difficult problem of securing unilateral privileges in direct negotiations with foreign countries. A favorite tactic used by the airline in Latin America was to acquire or form subsidiary companies in the various countries. These subsidiaries enabled Pan American to operate into the major terminals, and they acted as local "feeders" for the international service. CNAC could serve these functions in China.[8]

Trippe began negotiations with Curtiss-Wright early in 1933. William D. Pawley, Curtiss-Wright's representative, alluded to plans to supply modern aircraft to its "valuable property" and to develop new routes in China. Although Pawley has stated that such plans did exist, little evidence of them could be found in China. When Pawley sailed for Shanghai in January 1933 to discuss the factory proposal with the Nationalist government, Thomas Morgan took charge of negotiations. Trippe and Morgan reached agreement on March 31, and signed a contract the following day.[9]

Pan American acquired the American interest in CNAC in exchange for 3,000 shares of common stock, then valued at $28 a share. In addition, Curtiss-Wright may have been given an option to purchase a further 10,000 shares of Pan American stock at $25. According to one unverified report, Curtiss-Wright exercised this option prior to March 31, 1935, at which time Pan American stock had a market value of $39 a share. For accounting purposes, Pan American recorded its investment in CNAC at $282,258.69. It placed the actual value of the company at $165,000 worth of "obsolete planes, spare parts, and a very small and dwindling cash balance."[10]

Harold M. Bixby, Pan American's Far Eastern representative, arrived in Shanghai shortly before the arrangements to purchase CNAC were concluded. Bixby would remain in China, except for trips home, during the next four years. Thereafter, as a vice president of Pan American, he would have an influential voice on all matters affecting the parent company's relations with its Chinese subsidiary. "Trippe had the utmost confidence in Bixby," Charles Lindbergh has noted, "who was one of the most able officers PAA ever had."[11]

A person had to possess at least a touch of the romantic to become involved in aviation during the early 1930s, especially aviation in China. Bixby was a romantic—perhaps *visionary* is a better word—although his appearance belied it. Photographs of Bixby reveal a man of distinguished bearing, with a high forehead, strong chin, spectacles, a neat mustache, and usually dressed in a conservative business suit, who seems somehow out of place when depicted against an exotic oriental background.

Bixby was born in St. Louis, Missouri, in 1890. After graduating from Amherst in 1913, he returned to the Midwest and a position with a local bank. By the mid-1920s, Bixby had risen from clerk to vice president of the State National Bank of St. Louis. A leading figure in the Chamber of Commerce and active in all manner of civic affairs, the romantic in Bixby showed in his enthusiasm for flying. When a young air mail pilot named Charles Lindbergh sought financial support for his dream of a solo flight across the Atlantic, he found a sympathetic ear, and the necessary funds, from the outwardly staid banker. The success of Lindbergh's venture turned Bixby from finance to aviation. He joined Pan American in the early 1930s and quickly rose to a position of responsibility. "He had a face and a smile you trusted from the moment you saw him." Lindbergh recalled, "and the more you saw him, the more he confirmed your trust. He had a quick and perceptive mind, excellent judgment, and a wonderful sense of humor. And he had fundamental wisdom."[12]

Bixby took stock of Pan American's latest acquisition shortly after he reached China. He found the airport, located about five miles south of downtown Shanghai and adjacent to the village of Lunghwa with its famous seven-story pagoda. Until 1932, CNAC had been confined to a small area on the banks of the Whangpoo river, next to a military camp. When the soldiers had left after the Shanghai Incident, the city had taken over the

PAN AMERICAN AND PROSPERITY   75

grounds for a municipal airport and CNAC had erected a small hangar on the field.

CNAC's equipment left much to be desired. Of the airline's complement of five Stinsons, Bixby found four out of commission for repairs or rebuilding. The five Loenings were in good flying condition, although they were not very comfortable for passengers. Noise inside the cabin was terrific, and travelers had to be issued cotton to plug up their ears. Only the vibration matched the noise level in degree of discomfort. The airlines had reduced passenger capacity from six to four, in order to give the cramped occupants additional leg room and permit the transport of additional mail.

Stinsons operated service to Peking on a twice-weekly basis. Loenings flew daily except Monday between Shanghai and Hankow, and two round trips a week from Hankow to Chungking. The airline averaged 50,000 miles a month of scheduled operations, and lost $.25 a mile.

CNAC employed seven fully qualified pilots, six Americans and one German national. Chinese, both native and American born, flew as copilots. The training program for these individuals had not made much progress due to lack of time, equipment, and interest.

Ground personnel included Bond, chief pilot Allison (who also took regular turns on the flight schedule), chief mechanic Oscar Wilke, four American mechanics, and a staff of Chinese. Communications and weather reporting facilities were manned by Chinese. As CNAC's aircraft lacked radios, weather reports and other messages were received by pilots before departing Shanghai and at stops en route.[13]

Following this depressing survey, Bixby met with CNAC's Board of Directors. They welcomed him to China, then proposed a motion to declare the airline insolvent. The Chinese obviously sought to impress upon Bixby the desperate need for funds, with the strong implication that Pan American would be a better source of capital than the Nationalist government. If the Chinese had hoped for a "soft touch," they were to be disappointed. Experienced in dealing with Latin American regimes, Bixby had no intention of opening the coffers of Pan American to the Chinese. He persuaded the board to withdraw the motion.[14]

Having crossed the first hurdle, Bixby turned to his primary concern in China: CNAC's role in Pan American's projected transpacific service. Under the contract of 1930, CNAC had until July 8, 1933, to begin operations on the Shanghai-Canton route. "The preservation of this franchise," a Pan American official later testified, "was vital because it afforded [Pan American] an opportunity to secure a foothold in Asia for its trans-pacific service, as well as access to Shanghai,—the commercial center of the Far East." Pan American wanted to operate the Shanghai-Canton route with its own aircraft and crews, thereby preserving the "American character of the operation and making the line an integral part of the trans-Pacific service. Developmental and operating costs could then be considered when requesting a subsidy from the American government."[15]

The Chinese government vetoed the use of Pan American aircraft for the Shanghai-Canton route. Nanking steadfastly refused to grant cabotage rights to any foreign company. Such a concession would not only violate the principle of majority Chinese ownership, it also would mean that all foreign governments, including Japan, could claim equal privileges under the "most favored nation" clause of existing treaties.[16]

Bixby and the Chinese authorities managed to arrive at a provisional solution to this difficulty. Pacific American Airways, a wholly-owned subsidiary of Pan American, would operate the Shanghai-Canton service under charter to CNAC. This arrangement proved abortive, however, and the new aircraft which Pan American brought to China would carry CNAC markings. As always, money was a problem, and the two parties could not agree upon financial arrangements. Although Bixby wanted to defer operations until the point was settled, pressure of time forced him to push ahead while negotiations continued.[17]

Pan American mounted its expedition to China in late May 1933. Two modern Sikorsky S-38 amphibians were loaded on board the Danish freighter *Gertrude Maersk* in Savannah, Georgia. Proclaimed "the world's safest airplane," the S-38 had an unusual configuration, with its tail group on booms. The twin-engine amphibian was 40 feet long, had a wing span of 72 feet, and a maximum gross weight of 10,480 pounds. It carried a crew of two, and could lift eight passengers over a distance of 600 miles at 110 mph. Personnel from Pan American's Miami Division who would accompany the aircraft included Paul Groeger, former submarine commander and navigational expert, pilots George Rummel and Robert Gast, copilot/radio operators William Ehmer and Hugh L. Woods, chief mechanic Zigmund Soldinsky, and radio engineer Ivan Carlson. Pan American picked William S. Grooch to head the party.[18]

Grooch had pioneered service to Latin America for the New York, Rio, and Buenos Aires Air Lines, an ill-starred company which Pan American subsequently absorbed. When he arrived in New York from Rio to discuss the China project, the new operations manager found that preparations for the service had been fragmentary. Andre Priester, Pan American's chief engineer, "interrupted my work several times a day to lecture me on safety-first methods of operating," Grooch wrote. After several hectic days in New York, Grooch flew to the West Coast and joined the expedition onboard the *Gertrude Maersk*, which was refueling in the port of San Pedro, California. Priester had presented him with a copy of a book entitled *The Qualities of Leadership* as a farewell gift.[19]

The Pan American group reached Shanghai on June 26, twelve days before the deadline for start of the Canton service. Mechanics hurried to assemble one of the S-38s, sweating and swearing in the Whangpoo's oppressive heat and humidity. Grooch test flew the aircraft on July 1. Two days later, Bixby and Bond joined him on what was planned as a leisurely survey flight to Canton. Mail would be carried on the return trip, thereby fulfilling the terms of the contract.[20]

Following a brief stop at Wenchow, Grooch alighted in the harbor of Foochow, tying up at the Pagoda Anchorage. It was here, Bixby noted, that "all of the old clipper ships used to take on their loads of tea preparatory to the race to England." The party spent the night at the home of the American consul, Lincoln C. Reynolds, an enthusiastic supporter of aviation in China. The next morning, Independence Day, they clambered back into their S-38 and flew on to Amoy and Swatow. With special permission from the British, Hong Kong was their next port-of-call. "Across the harbor I spotted Kai Tak airdrome," Grooch later wrote. "Motioning Ehmer to pump the wheels down, I dragged the broad field, then came in to a landing. We ran smoothly for fifty feet. Then the wheels broke through a thin crust to dig into deep sand. The bow struck the dirt with a jar as we stopped with the tail high in the air. There goes our mail contract, I thought. We'll never make Canton in time." Fortunately, damage proved slight and, with British assistance, the aircraft was repaired and left for Canton the following morning.[21]

Bixby spent July 7 making arrangements for the inauguration of mail service. He soon ran into trouble. The minister of communications had ordered the mail withheld until Pan American agreed to make financial concessions for operations of the Shanghai-Canton service. Refusing to be pressured, Bixby persuaded the local postmaster, a European, to send two bags of ordinary mail via air. The flight took off from Canton on July 8 and touched down in the Whampoo off Shanghai the same day. Although the Chinese government attempted a hair-splitting game that sought to distinguish between ordinary mail carried by air and air mail, it finally accepted the flight as technically complying with the provisions of the franchise.[22]

While preparations for regular service on the Canton route continued, Bixby scheduled a survey flight to Manila. This would be the third flight ever from the Asian mainland across the South China Sea to the Philippines. Grooch equipped one of the S-38s with an extra gasoline tank built into the cabin to extend the aircraft's normal cruising range of 600 miles, secured weather data for the trip, and arranged for an ocean-going tug to stand by in Hong Kong as a rescue ship. Bixby and Grooch took off from Shanghai on August 14 for Hong Kong. They made the 600-mile flight across the China Sea the next day, landing in the Agno River where it enters Linguan Gulf. After locating prearranged fuel supplies, they inspected landing sites in northern Luzon, then continued to Manila.

"In Manila," Bixby commented, "we made a thorough survey of landing areas appropriate for the operations of the Trans-Pacific service in which we hoped some day to engage and we also explored the procedure necessary to secure operating rights from the Philippine legislature." After several flights around the Philippines, the survey party returned to Hong Kong on August 29. As Bixby noted, "This was the first round trip ever made between Hong Kong and Manila."[23]

Financial arrangements for the Canton service remained to be settled. Pan American offered to supply the necessary equipment and improve ground facilities for the line if the Chinese government would grant $175,000 annually for three years as a guarantee against losses. Eventually, this guarantee would be repaid out of earnings. The Chinese countered with a demand for 20 percent of the gross passenger revenue and 40 percent of the mail receipts. Bixby balked at this proposal. Pan American hoped to obtain a subsidy from the American government for transpacific operations; the Canton route could not be included in the subsidy if the Chinese appeared to profit from the service. Also, such an arrangement might complicate Pan American's relations with Latin American governments. "This precedent established," Bixby wrote to the American commercial attaché in Shanghai, "would lead to similar demands from South American countries served and would involve a very large sum."[24]

Months of hard bargaining followed before the two parties signed a provisional operating contract on October 8, 1933. Pan American agreed that stations along the Canton route would be considered CNAC stations and be administered by CNAC personnel. All aircraft would carry CNAC markings. Pan American would bear the entire cost of the operation. CNAC would receive 20 percent of all domestic mail revenue and 7.5 percent of passenger revenue. The Ministry of Communications agreed to "loan" CNAC $7,500 monthly for three years, which would include the subsidy of $3,500 to be paid for operation of the Peking line. The loan would be repaid to the government out of 50 percent of CNAC's net profits over the life of the contract of 1930. Pan American further agreed to finance new ground and flying equipment for CNAC to a value of $200,000 and furnish an additional $25,000 for a new hangar and other improvements at Lunghwa.[25]

Bixby had many reservations about the agreement. In particular, he considered the revenue-sharing feature "unjust." He had consented to it, Bixby wrote to New York, "only after months of arguments and [it] represents one of the compromises we were compelled to make."[26]

Dr. Chu Chia-hua, minister of communications, shared Bixby's displeasure. The minister termed the payment of $7,500 a month an outright grant since he did not expect the airline ever to become sufficiently profitable to repay the money. Pan American, he complained, paid little attention to CNAC's other routes, and they had refused to come to China unless granted a subsidy. The minister said that CNAC's overhead was excessive, that the Americans were overpaid, and that many Americans should be replaced by Chinese. "Dr. Chu," the American consul general in Nanking reported, "was evidently thoroughly conversant with the details of China's aviation enterprise and [is] giving the matter his personal, earnest attention."[27]

Regular, twice-weekly, mail service to Canton began on October 24, 1933. After a month's successful operation, Bixby scheduled the first passenger flight for November 24. George Rummel and William Ehmer, resplendent in trim blue uniforms and white caps, were the crew on the inaugural flight. The passenger list, typical of CNAC's operations, included Lady Carlisle, niece of Sir Miles Lampson, British minister to China, who was bound for Hong Kong, and Lincoln Reynolds, American consul at Foochow, who had been ordered to return to his post because of reported disturbances in the province. Also on board were Mr. K. Schaefer of the firm of Kunst & Albers, M. H. Wang, commissioner of customs at Wechow, S. F. Chang, manager of Foochow Motor Sales Company, Dr. Conrad Hsu of Asia Electric Company, and Yang Zung-wo of Wenchow.

The ungainly S-38 lifted off the Wangpoo River at 6:15 A.M.

Ki Chun, director of C N A C, and Harold M. Bixby beside Ford trimotor, 1935

Ford trimotor over the Temple of Heaven, Peking, 1935

Thirty minutes later, Rummel reported fog over Hangchow Bay. He returned to Shanghai, waited until 8 A.M., then tried again. Flying at 1,500 feet, Rummel once more ran into a fog/haze condition over the bay. After losing visual contact with the water, he descended to 500 feet where the air seemed clearer. Rummel dropped lower and lower as visibility decreased. The yellowish, muddy water of the bay blended into the haze. Now scraping along at 200 feet, Rummel lost sight of the horizon as well as the water. He began a shallow turn to port. Catching sight of a strip of beach, he pulled back on the yoke. The aircraft struck the top of a 300-foot hill, fortunately in a climbing attitude instead of head-on. Even so, Kwangin, the goddess of mercy, must have smiled, because crew and passengers escaped with their lives. Lincoln Reynolds, who was injured most severely, suffered "a broken neck, broken finger, and a bottle of spinach soup which had been contained in Lady Carlisle's thermos bottle."[28]

Although Rummel's accident had a reasonably happy ending, everything went downhill for the Pan American group after November 24. There was constant friction between Grooch and Groeger. The Americans complained about the declining exchange rate. Grooch recalled a dinner party when Mrs. Gast, wife of one of the pilots, broke into tears as she told Bixby of her financial worries. Relations with Chinese officials of the airline worsened. Summer's cloying heat and humidity had given way to winter's cold and fog, and working conditions were miserable. "As the weeks dragged by," Grooch wrote, "delays began to have a serious effect on our personnel. Frequently a plane would return only a few hours before its next scheduled departure. Soldinsky and his crew would have to work all night in the rain or sleet to get it serviced on time to go out next morning. In order to start the engines we had to put a hood over them with a oil stove below it to thaw them out. The crew, cold, wet and miserable, were continually snarling at each other. They hated China. Each of them begged for a transfer to the States." In January 1934, Grooch experienced a heart-rending personal tragedy when his wife and their two children, boys of seven and five, leaped to their death from the top of the Washington Apartments in Shanghai. Grooch refused to be relieved of his assignments.[29]

On April 10, 1934, the remaining S-38 took off from Shanghai on the regular service to Canton. It carried three crew, Robert Gast, James Frick, and Ivan Carlson, and one passenger, a Mr. T. Yuemura. Thirty minutes after departure, Gast radioed that he was returning due to fog in Hangchow Bay. That was the last word ever received from the plane. Searchers found bits of wreckage identified as part of the aircraft. Gast's badly decomposed body was found floating in the southern end of the bay several months later.[30]

"Aircraft," Nevil Shute has commented, "do not crash of themselves. They come to grief because men are foolish, or vain, or lazy, or irresolute, or reckless. One crash in a thousand may be unavoidable because God wills it so—not more than that."[31] While the cause of Gast's accident can never be known with certainty, some contributing factors stand out. Grooch was not an effective leader, and Pan American erred in selecting him to head the operation. Bixby should have noted the worsening situation and taken measures to correct it. Certainly, he should have relieved Grooch after the tragic death of his wife and children. Pan American should have utilized to a greater extent the operating experience of CNAC's pilots. Above all, the pilots sent to China should have been given instrument flight instruction, an aspect of aeronautics that had been sadly neglected by the airline because of the nature of their previous routes and flying conditions. Pan American's preeminent achievement in the history of commercial aviation was its ability to fly long distances with regularity and safety. Meticulous planning and careful selection and training of personnel, among other things, accounted for this feat. All were lacking on the Shanghai-Canton route.

As a result of the disasters on the Canton line, Pan American personnel and operations were integrated into CNAC. Minister Chu had been urging such a course in the name of economy since the previous October, but Bixby had resisted, arguing the superior character of Pan American's operations. Now, he had little choice. Bixby sent Grooch home. Groeger became airport manager at Lunghwa. Bond assumed control of all operations, and Allison became chief pilot. Chinese copilots were to be carried on all aircraft. "We have tried," Bixby noted, "to place our American personnel in positions of responsibility and not subordinate to any Chinese." Reorganization meant a saving of $30,000 per year for CNAC, and $25,000 for Pan American.[32]

Two twin-engine, eight-passenger Douglas Dolphin amphibians were ordered for the Canton service, and by the summer of 1934 they had arrived in Shanghai, been assembled, and test flown. Allison set up an instrument training program for pilots. CNAC established additional radio and weather reporting stations along the route. Following careful preparations, service reopened on November 2, 1934, and it was to operate successfully and profitably for the next two years. Had it not been for the outbreak of the Sino-Japanese war in 1937, Pan American probably would have recovered its entire developmental costs of $850,000.[33]

On New Year's Day, 1935, Juan Trippe ordered preparations to begin for the transpacific venture. Pan American personnel sailed from San Francisco aboard the freighter *North Haven* in March to set up operating bases on the mid-Pacific coral atolls of Midway and Wake. With service scheduled to begin in the fall, Pan American had yet to acquire a terminus on the Asian mainland. Trippe wanted landing rights in Hong Kong, but the British refused to grant such privileges. The British also would not let CNAC land in Hong Kong unless the Chinese allowed British aircraft into Shanghai. This raised the problem of "most favored nation," which meant that Japan would automatically gain comparable privileges. "The root of the whole problem," the *Far Eastern Survey* pointed out, "as far as China is concerned is generally conceded to be her unwillingness to have Japanese planes landing within her borders."[34]

Juan Trippe adopted a brilliant strategem to solve the problem of securing a terminus in Asia. Pan American concluded an agreement with Portugal in January 1936 for transportation of mail between the Portuguese colony of Macao and the United

States via the Philippines. The agreement did not cover exchange of mail from China, as the Portuguese wanted reciprocal privileges which the Chinese refused to grant. Bixby toyed with the idea of making the connection between Canton and Macao by fast motor launch, but this proved unnecessary when Britain decided to open Hong Kong to Pan American and CNAC.[35]

The British authorities had come under heavy pressure from the commercial interests of the island-colony, who realized the economic advantages that would accrue to the terminus of the transpacific route. London had resisted until the agreement with Portugal brought to the fore the long-standing commercial rivalry between Macao and Hong Kong. "His Majesty's Government," the British ambassador in Washington informed the Department of State on June 11, 1936, "have decided not to enforce for the time being the normal requirements of reciprocity." Great Britain granted Pan American a five-year permit to use Hong Kong with the proviso that this privilege would be cancelled if the United States granted rights to a third party to fly the transpacific route and denied such right to Great Britain. At the same time, the British accorded landing rights to CNAC at Hong Kong without condition.[36]

There remained one final detail: the Chinese had to sign an international air mail contract for the exchange of air mail between China and the United States. Bixby had been working on this since early in 1935 but without much progress. "The officials of the National government and of CNAC," he explained to New York, "are not imbued with any of the idea of empire-building or the establishment of a system like PAA. On the contrary, they are traders." Government officials were not interested in CNAC beyond their own tenure of office, and they were reluctant to conclude any agreement for fear of criticism. The more he tried to press the Chinese, the greater became their caution. Bixby had decided to take "the Chinese point of view." He would be patient, he would be content to play a waiting game.[37]

Bixby took the "longest way round," but time grew short. Pan American commenced transpacific passenger service from San

Francisco to Manila in October 1936, and plans called for through service to Hong Kong in April 1937. Bixby flew to Nanking in January 1937 to make a last effort with the director general of posts. This official had been a thorn in Bixby's side for years. "His attitude toward us," Bixby noted, "was outwardly polite but inwardly non-cooperative. Nothing that we proposed ever received favorable consideration—either for the services within China or for the trans-Pacific route." After lengthy preliminaries of tea and compliments, the two men turned to the matter at issue. "No," reported Bixby, "he would not sign an airmail contract, the Chinese post office would not make use of the transpacific airmail service and no postage rates would be quoted to the public."

Bixby spent an hour trying to persuade the official, pointing out the economic and political benefits to China, but the director general remained unmoved. As the interview drew to a close, Bixby delivered his parting shot. Would the director general agree positively that China would not use the transpacific service? He would. Bixby then smiled and said he would cable the good news to New York. The puzzled official asked for an explanation of this sudden change in attitude. Bixby proceeded to give an elaborate and confusing account of Pan American's economic relationship with the American government. He said, in essence, that Pan American was paid for miles flown and that the airline would not receive any revenue for carrying Chinese mail; this went to the American government. If the Chinese did not want to use the service, that would be just fine. Pan American would get paid all the same, and it could use the additional space to carry passengers. Bixby said that he had simply tried to be conscientious, out of consideration for the United States government in attempting to persuade the Chinese to use the service.

"Of course," Bixby concluded, "it may be difficult for you to explain to the American Government why you are not using the service and it may also be embarrassing to tell high officials of China why they cannot answer by airmail the messages that they no doubt will receive from equally high ranking American officials via the first flight—but no doubt you have carefully considered such consequences and I need not mention them further. Thank you very much for your decision and I am delighted to be in a position to immediately cable my associates in New York." Bixby then walked out of the door.

One hour later, Bixby received word from the director general that he might wish to use the transpacific service after all. The two men signed the contract the next morning, January 19, 1937.[38]

On April 15, a "First Flight Tiffin," held at the American Club on Nanking Road in Shanghai, attracted several hundred foreign and Chinese businessmen and officials. Guests of honor included CNAC's managing director, the American consul, and W. L. Bond. Also in attendance were C. S. Vaughn, W. Chen, and C. H. Woo, the crew of the Douglas Dolphin that was scheduled to take off the next day to make the connection with Pan American's inaugural Clipper flight in Hong Kong. They were formally introduced and duly applauded. Then Julean Arnold, the commercial attaché, stood up and proposed a toast that spoke the great truth of the hour: "to Harold M. Bixby, who has done more than anybody else to make this service possible."[39]

Bixby had worked long and hard to make the Canton route a reality, but this was only a part of his accomplishment. During his four years in China, Pan American's representative played an important role in fostering CNAC's remarkable progress from a struggling regional air carrier to a prosperous major world airline.

— II —

Dr. Chu Chia-hua, the minister of communications, complained in November 1933 that Pan American seemed uninterested in CNAC's routes in central China. There is little doubt that CNAC's domestic service remained a distinctly secondary consideration for the parent company, except as a feeder to the Pacific Clippers. The American airline did not expect to make a profit from its relationship with the Chinese; nor was Pan American willing to underwrite CNAC's losses. On the other hand, CNAC did benefit from its association with Pan American. At least, as Bond pointed out, Pan American was an air transportation company and not a manufacturer. Whereas Curtiss-Wright occasionally sent inferior equipment to China at inflated prices, Pan American supplied aircraft to CNAC that were in excellent condition and at a reasonable cost.[40]

CNAC profited in other ways. The American company, noted one official of Pan American, "gave CNAC without cost the benefit of many years of PAA experience, valuable engineering research, operating experience and management." Also, the Pan American Supply Corporation made purchases for CNAC at the same commission charged other divisions of the parent company, which meant savings of from 10 to 40 percent on most items. Finally, there was the less tangible morale factor of CNAC's American employees. As one young pilot commented upon learning that Pan American had purchased the American interest in CNAC: "It means I have almost limitless possibilities for promotion with the Pan-American organization." This did not always prove true, and was to become a source of controversy, but many CNAC employees eventually moved into the parent company.[41]

Shortly after his arrival in China, Bixby wrote to Dr. Arthur N. Young in the Ministry of Finance: "I want you to know . . . that we are earnestly trying to be real partners with the Ministry of Communications in the development of China National Aviation Corporation to the end that that System may take its place among the great air transportation organizations of the world." Although Bixby's primary concern during his four years in China related to projects directly associated with the projected transpacific service, especially development of the coastal line from Shanghai to Canton and Hong Kong, he nevertheless took an active interest in the expansion of CNAC's interior routes. Indeed, under Bixby's command, service improved throughout China, while the quality of CNAC's equipment changed dramatically for the better.[42]

The contract of 1930 had named Chengtu as the terminus for CNAC's Yangtze Valley route. The airline had reached Chungking in October 1931 but had been unable to extend beyond that point due to unstable political conditions in Szechwan Province. Capital of the province and a city of nearly one million inhabitants, Chengtu offered attractive possibilities for air transportation. The city was linked to Chungking by a road that was hardly more than a path, winding for nearly 300 miles across plains and over rugged mountains. Sedan chairs, carried by four bearers, and wheelbarrows were the primary means of transportation. The journey took ten to fifteen days with overnight accommodations at Chinese inns famed for their variety of ticks, fleas, and lice. Bandits preyed on travelers, and those who could afford the expense were accompanied by a bodyguard of soldiers. Flying the direct route of 170 miles, aircraft could make the trip between Chungking and Chengtu in less than two hours.[43]

P. Y. Wong, CNAC's business manger, flew to Chungking in early May 1933 to make the necessary arrangements with Marshal Liu Hsiang to serve Chengtu. The warlord granted tentative approval for the project. Allison, Bixby, and Bond took off from Shanghai's Lunghwa airport in one of the venerable Stinsons on May 26 to survey the route and secure Liu's final agreement. Although the party received disturbing reports of civil war in Szechwan Province upon arriving at Hankow, they decided to continue up river. After a day's delay at Hankow due to fog, they took off on the morning of the 28th for Chungking, following the meandering track of the Yangtze River. Just above Ichang, Bixby caught his first sight of the awesome sixteen-mile-long Ichang Gorge. "The wild panorama which rapidly unfolded," he wrote, "the surging river down below—the precipitous cliffs—fantastic rock battlements like medieval castles—stretches of wooded mountains rising above the gorge and extending back on either side as far as the eye could see. It was so breath taking in its grandeur that it defies word pictures." Bixby concluded: "If flight over the Gorges of the Yangtze fails to restore a man's sense of values then he must indeed be an insufferable ass!"[44]

Allison landed the Stinson of Chungking's military airport, some twelve miles south of the city. Bixby, Bond, and Allison called at Marshal Liu's headquarters the next morning, May 29.

Following a bizarre breakfast of champagne and angel food cake, they were ushered into the presence of the marshal. Liu expressed his interest in the proposed service to Chengtu, but he said that it was not safe to proceed because Chengtu was under siege. The marshal finally agreed to wire the attacking and defending generals that the airplane carried only mail and should not be fired upon. Liu gave Bixby permission to leave but disclaimed responsibility for the fate of the survey party.[45]

Bixby and associates remained in Chungking for two days, awaiting improvement in the weather and replies to Liu's wires. Meanwhile, Allison studied maps of the terrain between Chungking and Chengtu. Actually, Allison located three maps, and they were all different. The weather finally cleared on June 1. Although there had been no word from Chengtu, Bixby decided to go ahead. He and Bond took turns as copilot on the flight, "a circumstance," Bixby wryly commented, "which makes Allison's feat of piloting us safely to Chengtu . . . all the more remarkable."

Upon arrival over Chengtu, Allison discovered that the only available landing site was the military parade ground, a very short field about 1,000 feet by 400 feet with a two-story building at one end and a 20-foot wall at the other. Allison throttled back on the Stinson's engine and flew low over several hundred soldiers assembled on the field. "we had decided," Bixby noted, "that if any of them aimed their guns in our direction, we would go back to Chungking." As no one pointed a gun at the airplane, Allison circled the field, came down into the wind and landed on the parade ground. A double row of soldiers with fixed bayonets immediately formed a ring around the Stinson. As Bond stepped out of the plane, Bixby reported, one soldier standing under the wing came to "present arms" with such alacrity that "he stuck his bayonet straight through the wing with a resounding thump which scared the soldier more than it did us." The group went into Chengtu for a friendly lunch with General Liu Wen-wei, the local commander and Marshal Liu's uncle, from whom they learned that the civil war had reached a stalemate. They flew back to Chungking late the same day without incident.[46]

Allison inaugurated CNAC's regular service to Chengtu on June 4, 1933, but only a few days later Nanking ordered the airline to discontinue the route. While no explanation was offered, Bixby believed that the probable reason was "to give the National Government officials the degree of face to which they were entitled and to show their authority over the provincial war lord, an authority which, up to that time, had been conspicuous by its absence." Actually, Bixby welcomed the delay. The small parade ground at Chengtu was a dangerous landing area. He advised the authorities in Szechwan that service had been suspended because of the hazardous landing facilities, and that it would be resumed upon construction of an adequate airport. "It all ended very happily," Bixby recalled, "when the completion of the airport at Chengtu just happened to coincide with the order from Nanking that we might proceed with the service."[47]

The Chengtu line proved an immediate success. Thrice-weekly service began on November 21, 1933, and traffic was so heavy that another weekly round trip had to be added to the schedule within a month.[48]

Hewitt F. Mitchell flew the Chungking-Chengtu line during its initial six months of operation. Through this young man's diary and letters, it is possible to view CNAC during this period from the perspective of a pilot. The material reveals a good deal about the character of the company's operations; it also portrays the type of person who succeeded in China.[49]

Selection of pilots posed a serious problem for the management of CNAC. It cost a lot of money to bring a pilot to China from the United States, and if he proved unsatisfactory, considerable time and expense had been wasted. The airline, especially when Curtiss-Wright held the American interest, had to rely upon the judgment of individuals who were not familiar—and often unconcerned—with the peculiar requirements of the operation in China. All the airline could do in many cases was to wire for the records of individuals being considered for employment, a hit-or-miss system at best. For example, in April 1933 CNAC asked Major Edward P. Howard, the Department of Commerce's aeronautical trade commissioner in Shanghai, to inquire into the backgrounds of two prospective employees, Burton Hall and Charles Sharp. Washington replied that both men had good records at Air Corps training facilities, had received extended duty after graduation, and had been assigned to pursuit squadrons. Hall and Sharp were hired. Sharp turned out to be an excellent pilot and went on to become CNAC's operations manager. Hall proved unsatisfactory and had to be relieved from duty within a few months of arrival. On occasion, CNAC hired locally, and usually with good results. Eric Just was the only German pilot to fly for CNAC. A member of Baron von Richthofen's "Flying Circus" during World War I, Just was representing a German aircraft manufacturer in the Far East when he sought and obtained employment with CNAC in the early 1930s. Later, he became Chiang Kai-shek's personal pilot. "There may be better pilots, and finer gentlemen than Eric Just," Bixby wrote, "but I do not know where you will find them."[50]

Allison was on leave in the United States in the fall of 1932 when he received word that the Peking line was to be resumed with American pilots. Before he returned to China, he hired two young Air Corps officers to fly the Stinsons. These were J. R. McCleskey and Hewitt Mitchell. Then twenty-five years old, Mitchell had graduated from Stanford University in 1930 as a mechanical engineer. While a student, he had taken flying lessons from Paul Mantz, the movie stunt pilot, who ran a small flying school in Palo Alto. Mitchell joined the Air Corps after graduation and was ordered to Randolph and Kelly fields for flight instruction. After winning his wings and 2nd lieutenant's commission, he was posted to March Field, California, where he flew Boeing P-12s with the 73rd Pursuit Squadron. There seemed to be little future in the Army Air Corps during the early 1930s and commercial pilot openings were few and far between, so Mitchell promptly accepted Allison's offer.[51]

Mitchell arrived in Shanghai aboard a Dollar Line ship on February 13, 1933, on a three-year contract. He flew the Peking service as copilot with Allison for five weeks, becoming familiar with the aircraft and the route. Together with McCleskey and Floyd Nelson, the third pilot for the route who had been hired in the Philippines, Mitchell rented a furnished apartment in Shanghai and began to settle into the routine of life in China. On his days off, the young pilot had tiffin at 12:30 at the American Club—"on account of the people I meet there"—and dinner in the European fashion at 8 or 9 P.M. He liked to read. He enjoyed the sights of Shanghai. "China," he wrote, "is really a fascinating country and I think the time here will broaden me to no small extent." He decided to learn to speak Mandarin. But he did not have much time for such activities, as Mitchell flew 125 hours in his first five weeks with C N A C. "I like the work very much," he commented, "and all in all am very happy with my new job."[52]

Mitchell would have an early breakfast in his apartment, arriving at Lunghwa airport in time for a 7 A.M. departure. The flight to Peking via Haichow, Tsingtao, and Tientsin took eight to ten hours, depending on weather and winds. He stayed overnight in Peking, usually at the Grand Hotel des Wagon Lits, sometimes at the home of the American military attaché, Colonel Drysdale. The few passengers over the route during the first two weeks of June 1933 were mainly Westerners—the wife of an Italian diplomat, Roy Howard of the Scripps-Howard newspaper chain, and so forth. On occasion, Mitchell undertook special errands. At one point, he obtained serum in Peking for a missionary doctor who was treating a sick child in Haichow.

The Stinsons, Mitchell reported, were "old but recently overhauled and in good shape." The airplanes were equipped with new tires—low-pressure Goodyear "airwheels"—during June. "They certainly are great to land on," he commented, "compared with the old hard tires." Flying in China at that time was under "contact" conditions; that is, the pilot had to have visual contact with the ground. The aircraft did not have radios, there was no weather forecasting, and only National Geographic maps as guides. Considerable fog hung over the Yangtze Valley in June, and Mitchell flew as low as 200 feet above the terrain, his "personal minimum," in an effort to get under the weather. "I am anxious to get thru on schedule a very high percentage of the time," he wrote, "as the 'higher ups' watch us and think more of a pilot who gets thru most of the time. Getting thru is mostly a matter of using your knowledge of the country, your compass, and looking around for the best route." Mitchell demonstrated his interest in his profession when he devised a new system for instantaneously ascertaining ground speed by use of chart and stopwatch.[53]

After 16 or 20 hours in the cramped cockpit of the Stinson, Mitchell needed a day or two to unwind after he landed back at Shanghai. He played squash or tennis, perhaps with Julean Arnold, the commercial attaché, or Randall Gould, editor of the *Shanghai Evening Post and Mercury*. He had dinner with friends, sometimes at the apartment, on occasion at the home of Chinese acquaintances, like General Dzu of the Central Bank. But there was too little time for such activities in early June when Nelson became ill and Mitchell had to fly extra trips. He flew 50 hours in one seven-day period. "My eyes and nerves are beginning to show the strain," he reported, "altho not as much as I had anticipated." Mitchell continued to shuttle back and forth over the Peking line through the summer. In November 1933, he went to Szechwan to begin the Chungking-Chengtu service.[54]

Isolated Chengtu was a far cry from cosmopolitan Shanghai. But as Mitchell was young, interested in his surroundings, and very busy, he made the adjustment without difficulty. Business boomed, and Mitchell soon had to fly four round trips a week instead of three. "I am always busy," he wrote in December, "having so much mechanical and other work to do here besides flying." But he found the job rewarding, "I feel a great deal of pride in this work," he wrote. "The general manager always refers to it as my line when writing to me."[55]

The aging Stinson usually had a full complement of four passengers. In accordance with company policy, Mitchell's Chinese copilot would give up his seat if there was a fifth passenger available. Most of the travelers were Chinese, usually merchants or officials, and they were usually airsick. "It is caused mostly from fear, I think. . . . they have jumped from sedan chairs and rickshaws to airplanes, but most of them take it well—smiling even though they are sick—and come back for more in many cases."[56]

Mitchell sometimes flew special charter flights. He carried from Chengtu to Chungking an attractive Chinese woman, suffering great pain from a severe compound fracture of the leg which had been set improperly by a local doctor and had not healed. She was to continue down river to see a specialist in Shanghai. Her trip would have been an agony of days by sedan chair. On another trip, Mitchell brought to Chengtu Whang Mosen, envoy of the Nationalist government to Tibet. The Chinese emissary had flown from Nanking to Chengtu—about 1,000 miles—in two days; his next 1,000 miles from Chengtu to Lhasa, Mitchell noted, would take four to five months by sedan chair. The diplomat carried one suitcase that weighed 110 pounds; it was filled with silver dollars, the only money that could be used beyond Chengtu.[57]

Mitchell carried a variety of light-weight, high-value cargo in addition to passengers. Once he flew a 55-pound parcel of musk, a rare perfume base, to Chungking; the cargo had originated in Tibet and was bound for Shanghai, and it carried $100 in postage. "They send it by air," he noted, "largely because of the robberies that often occur to surface mail."[58]

Sometimes the cargo was more melancholy than exotic. En route to Chengtu on a typically hazy, overcast day, Mitchell turned the controls over to his copilot and wrote in his diary:

In the baggage compartment is a small casket containing the body of little Homer Brown. Up until 2 months ago, he and his family lived next door to us in Chengtu. Every morning Homer (he was 2½ years old) and his amah (native child nurse) would be waiting for me in the company car. They would ride to the gate of the University, then walk back. Every morning they were there, as regular as clockwork, for motor cars are scarce in Chengtu, and it is a great privilege to ride in one. Homer was a husky, cheerful little fellow, and very much interested in the car and all about it. He and I were great friends. Then one day about two months ago, Homer's family left on a native boat for Chungking (it took them two weeks to get there). Homer became very sick and at Chungking, the doctor diagnosed it as spinal meningitus. For over 5 weeks, he made a wonderful fight, but yesterday it was too much for him and life left his husky little body. And now Homer is on his last ride, back to Chengtu where he will be laid by his little sister who died a few years ago.[59]

Mitchell resided on the campus of a Chinese university in Chengtu. As the city completely lacked any form of entertainment, he had ample opportunity to admire the beauty of the countryside. "This a very beautiful time of year," he wrote in the spring of 1934. "There are many rose bushes covering up whole sides of houses and full of blossoms; trees of all sorts have a good foliage started; fruit trees, pears, cherries, etc. are blooming, and flowering shrubs are in blossom." Visiting the countryside adjacent to the campus, Mitchell found "countless fields of mustard, Chinese beans (big flat beans) and wheat . . . just getting full growth and soon to ripen and be ready for harvest. The mustard and beans have been blossoming for three weeks or so now and have filled the air with rich odors even to the point of drowning out the objectionable odors common to all China."[60]

One week later, Mitchell had an undesired break in his routine. As he was coming in to land at Chungking, the left shock-absorber strut of his Stinson came apart, and its wheel swung free under the airplane. The wheel folded underneath the aircraft upon landing, causing the left wing tip and propeller to strike the ground. Damage was not severe but took time to repair, and Mitchell now had a week to enjoy the pleasures of dank, dismal, sunless Chungking while awaiting parts from Shanghai. He stayed with Jesse Poole at the compound of the Socony Vacuum Oil Company, and he went to see movies that were shown free to all Westerners by the American gunboat *U. S. S. Guam*. He attended a show—"a sort of musical comedy"—put on by the crew of a British gunboat at the Foreign Club. The time passed quickly, and Mitchell soon was back in the cockpit of his Stinson, flying to Chengtu.[61]

Mitchell liked the Chinese people, but he did not care for the government of Szechwan under Marshal Liu. "Everything is squeezed out of the people that possibly can be, but the people have no comeback," he observed. "Taxes are terrific, to the point of taking all the poor people's income." The Nationalist government had banned cultivation of opium, but Marshal Liu made his own laws in Szechwan. "The whole thing is a racket which the military run at the expense of the people, both financially and physically. They force the farmers to put in at least 50% of their land into opium. Then they make opium shops legal and charge them a high tax, which, of course is passed on to the smokers, and do everything to encourage smoking of the drug."[62]

Mitchell left Szechwan without regret in early May 1934, his six-month assignment completed, and returned to flying the Shanghai-Peking line. "It seems mighty good to get back to the old run again," he wrote, "even though it seems like an awfully long day."[63]

The days would soon grow shorter, as CNAC began to acquire modern equipment in 1935. Two Ford trimotors, purchased from Pan American, arrived early in the year. Mitchell reported that one of the aircraft was only two years old and had been equipped with new engines, controllable-pitch propellers and the latest flight instruments. "It looks like a brand new ship," he wrote, "in spite of the fact that it had 1900 hours on the Mexico City–Brownsville run of PAA. They certainly do maintain their equipment well."[64]

The big surprise came in late March when a brand new Douglas DC-2 was off-loaded at Shanghai. At this moment, the DC-2 was the most modern airliner in the world; the famous DC-3 would not make its first flight in the United States until December 1935. The DC-2 lifted fourteen passengers in very comfortable accommodations—magnificent compared to a Loening or Stinson—and flew them to their destination at 190 mph, an incredible speed in 1935. If nothing else, the DC-2's arrival was dramatic evidence that Pan American was more than meeting its commitments to its Chinese subsidiary, at least in terms of modern equipment.

The sleek and silvery DC-2 created all kinds of excitement with Hewitt Mitchell: "I have been definitely assigned to fly it," he reported, "and it will be a real experience to have so expensive and so modern an airplane to fly. Its cost is about U.S. $90,000, and it is considered to be the world's best ship of its class. As soon as it arrives, I plan to spend all my spare time at the field studying its interior as it is assembled."[65]

The DC-2 met Mitchell's high expectations. In early May, Mitchell made a round trip to Peking with a factory representative from the Douglas Aircraft Company. "Returned to Shanghai non-stop, a distance of 650 miles," he wrote, "in 3 hrs. 35 min. . . . and that against a headwind a good part of the way!" The aircraft impressed him in every way: "In spite of its large size and weight (18,200 pounds), I have been amazed to find that it has a very quick take-off and slow, short-landing characteristics. These things mean a great deal to us as we have restricted fields most places. Its speed is excellent at high altitudes, but rather poor (135 mph) at less than 2000 feet as the air is too dense to use the high pitch on the propellers below that altitude."[66]

For all of a year, Mitchell flew the DC-2 back and forth over the Shanghai-Peking line. In the spring of 1936, however, personal problems closed in on him; he allowed his contract to expire, returned to the United States, and took a position with American Airlines. He later joined Canadian Colonial Airways, becoming a check pilot in their New York-Montreal run. Recalled to military service in 1942, he helped establish the northern ferry route to England via Newfoundland, Greenland, and Iceland; and for a time he was based at Washington, D.C.'s Bolling Field, flying VIPs for the Air Transport Command. Assigned to Homestead Field, Florida, in 1943 as an engineering officer, one of his duties involved trouble-shooting the new Curtiss C-46, an engineering nightmare which had been plagued by engine fires, later traced to a faulty fuel system. On Sunday, August 8, 1943, Mitchell test flew a C-46 that had undergone wing modifications. An engine caught fire shortly after take-off, and Mitchell tried to bring the aircraft back to the field. He almost made it. On final approach, about 50 feet off the ground, the left wing collapsed and Major Hewitt F. Mitchell perished in the subsequent holocaust. He was buried with full military honors at Arlington National Cemetery.[67]

While flying the Shanghai-Peking line, Mitchell had commented on the poor state of landing areas along the route. The field at Haichow was a pasture, frequently filled with cows, donkeys, and people. Tsingtao's airport was a small piece of cleared land, surrounded by telephone and power lines. "In fact," he had quipped, "Tsingtao airport is the nearest like an American airport we have, because it is the only one that can be found by simply following the high tension wires to where they intersect!" Peking used a military parade ground, across which soldiers often erected overhead telephone lines without bothering to notify CNAC. These airports were typical of facilities throughout China. The entire country did not have a single hard-surfaced runway. If CNAC was to operate large, modern aircraft, new airports were necessary—and Shanghai was the obvious place to begin.[68]

CNAC's main base at Lunghwa was a military parade ground. When the soldiers evacuated the field at the time of the Japanese attack in February 1932, employees of the airline pulled down the barracks adjacent to the field, thereby removing a landing hazard and also insuring that the soldiers would not return. As part of its contract with the Ministry of Communications for operation of the Canton route, Pan American agreed to advance $25,000 for improvement of CNAC's facilities, which enabled the airline to construct a new hangar, completed in June 1934. CNAC also contracted for a new runway. A portion of the parade ground, 50 feet wide by 1,200 feet long, was dug and leveled to a depth of six inches. Hundreds of Chinese women with hammers broke up the bricks from the former barracks and placed them in the excavation. The crushed bricks were then covered by cinders and clay, and the whole mass rolled. Within a short time, grass came up through the crushed bricks. The result, Bixby reported, was "an exceptionally fine runway—resilient, dustless, and yielding enough to start airplane wheels rolling without 'scorching' the tires at the time of first impact." CNAC later added a comparable runway at right angles to the original but at considerably higher cost.[69]

Bixby realized that this work could set an unfortunate precedent; the Nationalist government, reluctant to spend funds for airport construction, would be content to see CNAC bear the financial burden of building new airfields. He therefore began a campaign to convince authorities of cities along the airline's route that improved facilities would bring immediate economic benefits and eventual financial return through user fees. Shanghai, under Mayor Wu Te-chen, responded by authorizing $250,000 for improvements at Lunghwa. The result was the finest airport in China, with two 4,000-foot hard-surfaced runways, completed in 1934. Nanking, Tsingtao, and other progressive cities followed Shanghai's lead. The Nationalist government, forever at odds within itself, did nothing. Chinese military pilots, operating from inadequate fields with heavily loaded airplanes, were to pay a high price for this neglect when war broke out with Japan in 1937.[70]

CNAC also improved its communications and weather reporting facilities during the years 1934–1937, and new radio direction-finding beacons were installed at Shanghai and Canton. Unfortunately, airborne direction-finding receivers did not prove entirely satisfactory, and CNAC was slow to adopt the excellent Telefunken equipment of the Lorenz system used by Eurasia.[71]

Inadequate weather information was a constant problem in China, and CNAC had to develop its own network of reporting stations. Initially, Chinese radio operators took elementary observations at stations along CNAC's routes for transmission to Shanghai. As these individuals were not trained observers, had no equipment, and could not speak English, the airline devised a simplified system of reporting. Generally, three prominent landmarks were selected, approximately one, three-to-five, and eight-to-ten miles distant from the observer, and these were labeled "X", "Y", and "Z". The radio operator, for example, could then report: "X" visible, "Y" dull, "Z" invisible. Although crude, the system worked fairly well with the relatively slow Loenings and Stinsons.[72]

Modern aircraft, however, equipped with radios for air-to-ground communication, and flying higher and faster, required more sophisticated weather data, and they required it more quickly. CNAC modernized its weather reporting facilities. Reports were now received on all surface conditions and on conditions in the upper air. The improved system not only contributed to the safety and regularity of the airline's operations, but it also brought direct economic benefits. Upper air readings alone, Bixby noted, were worth "far more than the cost of the service, for it frequently happened that a ten-mile head wind at a thousand feet became a helpful tail wind at five thousand feet." The resultant saving of gasoline and engine hours added up to a substantial sum.[73]

CNAC's balance sheet for the fiscal year ending June 30, 1935, showed the first profit in the airline's history. The Board of Directors wisely decided to defer dividends and invest the money in new equipment. CNAC purchased a total of three Ford trimotors and two Douglas DC-2s in 1935. Utilizing the credit facilities of Pan American, these aircraft were obtained without down payment. Passenger service in China soon attained a level comparable to the best service offered by American airlines, and travel time to points along CNAC's routes was cut in half. CNAC even began to look like an airline. The new Pilots' Manual ordered: "The pilot's uniform shall consist of a double breasted blue serge coat, blue serge trousers, black socks, black oxfords, bright blue four-in-hand necktie, white shirt and blue serge cap. The cap will have a gold braid band and the CNAC shield set in gold leaves.... The CNAC wings will be worn above the left coat pocket. During the summer months white duck trousers and a white cover for the cap will be worn." Pilots of the old Loening open-cockpit amphibians, however, were allowed to keep their heavy flying suits in winter and to wear white coveralls in summer.[74]

While CNAC underwent modernization, the airline reduced passenger fares in search of business. The 1,500-mile long Yangtze Valley with a population of 200 million was the commercial heart of China, and although increasing volume of mail carried by the airline indicated its great traffic potential, passenger bookings had been disappointing. Bixby blamed competition from river boats. "The finest river boats in China ply this route," he noted; "service is excellent, food, either Chinese or foreign, is good. Staterooms are large and clean, bunks comfortable, river smooth and scenery while not grand is calm and peaceful." The trip between Shanghai and Hankow took three days and cost $20. The journey could be flown in three hours, but it cost $65. In the summer of 1934, CNAC reduced its fare on the Shanghai-Hankow route to $50, with comparable reductions on other routes. The new rates were experimental, in effect from June 15 to September 15. The experiment proved a resounding success. CNAC experienced the busiest period in its history; aircraft were booked far in advance, and in many cases the airline had to turn away people. CNAC responded by making the new fares permanent. In 1935, as Ford trimotors and Douglas DC-2s came into service, the fare to Hankow again was reduced to $40, with comparable reductions on other routes.[75]

The years 1934–1937 also saw several projects for expanding CNAC's routes, prompted mainly by the Nationalist government's efforts to unite China under its authority. An attempt to establish closer relations with Tibet following the death of the Dalai Lama brought plans in 1934 for air service between Shanghai and Lhasa. While this scheme proved abortive, a more successful project involved service to Kweiyang and Kunming (Yunnanfu).[76]

A narrow pathway afforded the only means of direct communication between Chungking and Kunming, capital of Yunnan Province. It took twelve days by sedan chair to reach Kweiyang, capital of Kweichow Province, and another twelve days, across high mountains, to Kunming. The journey from Chungking to Kunming by air would take three hours. In 1935 Chiang Kai-shek undertook major campaigns in Kweichow and Yunnan against Communist forces that had been driven out of Kiangsi Province in central China. In order to strengthen ties with the local governments of the beleaguered provinces, the Nationalists granted CNAC a subsidy of $100,000 to develop an air route to Kunming via Kweiyang.[77]

Bixby and a party of company officials took off from Shanghai in the new Ford trimotor on March 25, 1935, to survey the projected route. In order to take on additional reserves of fuel, Bixby and Ki Chun, a director of the airline, remained in

Chungking while Floyd Nelson and crew continued on the Kweiyang. Nelson returned a few days later and reported heavy fighting in the area between the Communists and Nationalists. Bixby joined the survey party for another flight to Kweiyang on March 30. Attempts to reach Kunming, however, were thwarted by bad weather.[78]

CNAC inaugurated regular service with Ford trimotors to Kweiyang in April 1935 and to Kunming in July. Despite the great savings in time afforded by air, traffic on the route proved to be a disappointment, no doubt because of the unsettled conditions in the provinces. Still, as the government subsidized the line, it remained in operation for more than a year. Shortage of equipment finally brought an end to the service.

In March 1936, pilot Byron O'Hara ran out of fuel in a snow storm and crash-landed on a mountainside near Tengya in Yunnan Province. Crew and passengers escaped without serious injury, but the Ford suffered extensive damage. Later that same month, a second Ford, piloted by Charles Sharp, caught fire on approach to Nanking. Sharp landed safely but the fire could not be contained and the aircraft was destroyed. This left CNAC with only one Ford trimotor. One additional Ford was on order, but the airline did not have sufficient equipment to maintain its schedules. Service to Yunnan had to be suspended in September 1936.[79]

CNAC ran into problems of a different nature when the airline sought to inaugurate China's first international service. The Chinese government had for long been interested in developing an air link to Europe. When the Germans of Eurasia abandoned plans for a Nanking-Berlin route due to Soviet objections, the Chinese entered negotiations with French authorities for a connection with Air France at Hanoi. Initially, these conversations had made little progress. Like the British, the French wanted reciprocal rights to operate in China; the Chinese refused to grant the concession out of the certainty that Japan would demand similar rights. In November 1935, however, France decided to allow the Chinese to begin service to Hanoi without securing reciprocal privileges, a decision no doubt influenced by the success of Pan American's transpacific service.[80]

When the Ministry of Communications awarded the contract for the Canton-Hanoi route to CNAC, the militarists in the southern provinces of Kwantung and Kwangsi protested. Foreigners partially controlled CNAC, they said, and the contract should have gone to Southwestern Aviation Corporation, a small airline operated exclusively by Chinese.[81]

This nationalistic argument was largely if not wholly specious. Southwestern was owned jointly by the governments of Kwantung and Kwangsi. Its seven Stinsons and three Loenings were flown by military pilots based at the military field in Canton. The airline had inaugurated interprovincial service between Canton and Lungchow via Wuchow and Nanning in May 1934 but had abandoned the route by the end of the year. It currently operated service between Canton and Pakhoi. As South China remained the center of opposition to Chiang Kai-shek, the militarists pushed the claims of Southwestern in order to demonstrate their independence from Nanking. CNAC became caught in the middle.[82]

Allison conducted a survey flight between Canton and Hanoi via the French enclave at Fort Bayard in late November 1935 without incident. An attempt to inaugurate regular service on February 14, 1936, misfired when the airplane was unable to proceed beyond Fort Bayard due to bad weather. Cecil Sellers flying a Douglas Dolphin amphibian arrived in Canton from Shanghai on February 27 for a second attempt. This time local authorities prevented the aircraft from leaving for Hanoi. CNAC instructed Sellers to return to Shanghai and suspended service until Nanking and Canton could settle their dispute.[83]

The action of the Cantonese dealt a sharp blow to the prestige of the Nationalists. Nanking clearly would have to respond to this challenge, but Chiang wanted to avoid trouble with the southern faction until he ended the campaign against the Communists. The Nationalist government, therefore, swallowed its pride, withdrew the contract from CNAC, and awarded the route to Southwestern. The Cantonese victory proved a Pyrrhic one.

Buoyed by their easy triumph over Nanking, the southern dissidents threatened another declaration of independence. With the war against the Communists progressing satisfactorily, Chiang moved troops to the borders of Kwangtung and Kwangsi. The revolt collapsed from within when most of the Cantonese air force defected to the Nationalists. As a sop to the vanquished southerners, Southwestern was allowed to continue service to Hanoi for a time. The airline went out of business in 1938.[84]

Despite the setbacks on the Yunnan and Hanoi routes, CNAC basked in the warm sun of success during 1936–1937. The airline had made enormous progress since the arrival of Pan American in China. By the spring of 1937, CNAC had in operation or on order four Douglas DC-2s, one Sikorsky S-43 amphibian, two Douglas Dolphins, two Ford trimotors, four Loenings, and five Stinsons. There were 34 pilots and copilots, and a trained staff of ground personnel. Between 1929 and 1936, CNAC flew 5,538,974 miles and carried 838,271 pounds of mail and 46,404 passengers. The airline had compiled an excellent safety record, with only four passenger fatalities. Despite heavy payments for new equipment, the airline was showing an increasing annual profit and had $15,000 in the bank. Dai Enki, CNAC's managing director from 1933 to 1937, credited this progress "to the wise and far-sighted policy of the Board, the sincere co-operation of the American associates, and the untiring efforts of all staffs of this corporation." There is no reason to disagree with him.[85]

While the future seemed bright, there were growing tensions beneath the surface that threatened to tear the airline apart. The Chinese applied growing pressure for the use of its nationals in CNAC's operations. For example, when Charles S. Vaughn, one of CNAC's ablest pilots, was about to return to the United States on leave, Dai Enki insisted that his contract be terminated and a Chinese replacement hired. Bond refused and took the matter to K. C. Huang, chairman of the board of directors. "I said," Bond recalled, "that I was not just defending Mr. Vaughn, I was also defending the sanctity of the contract which provided that the American partners would have charge of operations." When

Huang supported Dai Enki, Bond demonstrated one of the reasons why he was so successful in dealing with the Chinese. He suggested that the two men go to Nanking and lay the matter before Chiang Kai-shek. "I knew," Bond continued, "that Mr. Huang spoke fluent English, French, and German but almost no Chinese, and I knew very well that he would never go to see the Generalissimo and have to use an interpreter. Mr. Huang said that the matter was not that important. I apologized for my seeming stubbornness and eased out. Vaughn went home on leave *and returned* in good standing."[86]

More serious problems arose over the use of CNAC's aircraft at times of national emergency. During the trouble with Japan in the northern provinces in 1933, Chinese authorities asked CNAC to fly machine gun ammunition from Shanghai to Peking. Bond pointed out that such a mission would jeopardize the commercial character of the airline and violate laws that prohibited American citizens from engaging in unneutral activities. Furthermore, Japan had been notified through the American consul of the commercial status of the company, and, although the Japanese commanded the air over Peking, they had not bothered CNAC. Apparent Japanese recognition of the airline's non-belligerent status, Bond argued, was more important than the transportation of one cargo of ammunition.[87]

The Chinese did not press the issue; however, the matter came up again in April 1935 during the survey expedition to Kweiyang when a CNAC pilot was ordered to fly bombs from Chungking to Kweiyang in support of the drive against the Communists. Bixby demurred for two reasons: "First, the operation was an extremely hazardous one in that the landing fields at both places were small and the carriage of bombs, particularly with the percussion caps attached, is at best a highly hazardous undertaking. In the second place, we had repeatedly emphasized to our Chinese associates the necessity of preserving the commercial status of CNAC and thus make it possible for the American pilots to continue in the service of the Company in time of emergency." With respect to Bixby's second point, the Chinese argued that the Communists were bandits, thus there would be no violation of American law, which only dealt with international wars. Deciding not to contest the legal issue, Bixby offered to give the pilot a leave of absence if the Chinese could persuade him to carry the dangerous cargo, and to release the plane for use by the military. By this time, other arrangements had been made, and the crisis passed.[88]

The position of both sides in these disputes is understandable. Even granting the lack of time and equipment, the Americans were slow to train Chinese pilots. By the spring of 1937 —after a passage of seven years—only four Chinese had been advanced to command positions, and three of these were American-born. On the other hand, the Chinese government had done little to provide commercial pilot training for its nationals. Pressure for use of CNAC during time of emergency raised the question of whether or not majority Chinese ownership meant anything more than agreement on paper. Other nations considered their commercial air carriers an adjunct of the military during times of crisis. But Bixby was no doubt right that given the weak position of China vis-à-vis Japan, retention of the commercial character of CNAC served a more broad and flexible Chinese interest.

In any event, the undercurrent of tensions between the Chinese and Americans rose to the surface during 1936 and 1937. Chu Chia-hua, the tough but capable minister of communications, lost his position in a cabinet shuffle in December 1935. Bond reported in June 1936 that the acting minister Yü Fei-peng, seemed in league with the National Aviation Commission, a military organization that was seeking to control all aviation in China. This portended a replay of the old drama last performed in 1929–1930. Yü transmitted instructions from the commission ordering CNAC to transfer its head office and equipment to isolated Chengtu, a move that would have completely disorganized the airline. Although Bond managed to evade this incredible order, harassment of CNAC continued. At one point, the Ministry of Communications ordered the airline to qualify Chinese pilots in the new Douglas DC-2s within six months. Bixby pointed out that "pilots cannot be made by legislation" and, after considerable argument, won his point. Instructions then came down to write all purchase orders in Chinese. Bixby explained that if he ordered twelve cylinders from Pan American's purchasing department, a translation by a local interpreter would likely come out "twelve pieces fire pots." The Chinese compromised: purchase orders would be written in both languages. The minister of communications pressed CNAC to build a hangar at Chengtu, which would be turned over to the Aviation Commission; the airline should contribute $100,000 for improvement of Nanking's airport; and so it went.[89]

Concerned about these developments, Bixby flew to Nanking in March 1937 to seek the advice of Ambassador Johnson and Consul General Peck. Bixby emphasized the intense pressure applied on the airline in recent months, and he expressed apprehension about the future of the American interest in CNAC. Could the diplomats use their personal and informal contacts to find out what the Chinese were up to so Pan American could plan accordingly? Peck suggested that T. V. Soong and the China Development Finance Corporation might wish to purchase the American share in CNAC. Bixby said he was interested in this idea but he wondered how the American government would feel if Pan American sold out. It would be a sign, Johnson replied, that the Chinese were able to conduct their own affairs.[90]

Two months later, in May 1937, Dai Enki resigned—or was forced out—as managing director of CNAC and was replaced by Lem Wei-shing, a colonel in the Chinese Air Force. Colonel Lem, reflecting the military's old jealousy of CNAC, let it be known that, sooner or later, the airline would be nationalized. As the Chinese government already owned 55 percent of the company, Lem's meaning was clear: the Sino-American partnership faced a crisis.[91]

— III —

Pan American's acquisition of CNAC in 1933 meant a new beginning for commercial aviation in China. Following a shaky and tragic start, the Canton route was solidly established as an integral part of the transpacific service. The Yangtze Valley line reached Chengtu in the far interior, and the Peking route, after its hesitant beginning under Curtiss-Wright, became a reality. New equipment and modernized ground facilities thrust CNAC into the ranks of the world's major airlines. Traffic increased on all routes; chronic deficits turned to profits.

CNAC prospered as an economic enterprise, but, as Harold Bixby pointed out: "CNAC is not a business organization. It is political." By 1937, the future of the airline was again in doubt, as factions within the Chinese government battled for control of commercial aviation. Decisions made in Nanking or Washington, however, were not to determine the fate of the airline; Tokyo was soon to cast the deciding vote.

CHAPTER FOUR
CHINA'S LIFELINE
1937–1941

— I —

CHIANG KAI-SHEK'S program of political unification and economic reconstruction made remarkable progress during the years 1933–1936. Opposition to Nationalist authority declined in 1936 to its lowest point since the founding of the Republic. The Cantonese faction, a constant thorn in the side of the central government, had been humbled after the defection of their air force to Nanking, and the Communists had been pushed into the remote areas of the country. Even the kidnapping and subsequent release of Chiang in December 1936, followed by the formation of a Nationalist-Communist "united front" against Japan, failed to undermine the Generalissimo's power and prestige. "His position and that of the Central Government," judged the authoritative *Survey of International Affairs*, "appeared at the end of the year [1936], to have survived successfully the assaults which had been delivered from so many different directions . . . and to have emerged, in fact, stronger than ever."[1]

The Nationalists recorded comparable gains in economic affairs. Improved and extended railroads and motor roads mitigated, to some extent, the chronic problem of inadequate communications. Foreign investment, attracted by the evident stability of the central government, assisted industrial development, especially the growth of light industry. Monetary reform promised a sound currency. As financial adviser Arthur Young later wrote: "After a turbulent decade, the outlook was bright for an era of unprecedented progress in China, if only the country could remain at peace."[2]

CNAC had played a significant role in the political and economic advances of these years. The airline afforded fast and efficient transportation for mail, priority cargo, government officials, and Chinese and Western businessmen. It forged a link between the Yangtze Valley, center of Nationalist power, and the outlying regions of China—north to Peking, west to Chengtu, and south to Canton. Paradoxically but inevitably, CNAC's success was leading toward its demise, at least as a Sino-American partnership. China's growing strength intensified nationalistic sentiment throughout the country, and the airline became one of the targets of this heightened feeling. The government made clear to Pan American in 1937 that CNAC would be allowed to expire in July 1940, when the ten-year contract between the Ministry of Communications and the American partner came up for reconsideration. The Chinese planned to exercise their option and purchase the American share of the company's assets. But this was not to be. Within a short time, the Chinese would need the airline as they had never before needed it—and they would need Pan American's expertise to keep it operating.[3]

"If the country could remain at peace," Arthur Young had written; but 1937 brought war, not peace. An uneasy truce had existed between Japan and China since the spring of 1933. Employing both subtle and overt pressure, the Japanese had sought to consolidate their dominant position in northern China and to extend their influence throughout the country. The Chinese had resisted, passively at first; but as the nation grew in strength, its resistance became more overt and militant. In July 1937, Japanese and Chinese troops clashed at the Marco Polo Bridge, near Peking. The incident appeared at first no more serious than previous skirmishes between the two parties, and it seemed that the dispute might be settled within a few days. Both sides displayed new attitudes in the summer of 1937. A frustrated Japan, intent upon chastising an old enemy, faced a stronger and prouder China. Heavy fighting broke out in late July, as the two governments moved fresh troops to the border area. By early August, the incident had broadened into a war.[4]

Officials of CNAC were not unduly concerned over the trouble in the north. They viewed the fighting as merely another episode—albeit, a major one—in a long series of such disputes that would be resolved as in the past, by negotiation. The airline continued its operations to Peking during July without incident; the Japanese seemed prepared to honor CNAC's non-belligerent status, as they had before. Even the intensified fighting that erupted at the end of the month failed to shake the belief, shared by most Old China Hands, that negotiations would soon follow. Certainly, Shanghai was not in danger.

On August 9, 1937, a confused incident outside Shanghai resulted in the deaths of two Japanese sailors and a Chinese soldier. Accusations and recriminations followed, and the situation grew explosive. August 13 brought a serious clash between Japanese and Chinese troops. Walter C. ("Foxie") Kent, a pilot for CNAC who had been a member of the Jouett Mission, heard rumors on Saturday, August 14, that his former students from the Central Aviation School would attack the Japanese flagship *Idzumo*, anchored in the Whangpoo River, adjacent to the International Settlement. Kent and William Hunt, an American businessman, decided to watch the show from atop an eleven-story office building located behind the British Consulate in downtown Shanghai. "I was fairly boiling with excitement," Kent later wrote. "Here was a chance to see in action what our group [the Jouett Mission] had worked to build up —the participants would be men I'd helped to train, many of them friends of mine. I'll swear at the time I thought of the coming fracas mainly as a demonstration of military technique and not in terms of flesh and blood."[5]

Kent and Hunt waited for two hours on the rooftop, watching normal Saturday traffic along the Bund, the main thoroughfare in the International Settlement. Hunt had an appointment to meet Mrs. Theodore Roosevelt, Jr., at the Cathay Hotel. As he began to leave, six Chinese aircraft broke through the thin overcast that covered the city. Kent was elated: "Chinese bombers! There was the wing insignia, familiar to me as my own initials—Lord, what a kick it gave me!" *Idzumo* opened fire, scoring a hit on one aircraft. The remaining bombers struck shore batteries near the warship. Six more planes appeared, this time flying a course across the wind. Kent watched as the aircraft drifted over the International Settlement. He stood frozen as eight bombs "seemed to float as slowly as feathers" toward the ground in front of the British Consulate. When the explosives struck, it appeared as if the entire Palace Hotel—a six-story building at the corner of Nanking Road and the Bund—rose in the air; a sheet of flame enveloped the adjacent Cathay Hotel. Kent and Hunt rushed downstairs to see if Mrs. Roosevelt had been injured. "Just as we turned," Kent reported, "I had my first sight of the human—not the military—angle of war. Down the side street a coolie woman was running—her face a mask of horror and grief, in her arms a little girl of about two years; the baby's entire face was blown away. The woman's features writhed in anguished grimaces; tears poured over her cheeks. I hope I shan't keep on remembering it as I do now."

Kent reached the main street only to find more horror. "The Bund was a shambles; hundreds of people screaming, running, falling beneath stampeding feet. The traffic officer, neatly decapitated, lay quietly on his back with not even his uniform damaged. A coolie, with his whole calf torn away, dazedly jammed his hand into the hole, but with every heartbeat blood spurted like a fountain." Arriving at the hotel, the two men found the front door barred, and they had to enter through a side window. "The lobby was thick with smoke; great pools of blood smeared the magnificent Oriental rugs; people rushed about screaming, falling, rising and falling again—some wounded, some singed by fire from the explosions; some, I think, unconscious from shock and concussion." Somehow, in the pandemonium, Hunt learned that Mrs. Roosevelt had gone out just before the bombing.

Kent left to find his wife, who was seriously ill in a hospital after having given premature birth to their first child. He drove down Foochow Road toward Avenue Edward VII, the boundary between the International Settlement and the French Concession. As he neared the crowded intersection of Tibet Road and Edward VII, two bombs landed some 200 yards ahead. "A great, pyramid-shaped mass rose straight up in the air," Kent reported, "with solid sheets of flame shunting sideways. Bodies soared like skyrockets; heads, arms, legs, scattered back to earth; some seemed literally to splatter like too-ripe fruit against the side

How cargo was brought from the Gobi desert: Peking:1935
(J. R. McCleskey and the station manager are astride the camel)

Douglas Dolphin, 1936 (E. M. Allison in bow)

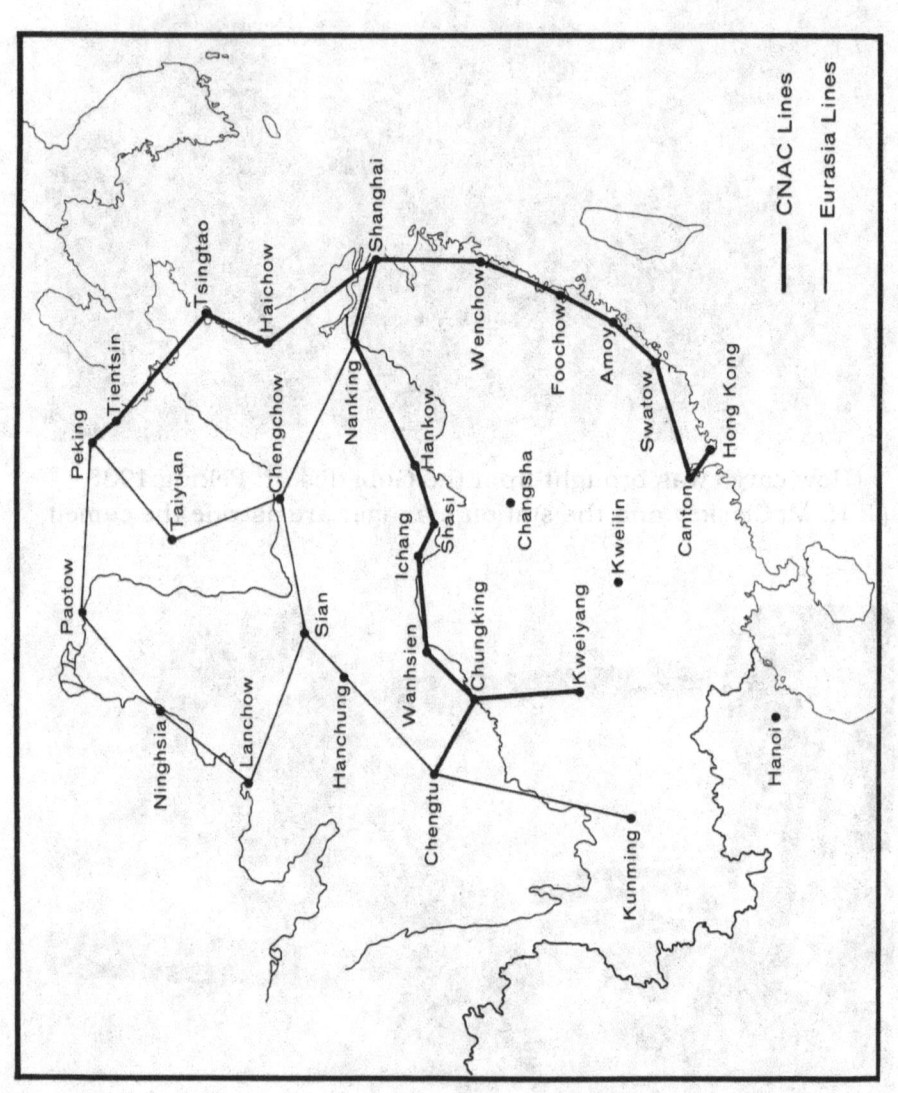

Air routes, 1937

of buildings. Ghastly fire flared suddenly all about; it was from automobiles with gas tanks punctured by shrapnel. In a few seconds they'd burn to ashes, before wounded or unconscious occupants could escape." He continued: "Can you believe that 1053 were killed that night, and next day it took thirty-seven trucks to haul away mangled remains? All over the street and inside stores and buildings, heads, arms, legs, and fragments of flesh were scattered like ghastly confetti." Kent's figures were low; actually, 1,740 were killed and 1,873 injured in the holocaust.

Kent managed to evacuate his wife and infant son, enclosed in an incubator, to Manila via sea. "The Shanghai we got out of yesterday," he wrote on the ship while en route to the Philippines, "is as near to my idea of hell as human eyes can bear to see."[6]

CNAC became swept up in the confusion that attended the outbreak of fighting in the Shanghai area. While Kent watched the bombing of the city, Charles L. ("Chuck") Sharp was piloting a DC-2 over Hupeh Province enroute to Nanchang. The Ministry of Finance had chartered the aircraft to carry banknotes to Shanghai. After Sharp landed at Nanchang, he found military officials swarming around the aircraft. They ordered him to fly bomb racks and machine guns to an air force base near Hangchow. Sharp said no; CNAC was a commercial airline, he was an American citizen and a neutral. The military officials threatened to shoot if he did not follow their orders. Sharp flew the cargo to Hangchow at gunpoint.[7]

When Bixby learned of this incident the next day, he pointed out to Managing Director Lem "that our American pilots can be a real help to China in maintaining communications in the present emergency. They are as willing and anxious to do their part as we are to have them cooperate." But the commercial status of CNAC had to be maintained. Personnel could not engage in military operations without violating American law. "All American pilots in the employ of CNAC," Bixby concluded, "have been instructed to remain on the ground until safeguards of a character satisfactory to us have been taken to protect American pilots in the future against unauthorized and illegal acts of the nature experienced by pilot Sharp."[8]

Colonel Lem replied to Bixby by commandeering several aircraft that were at Nanking and replacing the American crews with Chinese military personnel. On August 16, Japanese naval authorities advised the American consul in Shanghai that CNAC would no longer be considered a non-belligerent commercial enterprise. The consul delivered the message to Bixby, informed him that the airline's personnel had already violated American neutrality law, and that their continued service with CNAC would constitute further violations.[9]

Faced with seizure of the company's aircraft by the managing director, threats from the Japanese, and the disapproval of the State Department, Bixby had no choice but to withdraw all American personnel. Force of circumstance, he announced on August 22, had changed CNAC from a purely commercial to a semi-military organization. Under existing law, the Americans had to leave under penalty of fine and imprisonment. "There has been talk," he concluded, "about a break between Pan American Airways and the China National Aviation Corporation. That is complete rubbish. The planes are being used for semi-military purposes and in a time of national emergency I think that any Government would feel free to make use of such a service operating in its territories." He left undefined the relationship between the American partner and the Chinese partner during time of war.[10]

Bond was on leave in the United States when war broke out in China. After the fighting in Shanghai, he went to Pan American's offices in the Chrysler Building at 42nd and Lexington in New York for discussions with Stokely Morgan, head of Pacific operations, and Juan Trippe. Trippe stressed Pan American's desire to follow American foreign policy; it seemed impossible to continue operations in China under present circumstances. Aircraft, personnel, and as much of the company's funds as possible should be flown to Manila to await developments. Trippe offered Bond a position in New Zealand, the terminus of a new transpacific route Pan American had inaugurated from Hawaii in early 1937. Although the offer was tempting, Bond declined; he felt responsible for the fate of CNAC and wanted to return to China. "I told Mr. Morgan," Bond recalled, "that I was leaving for Hong Kong at once. He said that he would not try to stop me but reminded me that I was giving up something very good and was risking my future with the company. I said that I realized that but I still thought I was obligated to go. He only repeated that he would not try to stop me."[11]

Bond was soon on his way halfway around the world to Asia. He flew by domestic airlines to San Francisco, a flight of eighteen hours, where he boarded one of Pan American's Martin M-130 Clippers. The flight to Hawaii was an overnight one and took almost another eighteen hours. After a night in a hotel in Honolulu, he was off to Midway Island for another overnight stop. He reboarded the Clipper the next day and flew to Wake Island, where everyone—flight crew and passengers—spent the night. He reached Guam the next day. The following morning he was off for Manila, which he reached that evening, seven days after he had left New York City. There remained the flight across the South China Sea to Hong Kong via the connecting Sikorsky S-42 Clipper. Although the trip may seem lengthy in an era of jet aircraft, in 1937 Bond had made a remarkably rapid journey. The alternative route, by rail across the United States and steamship across the Pacific, would have taken almost a month.

Despite the rigors of the journey, Bond reached Hong Kong in late August "fresh and fearless and ready and willing and able to save China for the Chinese—and not the least bit discouraged. I damn soon was." Allison met Bond at Kai Tak's moorings for marine aircraft. The Chinese had the airplanes, Allison said, and American personnel were awaiting transportation—better described as evacuation—to Manila and the United States. Bond criticized Allison for mishandling operations during his absence. Allison protested that he had done all he could in an impossible situation. "I agreed," Bond noted, "that it was a tough situation, but insisted he should have gotten the 'planes and as much equipment as possible out to Hankow and then decide what could be done—go home if necessary." Allison, according to

Bond, "got angry as hell." The two men, who had worked so well together for five years, parted company.[12]

Bixby arrived in Hong Kong from Manila the next day. He told Bond that CNAC was finished. The Chinese considered the departure of the American personnel an act of treachery; Pan American had deserted China during its hour of need. With thoughts of Auckland, New Zealand, in mind, Bond was certain that "I had burned my bridge behind me and there was a stone wall in front of me."[13]

In the months ahead, Bond fought to reestablish the American partnership. He tried to see T. V. Soong, but the minister would not grant him an interview. Bond then sent a memorandum to Soong, with a copy to Madame Chiang Kai-shek, stressing the continued value of the airline to China if operated as a non-military enterprise. The Americans would return, Bond insisted, but not until Colonel Lem was replaced, and the Chinese government guaranteed that there would be no further effort to use CNAC as a military auxiliary to the air force. It would be in China's best interest to continue the relationship with Pan American, whose officers had valuable connections with officials of the American government. In any event, he predicted that Chinese personnel would prove incapable of running CNAC.[14]

Bond sat back to await developments. After the airline's operations ground to a halt under the inept management of the Chinese military, W. H. Donald, an Australian-born adviser to the Chiangs, paid a visit to Bond. Donald said that the government was prepared to guarantee the commercial status of CNAC. What is more, Bond should submit a list of three names, from which Madame Chiang would select a new managing director. Finally, the contract with Pan American, due to expire in July 1940, would be renewed for an additional five years.[15]

Bond flew to Manila and explained the situation to Bixby, who then called Juan Trippe over the transpacific telephone. In order to secure Pan American's consent to renewed American participation and to avoid problems with the State Department's lexicon of legalisms, Bond resigned from Pan American and became an employee of the Chinese government. American personnel who agreed to return to China would do likewise. Trippe agreed to this novel arrangement.[16]

Bond had an interview with Generalissimo and Madame Chiang in mid-December 1937 to confirm the agreement with Donald. Bond had submitted the names of Ho Chi-wei, Dai Enki, and P. Y. Wong for managing director. Ho was Bond's first choice; he had proved a capable managing director at the time of the Shanghai Incident in 1932, and his brother was the minister of war. Dai Enki, the second choice, had been an outstanding managing director of the airline during the years 1933–1937. Madame Chiang, however, selected Wong, a graduate of the Wharton School of Finance in Philadelphia and business manager of CNAC under Dai Enki. "As it turned out," Bond noted, "I am sure he was the best for the times and conditions. Also he knew that he had received his appointment because of my recommendation although I never told him." Bond apologized for any "misunderstanding" that had occurred during the confused and turbulent days after the Marco Polo Bridge incident, and he pledged Pan American's continued support to China.[17]

During the winter of 1937–1938, Bond sought to retrieve the services of Americans who had left China the previous summer. Only Harold Sweet had defied the State Department and Pan American by staying with CNAC. Meanwhile, many former employees of the airline had sought and found safe havens with Pan American's growing empire. McCleskey joined Panagra, while Vaughn flew a Sikorsky S-42 on the Manila–Hong Kong stub of the transpacific route. Allison took a job as adviser to the Chinese Commission on Aeronautical Affairs. Sharp and Woods, two veteran pilots, had been offered positions with Panagra as copilots. Displeased because less senior men, who were married, had received captaincies, they decided to return to China when CNAC resumed operations. Robert W. Pottschmidt, who had flown the Shanghai–Peking line before the war, rejoined CNAC in June 1938. Other personnel were hired locally, such as Royal Leonard, personal pilot for various high officials in the Chinese government.[18]

CNAC had to develop an entirely new route structure when

it resumed operations in the spring of 1938. The Yangtze Valley from Shanghai to Nanking had fallen to the advancing Japanese, and the Nationalist government had transfered their capital to Chungking, some 1,500 miles into the interior. CNAC joined the Nationalists in exile. The airline found that facilities at Chungking were dismal. The city's airport, located on a small island in the Yangtze River, had a runway of only 2,000 feet, barely adequate for large Douglas airliners. Also, the rising waters of the muddy Yangtze frequently flooded the field during the middle months of the year. Japanese air attacks forced CNAC to seclude its storage and overhaul facilities in a deep cave halfway up the cliff upon which Chungking was built.[19]

CNAC operated flights east, south, and west from China's wartime capital. One route ran to Hankow, 440 miles to the east. A shorter line followed the Yangtze westward to Luchow and Suifu, then curved northward to Kiating, a total of 225 miles. A third route ran due south for 225 miles to Kweiyang in central Kweichow Province, thence westward 260 miles to Kunming. The airline's most important—and most profitable—route extended 770 miles to the southeast and connected Chungking to Hong Kong via Kweilin.

Operational problems abounded as the airline sought to reestablish itself, but these difficulties paled in comparison to the new hazard that lurked in the skies over China.

Captain Hugh Woods took off from Hong Kong's Kai Tak airport shortly after 8 A.M., August 24, 1938, for Chungking in a DC-2 named *Kweilin*. He carried a full load of fourteen passengers. A few minutes after crossing the boundary of the Colony, while climbing through 6,000 feet on a course of 297°, Woods sighted eight aircraft ahead and above. Woods had run into similar flights of Japanese military aircraft on previous occasions, and he was not unduly concerned. CNAC was again a purely commercical company, and the Japanese seemed prepared to return to the status quo ante bellum and treat the airline as a non-belligerent. The DC-2 had an unmistakable silhouette; *Kweilin* had "CNAC" painted in large black letters on the upper and lower surfaces of the wings and the Chinese characters for mail on the fuselage.

Although Woods did not expect trouble, just to be safe he turned back toward the border of British territory. After the Japanese planes disappeared, Woods resumed his original course. As he reached the western end of the bay between the territory of Hong Kong and the Chinese mainland, north of Macao, five Nakajima pursuit planes swooped down on *Kweilin*. Woods put the DC-2 into a steep dive and headed for a small patch of clouds some 5,000 feet below and to the left. Unfortunately, the clouds covered the tops of several small mountains. "I went to the edge of these clouds," Woods noted in his report of the incident,

and was in there for a few seconds and emerged on the other side. Directly ahead of me all was clear, so I started to turn to re-enter the clouds when I heard machine-gun bullets striking inside the control room. I immediately started descending in a tight spiral. During this spiral I could see the shadow of my 'plane, also the shadow of another 'plane directly at my rear. The terrain immediately underneath consisted of small rice paddy fields surrounded by dykes. I considered it extremely hazardous to attempt a landing on land due to these dykes, so I headed for a river a short distance to my right. I shut off the engines, cut the motor switches, and disconnected the battery, and glided into a landing on the water. During this time the plane was being struck by machine-gun bullets. The 'plane was landed safely near the right-hand side of the river. By the time the water cleared from the windshield, however, the current had caught the 'plane, and swept it into the middle of the current.

Woods found that none of the passengers had been injured. He raised the emergency hatch cover in front of the cockpit and looked skyward as Japanese aircraft came down to strafe the crippled *Kweilin*. Woods ordered the copilot and radio operator to get the passengers into the water. Then he jumped into the river and began to swim toward a sampan, tied up on the shore opposite the aircraft. He continued:

It was not until after I started swimming that I noticed the current was so strong. I estimated it later about four or five knots. As I was progressing toward shore several Japanese 'planes dived on me and machine-gunned me. At first I submerged myself when they started shooting, but later became so exhausted I could not do this. Many bullets came extremely close; so close in fact that it left no doubt as to whether they were aiming at me or the ship. After what seemed an endless time, I reached the shore in a state of complete exhaustion. . . . It was probably over an hour before I could stand. I was violently ill at my stomach."[20]

Meanwhile, the DC-2 half-submerged, floated downstream. Japanese fighter planes continued their attack. Only two people survived besides Woods: the radio operator and an official of the Ministry of Finance. Fourteen died, including Wong Yu-mei of the Central Bank of China, Dr. Liu Chung-chieh, former minister to Berlin, two women, and two children. Nine of the bodies bore machine-gun bullet wounds.[21]

CNAC had the dubious distinction of losing the first commercial airliner in the history of aviation to hostile aerial attack. Although later denied by the Japanese, there seems little doubt that the attack had been premeditated.

This unprecedented destruction of a commercial aircraft created a major diplomatic incident in the summer of 1938. The Department of State, which had adopted a more tolerant attitude toward CNAC after the Japanese attack on the gunboat *Panay* in December 1937, instructed Ambassador Joseph C. Grew in Tokyo to make a formal protest to the Japanese Foreign Office. "You may state," Secretary Hull advised, "that the attack upon the plane has aroused public feeling in this country. You should point out . . . that not only was the life of an American national directly imperiled but loss was also occasioned to American property interests . . . . You should express the emphatic objection of this Government to the jeopardizing in this way of the lives of Americans as well as other non-combatant occupants of unarmed civilian planes engaged in clearly recognized and established commercial services over a regularly scheduled air route."[22]

Grew delivered the note on August 26. Five days later, the foreign minister answered. The Japanese planes, the reply stated, had attacked only because they had suspected the unidentified aircraft of military activities; they had not fired after the plane had landed in the river; furthermore, as "the company to which the aircraft in question belonged, being a Chinese juridical person, the incident is not one which involves Japan directly with a third person." In short, the United States should mind its own business.[23]

Secretary Hull dismissed as improbable the tale of mistaken identity. Also, "the incident in question was and is of material concern to the American Government and people." Hull then took the occasion to raise the issue of continued attacks by Japanese military forces upon American property interests in China and the danger to American citizens. He concluded:

> The American Government therefore feels impelled to call attention of the Japanese Government to the urgency of there being taken steps effectively to implement the Japanese Government's repeated assurances with regard to the rights and interests of American nationals, and more especially of there being taken such steps with regard to the operation of Japanese military planes as may remove the possibility of attacks by such planes upon the lives or property of non-combatant civilians in circumstances where such attacks will jeopardize the lives and interests of American nationals.[24]

The incident died at this point. The State Department went on its pedantic way to other protests as Japanese aircraft attacked without discrimination American property in China. CNAC, for its part, assumed that its aircraft were no longer protected by the commercial character of the company's operations. This did not mean an end to service, it merely meant that CNAC would have to exercise more caution. For example, service to Hong Kong, which had been suspended after the *Kweilin* incident, resumed on an irregular night-time basis in October. [25]

Late August 1938 brought a new Japanese offensive in the Yangtze Valley, as the Imperial Army drove beyond Kuikiang toward Hankow. On September 28, the key position of Tenchiacheng fell after a bitter two-week battle, opening the route to Hankow. A second Japanese force of 30,000 men landed at Bias Bay, some 50 miles northeast of the Pearl River, on October 12. The Chinese offered only light resistance, and Canton capitulated on October 21.[26]

The day Canton surrendered, Bond received an urgent message from the minister of communications requesting CNAC to evacuate high government officials from Hankow. As the city was under constant aerial attack during the day, evacuation would have to be accomplished at night. Hankow possessed night-flying facilities, but Chungking did not. Bond therefore made arrangements on October 21 to install floodlights and lanterns at Chengtu. Bond's evacuation plan called for two DC-2s to take off from Chungking in time to arrive at Hankow shortly after dark. The two aircraft would leave Hankow for Chengtu, then return to Hankow in time to make a second trip just before dawn, landing at Chungking in daylight. This ambitious program involved a total distance of 2,100 miles or about 14 flying hours.[27]

Charles Sharp and Royal Leonard, the only two pilots qualified to fly at night, took off from Chungking shortly after 5 P.M. on October 22 and landed at Hankow after dark. They departed for Chengtu with fifteen passengers each at 9 P.M. Snow and ice were encountered over the mountains en route to Chengtu, and Bond's careful schedule began to break down. Sharp managed to make a second trip to Hankow, leaving for Chungking just before dawn. But Leonard did not arrive over Hankow until daylight. He found an air raid in progress and headed for Ichang. Leonard did not get back to Chungking until noon on the 23rd, after having flown nearly 16 hours during the previous 24-hour period. Despite Leonard's protests, Bond ordered him to bed. Sharp alone would continue operations to Hankow that night.

The weather worsened during the 23rd. Bond wired Hankow that there would be only one flight that night: Sharp would arrive after dark and leave for Chungking before dawn. Receiving a "frantic reply" from the minister of communications, Bond decided to fly into Hankow with Sharp and explain the situation to the minister. The weather en route to Hankow was rotten. "We had a bad icing condition," Bond reported, "with the temperature only 3 degrees above freezing. If we had pulled up, as we would have to do at night, it would have been difficult." Sharp landed the Douglas at 8 P.M. "The field presented an eerie but interesting spectacle," Bond wrote. "It was a particularly dark night and only small lanterns and flashlights were allowed. The field had been heavily bombed recently and none of the holes were being filled up. All over the field were gangs of coolies digging and we were told that they were mining the field." Bond made his way into the city. Hankow "was crowded with Chinese soldiers but there was no semblence of order at all. Many of them looked in the dark like convalescent wounded. There were no guns or armed troops nor was there any disorderly conduct that I saw. Only hopeless confusion."

Bond located the minister of communications, explained the situation, and promised to make a maximum effort the following night. Both DC-2s would be used, operating into Ichang, only 190 miles away, instead of Chengtu. Also, two Commodore flying boats that had recently been acquired from Pan American would attempt a trip at dawn. Bond then closed up CNAC's operations, arranged for the transfer of gasoline reserves by steamer, and returned to Chungking with Sharp before dawn.

Sharp and Leonard flew one trip to Ichang the night of October 24, as Japanese troops approached the gates of Hankow. Sharp returned to Hankow and found Chiang Kai-shek and his party stranded at the airport. Eric Just, a former CNAC pilot now flying for the government, was supposed to have flown Chiang to Hengyang, but Just had objected to landing at Hengyang at night because he was unfamiliar with the field. Allison, flying a DC-2 for the Ministry of Communications, had replaced Just; however, he had been forced to return to Hankow after a malfunction in the electrical system. Allison appealed to Sharp to evacuate Chiang and party, and Sharp wisely agreed. "Sharp said the Madame seemed very pleased." Bond commented with considerable understatement, "and when they landed at Hengyang she thanked him for herself and the Generalissimo for his aid. It was a good break for CNAC and Sharp used his head." One wonders if Chiang, while he waited at the airport, recalled his first experience with CNAC on Christmas Day 1930, when Station Manager Ott refused to hold a Loening for the Generalissimo.

Sharp returned to Hankow from Hengyang and took off before dawn for Chungking. In the meantime, Leonard had made a second trip to Ichang. At dawn, October 25, the two Commodore flying boats took off from Hankow. Moon Chin, an American-born Chinese, returned in a Commodore that afternoon for eleven members of CNAC's staff. Chin reported Hankow on fire and Japanese troops entering from the north. Deciding that it would be too dangerous to wait until dawn, he took off shortly after sunset, although this meant a hazardous night landing on the river. "It was his first night flight," Bond reported; "he came in on a flat power glide with his copilot hanging out the window watching the river and Moon peering ahead for sampans or junks. When they seemed to be about eight or ten feet off the water the copilot yelled and Moon pulled back on his throttle and eased back on his stick and shut his eyes and prayed to Buddha." The big flying boat alighted safely.

CNAC had fifteen flights out of Hankow before the city fell to the Japanese, evacuating 223 people. "The men all did a fine job," Bond concluded, "and I am sincerely proud of them, but no one could keep that up long. I don't see how they accomplished as much as they did."[28]

The Japanese now controlled all the major cities and lines of communications in northern and central China, and the whole Chinese seacoast from the Taku Bar to Canton. Isolated in the interior, the Nationalist government retained only slender ties with the outside world. "I think we may say that one period of the war is ending," Bond wrote after the fall of Hankow,

and the future may be difficult. It certainly looks bad for China now but actually it seems to me it is not really as bad as it was after the fall of Nanking nearly a year ago. It is true the Chinese are worse off, but so are the Japanese much worse off. They are getting further from their base, apparently they are really beginning to feel the pinch, and they have no more big important town or objectives they can work toward with the feeling that if they can take that their situation will improve. . . . If the Chinese will just hold on, I believe they have a good chance to get very favorable peace terms. I think the Generalissimo will certainly keep up the fight. It all depends on how China unites behind him.

Bond then turned to the prospects for CNAC: "It is not a very pleasant outlook but at least CNAC is still fairly well organized and is a going concern with a little reserve. I think CNAC will probably go back into the red again before long but by doing a lot of drastic reorganizing when it becomes necessary we will manage to hold on. CNAC takes a lot of licking."[29]

— II —

As Bond predicted, the war in China entered a new phase following the fall of Canton and Hankow in October 1938. The Japanese established puppet governments in the occupied areas of China and sought the economic integration of these regions into their so-called New Order in East Asia. For a time, Japan attempted to settle the China Incident by applying a combination of military and political pressure on the Nationalist government. When this failed to shake Chiang Kai-shek's will to resist, the Japanese tried to strangle the Nationalists by cutting all supply routes to China.[30]

Survival became the policy of the Chinese government; in order to survive, communications with the outside world had to be maintained. The primary supply route to China during the first nine months of 1938 had run from Hong King to Hankow via Canton. Between May and September, 90,000 tons monthly had traveled over the Canton-Hankow railroad. When the Japanese seized Canton and thus severed this route in October 1938, most supplies moved to China along a rail line that extended from the port of Haiphong in French Indochina, through Hanoi, to the border town of Laokai in the northwest. Material was then trans-shipped via a meter gauge line that crossed mountainous terrain to Kunming. Tonnage over this 500-mile route rose from 5,000 a month in 1938 to 15,000 a month in 1940. Two additional routes brought lesser quantities of supplies to China: a long and difficult line of communications by motor track reached to Outer Mongolia and the Soviet Union through Chinese Turkestan, while a precarious land route of 715 miles extended from Kunming to Lashio, Burma. This latter route—the Burma Road— opened for traffic in December 1938. Due to a shortage of motor transport and inefficient management, it carried only 5,000 tons a month during 1940, far below peak capacity and less than the Hanoi-Laokai rail line through French Indochina.[31]

Travel along the major supply routes to China was slow and uncertain, suitable only for bulk cargo. Air transportation via CNAC and, to a much lesser extent, Eurasia, provided the sole means of rapid communications for officials and priority cargo. Some 1,500 miles deep in the interior, Chungking was only hours away from Hong Kong by air. Connections with Imperial Airways and Pan American brought London and San Francisco within a week of the Chinese capital. Important Chinese officials could travel to the major cities of the Western world with relative ease in their search for assistance. Visitors inbound to China, such as Lauchlin Currie, President Roosevelt's administrative assistant who was sent to China in early 1941 to examine the military and economic situation, traveled via CNAC. So did sympathetic journalists, like Ernest Hemingway and his wife, Martha Gelhorn. CNAC carried banknotes and medical supplies into China; tungsten, bristles, and other high-value exports were flown to the outside world. Air transportation, observed one writer, is "one of the basic factors in the ability of nationalist China to continue its existence as an independent nation."[32]

China's aerial lifeline was little more than a slender thread during the period 1939–1941. CNAC, Theodore White pointed out, "is one of those peculiar enterprises whose capital value in dollars and cents might barely equal that of a large American department store; but whose actual value in the war for the control of Asia can only be weighed by history." The airline in January 1939 had only seven large aircraft in operation: two DC-2s, one DC-3, one Ford trimotor, two Consolidated Commodore flying boats, and one six-passenger de Haviland Dragon Rapide. By 1941, after losses and replacements, CNAC could muster three DC-2s, three DC-3s, and three Curtiss Condors. With this handful of airplanes and an equally small group of pilots, CNAC maintained China's vital internal and external communications.[33]

CNAC's most important route by far connected Chungking and Hong Kong. Harold Sweet had inaugurated irregular service on this line during the winter of 1937–1938. Twice-weekly service began in the spring of 1938. Following the attack on *Kweilin*, CNAC switched to night operations into the British colony. Heavy traffic led to service four times a week in January 1940. Space on every flight was booked months in advance. Besides passengers, CNAC airlifted nearly 9,000 pounds of cargo a week into China.

This air service to Hong Kong was a hazardous undertaking, and it was unique in the annals of commercial aviation. The route was 770 miles long; approaches to and departures from Hong Kong had to be flown at night—hopefully in bad weather. Japanese fighter planes were a constant menace, and a forced landing almost anywhere en route meant capture. "Airline flying by night over China has no parallel," Royal Leonard, one of the pilots who flew the route, has written. "There are no intermediate fields, and there are no airway beacons so common in America. Also no lighted cities, because planes heard at night are taken as Japanese. Radio communications are restricted, weather reports almost unavailable. There is a further hazard of running afoul of the Japanese. Approaching Hong Kong, CNAC's route then actually went over some of the Japanese bases."[34]

Navigation required expert technique, especially when powerful Japanese radio transmitters interfered with the necessary radio signals for an instrument approach to Hong Kong. Leonard has described the normal procedure as follows: "We used the German [Lorenz] method of radio navigation. It was a matter of winding a handle and pointer on a dial that turned a loop overhead in the direction of any radio we chose. One side was the A (·-) signal of the Morse code, on the other the N (-·) signal. When the [antenna] loop was pointed directly toward the station contacted there was a T (-) signal. We then drew a bearing line on our map. By holding such a course and checking the bearings at intervals it was possible to spiral down. We used to say: 'I think I'll spiral down on a phonograph record when I get to Hong Kong.'"[35]

Passengers bound for Chungking usually arrived at Kai Tak

airport after midnight, not knowing when or if the airplane would depart. A clear night usually meant cancellation; clouds and fog were a good sign that the trip would operate. "It was a spooky business for the poor ignorant passengers," one frequent traveler recalled, "however cordial their relations with the pilots (and most of us knew them well). I was never shot at but we had some close calls." Between October 1938 and December 1941, CNAC operated the Chungking–Hong Kong service without accident; this not only attests to the skill of the airline's pilots, it also suggests the existence of a benevolent Sino-American diety.[36]

CNAC developed other international routes during 1939. The airline inaugurated service from Chungking to Hanoi via Kunming in March. This line had special importance because it enabled CNAC to acquire gasoline, a critical item of supply that restricted the airline's flight operations as much as lack of equipment. Despite pressure from the Japanese, Air France for a time permitted CNAC to carry full tanks of fuel into China.[37]

Another new route extended into Burma. An agreement between Great Britain and China, signed on January 25, 1939, permitted reciprocal air service between Chungking and Rangoon via Kunming and Lashio by CNAC and Imperial Airways. CNAC flew several survey flights during the spring and summer of 1939, but inadequate landing facilities at Lashio and the monsoon weather delayed scheduled service until October.[38]

CNAC continued to face frightful difficulties in conducting aerial activities and had to pay a high price for maintaining services in war-torn China. An especially tragic loss came on October 29, 1940. Walter Kent, the red-headed Louisianan who had watched the bombs fall on Shanghai in 1937, was en route from Chungking to Kunming on that day. Kent had taken Royal Leonard's regular trip, as he wanted to be in Hong Kong to celebrate his thirty-seventh birthday on October 31 with his wife and three-year-old son, who were scheduled to leave for the United States the next day. Kent's aircraft was the DC-2 *Kweilin*, which had been salvaged from the Pearl River following Woods's ill-fated encounter with Japanese fighters in August 1938. Ten passengers were on board in addition to four crew members. About 100 miles northeast of Kunming, Kent ran into a flight of five Japanese fighter 'planes and landed at a small emergency field near Changyi. The Japanese spotted the Douglas and began a series of strafing passes as the airliner taxied off the runway. On their first pass, Kent was hit in the back by a 20-mm shell and died instantly. The other crew members evacuated the passengers as the left wing of the aircraft caught fire. They were machine-gunned while crossing the field in search of shelter. Nine of the fourteen persons on board the DC-2 were killed, two suffered wounds, and three escaped unharmed. The Japanese government dismissed subsequent American diplomatic protests.[39]

The impact of Kent's death shook and almost shattered Bond's determined optimism. "I don't know what the answer to all of this is," he confided to Allison; "the situation out here is gradually getting worse and worse. . . . I wish there was some way I could get out of this. I feel I have done my part. I have a wife and child and if you saw Kitsi [Bond's wife] on her way home she probably told you we are expecting another. That is if her constant worry about me out here doesn't cause a mishap. Well, it is no use to worry about it. If I don't like my job I can quit and if I haven't guts enough to quit I had better stop talking about it."[40]

Other losses followed. Bernard Wong in a Ford trimotor crashed in mountainous terrain near Kian in Kiangsi Province on January 20, 1941. The next month, Joy Thom in a DC-2 struck the top of a 7,000-foot mountain in southern Hunan. The crews perished in both instances; fortunately, neither aircraft was carrying passengers.[41]

CNAC went to great lengths and displayed incredible ingenuity to keep its dwindling supply of aircraft in service. For example, in May 1941 Japanese fighters intercepted Hugh Woods in one of CNAC's new DC-3s while en route from Chungking to Chengtu. He made a forced landing at Suifu as the Japanese dived to attack. Although crew and passengers escaped without injury, Japanese bombs blew the right wing off Woods's DC-3. The 24,000-pound airplane had to be moved from the airfield as soon as possible in order to escape damage from a second strike. CNAC did not have a spare wing section in stock for a DC-3; however, a slightly smaller DC-2 wing was available in Hong Kong. No one really knew if a DC-3 would fly with a DC-2 wing, but it seemed worth a try. The spare wing section was lashed to the fuselage of a DC-2 for the 860-mile flight from Hong Kong to Suifu. While the aerodynamic effect of this strange configuration could not be predicted, CNAC's engineering staff believed that the aircraft could be controlled in flight—theoretically, at least. Harold Sweet, an expert pilot with more courage than good sense, volunteered for the trip. Fortunately, the aircraft flew normally, except for a slight longitudinal instability and some buffeting.

While Sweet was en route to Suifu via a refueling stop at Kweilin, a gang of coolies pushed the damaged DC-3 three miles down a highway and hid it in a clump of trees. Japanese bombers arrived over Suifu to complete their work just as Sweet approached the area. Sweet avoided the Japanese planes by landing at nearby Chautong. After the bewildered Japanese had left Suifu without locating the camouflaged DC-3, Sweet flew into the airfield with the spare wing. The new wing and the damaged aircraft were mated, and with only a little ingenuity and effort. The aircraft, rechristened a "DC-2½," was then flown to Hong Kong for permanent repairs. The "DC-2½" performed well on the flight, pilot reported; she needed no more than full aileron-tab setting for stability.[42]

Despite equipment shortages, inadequate gasoline supplies, and Japanese harrassment, CNAC continued to prosper during the years 1938–1940. In 1938 the airline flew 810,910 miles, carried 14,505 passengers, and airlifted 477,819 pounds of mail and freight; in 1940 CNAC flew 1,005,000 miles, carried 16,432 passengers, and airlifted 1,277,000 pounds of mail and freight. Revenue in terms of Chinese dollars increased by 35 percent during this period, although the gain was negligible in terms of American dollars because of wartime inflation in China.[43]

CNAC's morale remained excellent, even if there were moments of depression such as Bond experienced following Kent's death. Charles Sharp, perhaps the most expert of the airline's superb flying staff, was a tough but extremely capable operations manager, and, as one pilot later wrote: "His foresight, determination and leadership during the most critical and discouraging periods must not be overlooked." Hugh Woods, the chief pilot, was outspoken, demanding, and respected. Pilots like Robert Pottschmidt, William McDonald, Royal Leonard, Frank Higgs, Hugh Chen, and Moon Chin flew hours under the most trying conditions with a professional skill and courage rarely if ever equalled by any group of commercial pilots. The maintenance staff performed miracles to keep CNAC's aircraft flying. Relations with the Chinese managers had never been better. Managing Director P. Y. Wong, Bond commented at one point, "is the best friend that the American partners and the American personnel have ever had, and he is plenty able." Above all, stood the indomitable spirit of W. L. Bond—the man who refused to quit even in the face of what often appeared to be a hopeless situation. More than any other person, Bond kept CNAC going through these difficult years.[44]

— III —

The most important development for CNAC in 1940–1941 was the beginnings of extensive freight operations. The airline pioneered freight service in China before the Japanese attack on Pearl Harbor in December 1941; it also laid the foundations for a freight line between India and China, a route that was to become China's main—and at times only—link to the outside world. The freight service originated in response to increased Japanese pressure on China's supply routes in 1940.

In September 1939, Germany attacked Poland, and Europe soon became caught up in the conflagration of World War II. Following a period of "phoney war," the *Wehrmacht* lashed out against France in the spring of 1940. Hitler accepted the French surrender on June 22 in a small clearing outside Paris, as a German band played "Deutschland über alles." The *Luftwaffe* prepared for an aerial assault on beleaguered England, the prelude to a planned invasion of the British Isles.

Japan sought to take advantage of the situation in Europe and tighten the noose around China's neck. The Tokyo government in June 1940 demanded that Great Britain close Hong Kong and Burma to Chinese material. The American consul general in Chungking informed Bond "that he had heard, unofficially but reliably, from the British that the Japanese are demanding that either CNAC be stopped running into Hong Kong or that the many Chinese officials who are constantly going back and forth be made to leave the Colony." Although British authorities resisted the pressure against Hong Kong, they did agree in July to close the Burma Road for three months. More bad news for China came in September when Japan forced the French Vichy government to accept occupation of northern Indochina by the Imperial army. The Japanese thus severed the vital rail link and air service between Chungking and Hanoi. Also, Japanese aircraft based in Indochina were now within 175 miles of Kunming. "Just how we will solve these problems," Bond wrote, "I do not know, but I think we will work it out someway so that we can maintain a reasonably satisfactory service and stay in business."[45]

The Chinese government, for once, had anticipated these problems. Early in 1940, before the German attack on France, the Ministry of Finance developed plans for an air freight service between China and the outside world to augment existing lines of supply. Ernest Allison, now an employee of the Chinese government, had gone to the United States to inspect several Curtiss Condor aircraft that had been offered for sale by Charles H. Babb Company, a southern California used-aircraft dealer. The huge, obsolete Condor biplanes, commercial versions of the bomber used by the Air Corps during the 1920s, were slow, but they could carry a payload of 3,000 pounds. Babb had five of these aircraft and hoped to acquire two more. Originally intended for service during the Spanish Civil War, the planes had been stranded in Mexico. They had sat on the piers at Tampico, exposed to the sun and salt air for more than a year, and they were in poor condition when purchased by Babb and shipped to Glendale, California.[46]

Aircraft, especially large cargo aircraft, were in very short supply in 1940. Despite the condition of the Condors, Arthur Young recommended to Finance Minister H. H. Kung that the seven aircraft be purchased for $400,000, which would include renovation, spare parts, and shipment to China. Young estimated that seven Condors could transport monthly 350 tons inward and 385 tons outward between Lashio or Hanoi and Kunming at a cost of $263 per round trip ton. This figure compared favorably to the $242 per round-trip ton by motor transport over the Burma Road. He further recommended that CNAC operate the service on a cost-plus basis.[47]

After some discussion, Minister Kung approved purchase of the aircraft—only five were available—and agreed that CNAC should conduct the operation. The Condors arrived from the United States in the summer of 1940. Following extensive modifications, test flights took place at the end of the year. Their performance proved disappointing. Bond reported: "The most important result so far discovered is that it takes 55 minutes to climb to 15,000 feet from sea level, with a crew of two, full tanks of gas, and 1,466 kilograms [3,225 pounds] of cargo. Also, 15,000 feet was the maximum service ceiling with this load, and with open throttles, permitted for cruising at this altitude, the indicated speed was 90 miles per hour, or approximately 120 miles per hour actually. The single-engine performance with full cargo has not been tested fully, but we know it will be much below 15,000 feet." The Condors had been acquired for a projected route from Hanoi to Kunming, transversing comparatively flat terrain. By late 1940, however, Japanese control of northern Indochina ruled out use of this route. A more northerly route from Burma to China involved flight altitudes of up to 15,000 feet, for which the Condors were completely unsuited. "I went into the Condor deal last February and March," Bond concluded, "thinking they would be used from Hanoi to Kunming. Since then many things have changed, except the Condors."[48]

While the Chinese government began to plan more ambitious air transportation projects, an alternate use was found for the weary Condors. The Ministry of Economics signed a contract with CNAC early in 1941 to transport tungsten ore and tin bars from Nanshiung to Hong Kong, which meant a flight of some 200 miles over level country. Service began in March 1941 with ten round trips a month. Operations increased to 105 round trips in July. Between March and July, CNAC carried 644 tons of tungsten and tin to Hong Kong, and 488 tons of material, mainly Red Cross supplies, into China. "The Chinese government," Bond pointed out, "receives US$1,000 per ton for wolfram [tungsten], out of which they will pay us US$300 for transportation. The cost of this wolfram up to the time it is delivered to CNAC planes in China is in National Currency. The great need of the Chinese today is for foreign exchange. On this transaction with CNAC they will obtain approximately US$700 per ton." According to Bond's estimate, the government earned more than $450,000 in needed foreign exchange from the freight service, a sum that exceeded the purchase price of the ancient Condors.[49]

CNAC also profited from the Condor operation, at least in terms of experience. This expertise would soon prove important because the Hong Kong–Nanshiung service was only the beginning of CNAC's freight line. Even before the Condors arrived in the Far East, plans were being developed for a massive airlift of goods to China.

In July 1940, after the closing of the Burma Road, Minister of Foreign Affairs T. V. Soong submitted a request to Secretary of the Treasury Henry Morgenthau for American financial support. In order to maintain resistance against Japan, Soong asked for $50 million to support China's depreciating currency, $70 million for military supplies, and $20 million for transportation improvements. The latter sum included provisions to develop an air route from Lashio in Burma to Kunming "by purchasing and operating additional transport planes to be operated by the China National Aviation Corporation."[50]

CNAC had been flying from Lashio to Kunming as part of its scheduled passenger service between Chungking and Rangoon.

Japanese control of northern Indochina in September 1940, however, brought Lashio within easy range of Japanese fighters, and raised the possibility that the route of Kunming could easily be cut in the event of war between Japan and Great Britain. In November 1940, Bond looked into the feasibility of a more northern route to China, one that would be beyond the reach of Japanese fighters. He traveled by car from Mandalay to Lashio then by train to the town of Myitkyina, the northern-most terminus of the main line of the Burma Railway. He discussed the possibility of construction of an airport with the district commissioner and the commander of the British garrison at Myitkyina and received assurance of their support. Bond then returned to Lashio where he boarded one of CNAC's DC-3s, commanded by Hugh Woods, to make an aerial survey of the projected route.[51]

The aircraft proceeded up the Irrawaddy Valley to Myitkyina, where Woods selected a site for the proposed airport. He flew on northward beyond Fort Hertz, climbing 14,800 feet, then swung eastward over the Naga Hills to determine the height of the unexplored terrain. "Without landing," Woods recalled, "I proceeded on to Likiang Mountain and Tali Mountain to establish their exact position and altitudes as our maps were quite unreliable at that time, in fact, showed some of the territory over which we flew as unexplored and there had never been an airplane flown over this part of the World before. I then proceeded on to Chikiang and Suifu, and thence to Chungking." Although he did not know it at the time, Woods had flown the first trip over what was to become known as "the Hump."[52]

"Little of definite value could be told from one flight," Bond reported. "We know the country is high but can be flown in weather similar to what we had, but if the weather should be much worse, with bad cross winds or a bad icing condition, or if the tops of the clouds should be two or three thousand feet higher than we saw, then it would be extremely dangerous and costly and very nearly impractical." In any event, nothing could be done until the British built an airport at Myitkyina. Bond approached Sir Alexander Cochrane, governor of Burma, and obtained his approval for the aerodrome.[53]

While Bond traveled in Burma, T. V. Soong and Arthur Young were in New York for discussions with Juan Trippe, Harold Bixby, and other officials of Pan American Airways. Several conclusions emerged from these talks, which Young included in a memorandum in March 1941. China's non-military aviation requirements up to June 1942 were placed at 18 DC-3s, 3 for passenger service and 15 for cargo operations. First priority was for three passenger aircraft, one for use by Chiang Kai-shek and two for CNAC. The 15 aircraft for the air cargo service should be delivered at the rate of one a month beginning in July 1941, and two a month as soon as possible thereafter. "This additional equipment," Young wrote, "is needed for transport of supplies urgently needed for China's war effort, including import of materials that will aid in an eventual offensive against the Japanese forces. Also, it would facilitate the outward movement of export commodities, which provide necessary foreign exchange. At present China must rely almost entirely on the Burma Road, which is inadequate and liable to interruption by air attacks."

The best route for the air cargo operation, Young continued, extended from the rail head at Lashio to Kunming, a distance of 380 miles. Young estimated that 15 DC-3s could transport 800 to 1,000 tons a month over this route. In the event that the Lashio-Kunming line could not be operated safely due to Japanese air attacks, then the more northerly route from Myitkyina to Suifu—surveyed by Bond and Woods—could be used. "This route," Young pointed out, "is more difficult because mountains 12,500 to 13,500 feet high must be crossed, but would deliver supplies to an all-year river port."[54]

Bond raised one problem that remained to be solved. CNAC, he wrote, had at present 14 qualified pilots who had averaged nearly 110 flying hours during the month of February 1941. "Beyond this, we have absolutely nothing, and we have no idea where we can even try to get any more." Any proposal to acquire large numbers of aircraft for use in China under present conditions "is like building air castles in a vacuum." Bond agreed that "a properly organized and operated air freight service in China would fill a truly vital need." Also, he believed it would be possible to use the Myitkyina-Suifu route, if absolutely necessary. But if five DC-3s suddenly appeared tomorrow, "we would have to push them over in the corner and start paying dead storage on them." Bond concluded: "The vital need of China just now is more transportation, but this transportation is just as dependent on more flight crews as it is on more planes. At the moment the greatest need is for flight crews."[55]

While Bond looked for pilots, Young sought airplanes—and a way to pay for them; 18 DC-3s would cost $3 million. Juan Trippe stated that Pan American Airways was greatly interested in the further development of aviation in China and in China's stand against Japan; he would do everything he could to help, but Pan American was already fully committed for bank loans to finance CNAC's previous purchases. The Chinese government, he suggested, should apply to the Import-Export Bank or some similar source for a loan. Although Pan American was not in a position to endorse CNAC's obligations, Trippe said he would not object to pledging the earnings or assets of CNAC, if this proved necessary to negotiate a loan.[56]

The American government, as Trippe had emphasized, was a more logical source of funds for expanded air transport operations in China. Although Washington had not taken any action on Soong's request of July 1940, worsening relations between the United States and Japan led to plans for more active American assistance to China. In January 1941, President Roosevelt sent one of his administrative assistants, Dr. Lauchlin Currie, to assess the military and economic situation in China. "A consequence of my trip," Currie recalled, "was that I automatically became an 'expert' on China and an advocate at court. Within three days of my return [in March 1941] I was able to persuade the President to extend Lend-Lease to China and shortly thereafter I was appointed administrator of Lend-Lease for China while retaining my post at the White House as assistant to the President. I was nominally responsible to [Harry L.] Hopkins, but he did not interfere. For a year and a half, 'helping' China and pushing its claims against the thousand other claims for the scanty supplies of those days was my full time job."[57]

Bond arrived in the United States via transpacific Clipper in May 1941 for discussions in Washington between Currie, Soong, Young, Bixby, and officials of the China Defense Supplies Corporation, a newly formed Chinese purchasing and supply agency. On May 8, Bond presented to Soong a lengthy memorandum setting forth the details for an air freight service to China.

"The China National Aviation Corporation," Bond began, "for the past year has studied the problem of air freight transportation carefully and in great detail and has investigated many proposed and possible routes and flown numerous survey flights." These studies have indicated that "the best air freight route would be from Myitkyina in North Burma to airports on the so-called Burma Road in China in the vicinity of Yunanyi east of the bridge over the Mekong river." Myitkyina was the preferred western terminus for three reasons: it was the railhead for the Burma Railroad, it was far enough away from Japanese air bases to afford comparative safety, and the flying weather in the area was superior to Lashio, which was susceptible to heavy ground fogs. Delivery of cargo by air to Yunanyi would reduce the trucking distance from the railhead in Burma to Kunming from approximately 715 miles to 215 miles; also, it would by-pass the main bridges over the Mekong, which were subject to aerial attack. "In other words, the planes will deliver freight past the bottle neck. From there on it can be delivered more safely, surely and cheaply by surface transportation." Because of the shorter distance and resultant increased payload, Bond estimated that "one plane can deliver nearly three times as much cargo from Myitkyina to Yunanyi as it can to Kunming and with far greater safety." Bond continued:

There are many difficulties connected with this route of course. The country between Myitkyina and Yunanyi is high and rugged and the country west and north of this route, where the freight planes frequently would be forced to fly during air raids, is even worse. The weather is usually bad and the country is notoriously windy. Winds of forty to seventy miles per hour prevail most of the year. In clear weather flights would have to be at altitudes of from twelve thousand to fourteen thousand feet. To the west and north of course, but within seeing distance or about one hundred miles, are peaks and ranges more than seventeen thousand feet in height. However, we believe that with the exercise of proper care and training, all of these hazards can be controlled and once they have been controlled they in fact become safety factors, as the Japanese planes are not likely to go very far after our planes over that country in that weather.

For planning purposes, Bond assumed that 35 airplanes would be required. Because all aircraft and supplies would have to be transported 12,000 miles from the United States to China, Bond stressed efficiency of service. "The key to compact efficient operation of this kind is standardization. It starts with the airplane and engine and extends through spare parts, gasoline, overhaul maintenance, training supervision and flying." He recommended that only Douglas DC-3s be acquired. "Its maintenance requirements and payload and performance make it ideally suited for work in China. CNAC has flown many types of planes all over China and while we have not flown them all, we are sure we can do a highly efficient job of transporting air freight with DC-3s." It would be, he said, "a mistaken kindness and the height of inefficiency to send to China any varied and numerous types of planes which might appear to be more quickly available. It would simply doom the entire project to failure."

Qualified personnel were essential for a successful operation. "It will require pilots of experience and skill in handling multi-engine planes," Bond stressed, "and it will require men of responsibility, determination and character." Eight pilots would be needed for each five planes in operation. CNAC would conduct the training and familiarization program. Upon successful completion of the course, the men would be paid a base salary of $700 per month for 60 hours of flight time with premium pay for flying above 60 hours. Bond hoped that the American military services would be allowed to release men from active duty who were willing to volunteer for CNAC's air cargo line.

Bond placed the estimated capital outlay for a 35-plane operation at $6.7 million. At a minimum, each Douglas DC-3 could lift 60 tons per month inbound to China and 30 tons outbound, the outbound figure based on availability of cargo rather than capacity of the aircraft. Maximum figures would be 120 tons inbound and 60 tons outbound. Cost per ton for the minimum tonnage figure would be $206, and for the maximum, $103. This estimate included depreciation of the aircraft over a 30-month period. Bond preferred that payment to CNAC for operation of the service be tied to efficiency, and he suggested reimbursement for actual expenditures plus $20 per ton.

Bond concluded his report—the genesis of the wartime Hump route—on a note of cautious optimism: "It is important to remember that aviation operations in China are extremely difficult. They involve every obstacle known to aviation, such as prevailing bad weather, a route over some of the highest and most rugged country in the world, and the ground facilities are practically nil. In addition, the operation would be about twelve thousand miles from the source of most of their supplies, in a country nearly blockaded, and the operations are subject to constant air raids and enemy air attack. But CNAC has shown after nearly four years of such operations, that it can be done successfully."[58]

Bond presented his proposal to Currie on May 22, 1941, after it had been cleared by Soong. The following week, Currie outlined a comprehensive aviation program, covering military and transport aircraft, to the Joint Board, the agency charged with coordinating American supply activities. Currie's program included provisions for ten DC-3s, to be delivered prior to October 31, 1941, for inauguration of the Burma-China air cargo service. "I supported CNAC whenever and however I could," Currie recalled, "as I had the highest opinion of the efficiency and worthwhileness of the operation. This I attributed largely to W. L. Bond, the manager."[59]

The Joint Board accepted Currie's recommendations in principle, but no transport aircraft were available to implement the program. Later in the summer of 1941, the board reconsidered the aircraft production situation and agreed to supply ten airplanes to CNAC, five in February and five in March 1942.[60]

While the American government considered the project for

the air cargo service, CNAC sought aircraft for its domestic passenger operation, depleted by the loss of a DC-2 that crashed in Honan in February 1941 and the DC-3 that had been damaged by Japanese bombers at Suifu in May 1941. Currie promised two aircraft, but various difficulties prevented delivery. Pan American came to CNAC's assistance by taking one DC-3 from the Alaska Division and shipping it to China. "The PAA Superintendent in Alaska," Bond reported, "threatened to resign if this plane was taken from him as he was already short of planes, but I threatened to resign if CNAC did not get it."[61]

Bond toured aircraft factories on the west coast in July. The Douglas Aircraft Company, he reported, was completing three DC-3s a week. The somewhat smaller, but substantially faster, Lockheed Lodestars were coming off the assembly line at the same rate. Curtiss-Wright was ready to begin production of its large C-46. "Everyone is sympathetic, encouraging and cooperative," he wrote to the minister of communications, "and in about six or eight months the situation will be greatly changed and improved. The US government is really making a tremendous effort to increase production of airplanes but it is a tremendous task. Apparently no one realized how small our production was and [how] few our facilities were. New factories had to be built, new machinery made and more men trained. But this is all proceeding at a great rate now and by the end of the year tremendous results will be beginning to appear."[62]

Bond flew across the Pacific to China in the fall of 1941. While awaiting delivery of the promised aircraft, he urged the Chinese and British governments to push ahead with ground facilities for the air cargo service. Construction at Myitkyina was underway. Also, mainly due to Bond's efforts, an airport was being built at Dinjan in Upper Assam. In November 1941, he flew with Sharp, Young, and a party of British army officers from Lashio to northern Burma to survey progress. Sharp overflew Myitkyina, then landed at the partially completed airport at Dinjan before continuing over the Himalayas to Kunming. Work was coming along at points along the route, albeit slowly; but this did not appear to be a problem, as the DC-3s for the air cargo service would not be delivered and placed into operation for several months. There was ample time, or so it seemed.[63]

— IV —

CNAC performed magnificently during four difficult years, and Bond had good reason to be proud of what he had accomplished. On the verge of collapse after war broke out in 1937, CNAC not only endured, but it became a vital element in the continued survival of China.

Increasing Japanese pressure on China's supply routes after 1938 led to the first tentative experiments with an air cargo line. Even more important, CNAC laid the groundwork for the massive effort that would come after Pearl Harbor.

Unfortunately, Tokyo moved before CNAC was ready. As Bond was flying between India and China, elements of the Imperial Japanese Navy were making their way across the stormy waters of the northern Pacific for the rendezvous with history. CNAC—and the United States—were about to run out of time.

CHAPTER FIVE

OVER THE HUMP
1941–1945

— I —

MONDAY morning, December 8, 1941 (Sunday, December 7, east of the international dateline), found Bond in his apartment on Repulse Bay, Hong Kong. Fred S. Ralph, pilot of the Pan American Clipper that had recently arrived from Manila, telephoned before breakfast and reported that the British airport authorities had ordered him to leave Hong Kong at once. No reason had been given. "I told him," Bond later wrote, "I could not imagine what was in back of it but considered Hong Kong, in case of trouble, more dangerous than Manila." Bond recommended that Ralph drop his passengers, then return to Manila as soon as possible. Ten minutes later, Captain Ralph called with the news that Japan had declared war on the United States and Great Britain.

Bond drove from Repulse Bay on the southern end of the island to downtown Hong Kong, arriving just as the first air raid alarm sounded. Anxious to reach the airport across the harbor in Kowloon and finding the Star Ferry inoperative, Bond and four Canadian soldiers, who wanted to report to their units, commandeered a sampan. He arrived at Kai Tak to find half of CNAC's fleet in ashes. Japanese bombers had destroyed two DC-2s and three of the old Condors, and they had sunk Pan American's Clipper at its moorings. Two DC-3s and one DC-2 had escaped damage.

Bond realized that the surviving aircraft had to be moved immediately. A bulldozer flattened a section of fence, then a tractor pushed the planes into several vegetable patches along a road opposite the airport, where they could be camouflaged. While the work progressed, Bond sought to clear his actions with the airport staff. The British officials were not yet certain that there was a war on, and they refused to permit destruction of the fence; after all, it was Crown property. Bond kept the conversation going until the job was completed.

Bond remained at the airport throughout the day, preparing spare parts and other vital supplies for shipment. Twice, he had to interrupt the work and take cover as Japanese bombers made high-level attacks on the field. The last raid came over at 3 P.M. Eight bombs struck the airport; fortunately, they did little damage. Evacuation began that evening. The first aircraft, a DC-3 piloted by Frank L. Higgs, roared off Kai Tak's runway at 7 P.M. for Namyung, a small airfield about 200 miles north of Hong Kong. Harold Sweet took off in a DC-3 at 7:15 P.M., followed by Paul W. Kessler in a DC-2 at 7:45 P.M. All three aircraft carried the airline's staff, families, and equipment.

After seeing the aircraft safely on their way, Bond went to the Peninsula Hotel in downtown Kowloon to arrange for the evacuation of Chinese officials; Loy Chang and Hsi Teh-mou of the Central Bank could not leave that night, but K. P. Chen and A. Manuel Fox of the Currency Stabilization Board were willing to fly out. After Fox agreed to contact other members of the board and to get everyone to the airport by midnight, Bond returned to Kai Tak.

Higgs was first to get back from Namyung. Nervous British anti-aircraft units mistook the DC-3 for a Japanese bomber and sounded the air raid alarm. Higgs turned on his cabin lights and was identified before the batteries opened fire. Operators of the gasoline trucks, however, fled when the alarm sounded and did not return. CNAC's ground crew had to refuel by hand, a painfully slow process. Bond dispatched Higgs back to Namyung with staff and equipment after refueling. Kessler, who landed shortly after Higgs, also made a second flight to Namyung. Although engine trouble (later diagnosed as a burned-out piston) prevented Harold Sweet from returning to Hong Kong, William McDonald flew in from Chungking shortly after midnight with CNAC's remaining aircraft; he loaded aboard members of the Currency Stabilization Board, several bank officials, and a Chinese general, hurriedly took off and flew directly to Chungking. Higgs and Kessler, carrying staff and supplies, followed

C N A C's main passenger terminal, Shanghai, 1937

C N A C's fleet of DC-2s, Shanghai, 1937

DC-2 over downtown Shanghai, 1937

McDonald to Chungking after returning from their second flights to Namyung.

Bond returned to the Peninsula Hotel at 5:30 A.M., "pretty well tired out, with a bad cough and a game leg which I took to be a 'charley horse.'" He had no sooner crawled into bed when an air raid alarm sounded; he thought about taking shelter but was too exhausted to move. The all-clear came fifteen minutes later, followed by another alarm. The constant wail of sirens made it impossible to sleep, so Bond arose, had breakfast, then crossed the harbor to Hong Kong Island where he arranged for the shipment of vital records and company funds. He also called on Madame H. H. Kung, wife of the minister of finance, at the Glochester Hotel. Bond had telephoned Madame Kung the previous day and offered transportation to Chungking, but she had declined. "She was still uncertain as to whether it would be safer to go or to stay," Bond noted, "but I urged her to get out." Bond found many high Chinese officials, like Loy Chang, reluctant to leave Hong Kong, and he implored them to come to the airport. "However," he reported, "practically everyone seemed to think our efforts were too dangerous and were afraid that if they went over to the Kowloon side they might not be able to return to Hong Kong, which was considered a much safer place to be." Finally, Bond left Charles Schafer, Pan American's traffic representative, to coordinate passenger evacuation while he returned to Kai Tak to take charge of operations.

CNAC's transports flew in from Chungking at 10 P.M. The three aircraft made one flight to Namyung, then returned to Hong Kong for a second departure, this time for Chungking. Madame Kung and as many officials as could be persuaded to leave were carried on these flights. Plans to continue the evacuation were jeopardized when the airport manager advised that the field would be blown up the next day. Bond asked the manager to leave a short strip for CNAC's operations. When he agreed, a thoroughly exhausted Bond took off for Chungking with Moon Chin on the last plane.

After making plans with Sharp to operate Wednesday's flights into Hong Kong, Bond got to bed at 1:30 in the afternoon.

"I had been awake for over 53 hours," he wrote to Bixby, "and on duty practically the whole time. When I undressed . . . I discovered that I had broken several blood vessels in my left leg, which was badly swollen. My foot and ankle were as black as your hat and my leg was yellow. I stayed in bed until 8 the next morning, and felt much better."

When he awoke, Bond was told that permission to operate Wednesday night had been denied. He called upon the British ambassador, Sir Archibald Clark Kerr, and asked him to intercede with the authorities in Hong Kong. The ambassador contacted the governor of the Colony and obtained approval for two flights on Thursday night. McDonald and Higgs took off from Chungking at 4 P.M., but one hour out of Hong Kong they received a message from Kai Tak that the arrangements had been cancelled. The two planes diverted to Namyung where they took aboard the CNAC staff members who had been hastily offloaded there a few days before. With all on board, they returned to Chungking. The next day, Friday, December 12, Kowloon fell to the Japanese.

All together, CNAC had flown sixteen trips out of Hong Kong and had evacuated 275 persons. The airline was criticized later for showing preference to its own staff at the expense of government officials. "My answer to that," Bond replied, "was that we brought out every official we encountered . . . but I had been unable to persuade officials to come to Kai Tak or even to the Peninsula Hotel where we could get them. . . . Except for one Chinese general, who came to Kai Tak himself, I do not believe we would have evacuated any [government officials] unless we had definitely made all the arrangements and got them to the Airport. This, of course, was due partly to the fact that no one expected the situation to worsen so rapidly."

Bond took pride in "the splendid behavior of the entire CNAC staff." Every man, he wrote, "was in the place he was needed most and there he stayed." Sharp, who had coordinated flight operations, "was a wheel horse and was as steady as a rock." Higgs and McDonald had done most of the flying, with Kessler, Moon Chin, and Robert S. Angle. Hugh Chen, CNAC's first native-born Chinese captain, had volunteered to fly a single-engine Vultee trainer to Namyung. Although the aircraft lacked a radio, and the compass became inoperative en route, Chen successfully navigated with a pocket compass. Bond concluded: "Every man did his job."

Characteristically, Bond found fault only with himself. "All things considered," he told Bixby, "it was a bad show. CNAC got badly caught. We knew, of course, trouble was coming, and we had plans for evacuation that would have saved much more if we had had a chance. Orders were out to evacuate our spare DC-3 engines and they would have gone out Monday night [aboard the Condors], as well as a lot of our more important supplies. If you think this sounds like a lousy alibi, I would like you to know I think so too. After the hell broke loose we did out best to save the pieces." Bond did not know it at the time, but the United States Navy had not fared too well, either.[1]

The "pieces" saved consisted of three aircraft, personnel, and spare parts. Japanese aircraft attacked the DC-3 that had been grounded at Namyung with engine trouble on December 11. It did not burn because the gasoline and oil had been drained off, but it was struck more than 500 times by bullets. Bond wrote: "The engines were ruined and so were the props. Most of the instruments were shot to pieces, the tires, the control lines, landing gear and gas tanks." CNAC's maintenance staff made temporary repairs during the next few weeks. The most temporary involved use of a canvas awning and home-made glue to patch over the bullet holes in the wings and fuselage. So great was the need for aircraft that Sharp decided to fly the crippled machine to India for repairs.

Sharp's troubles began as soon as he left the runway at Namyung. As the landing gear came up, a damaged hydraulic pipe burst, and Sharp had to fly the 800 miles to Kunming with the gear down. Following temporary repairs to the landing gear, Sharp took off from Kunming for Calcutta, the nearest overhaul facility. En route, he ran into heavy rain storms. The patches covering the bullet holes gave way, resulting in an unearthy whistling sound. Some 350 miles later, Sharp landed in Lashio,

Burma. He found passengers, mail, and cargo awaiting shipment to India. Although the DC-3 hardly looked airworthy, the frantic passengers decided to cast their fate with Sharp rather than wait for the rapidly advancing Japanese. The final 600 miles to Calcutta were flown without incident, thus completing what Bond termed "the most spectacular and dangerous flight of this nature ever made by CNAC."[2]

CNAC resumed passenger and mail service on a restricted basis following the collapse of Hong Kong on December 25. Three trips a week were flown between Chungking and Lashio, with one flight going all the way to Calcutta. The airline also operated from Chungking to Chengtu twice weekly. "We hope to hold our schedules down to just this," Bond wrote, "as we have so little reserve." CNAC found enough reserve, however, to conduct a variety of special missions in December and January, including an airlift for the American Volunteer Group—Claire Chennault's Flying Tigers—from their training field at Toungoo, Burma, to their operational base at Kunming.[3]

The news was uniformly black for the Allies during the early months of the war in the Pacific. Japanese planes sent *H.M.S. Repulse* and *Prince of Wales* to the bottom on December 10, 1941, thereby eliminating the Royal Navy as a factor in the Far East. The Imperial Army launched a major operation in the Philippines; Manila was declared an open city on January 7, 1942. Japanese military units assaulted Borneo, Sumatra, the Celebes, and Java. Japanese troops swarmed out of French Indochina and into Thailand, followed by an assault on the Malay Peninsula. The great bastion of Singapore fell with a shock felt around the British Empire on February 15, 1942. The Japanese also planned to cut the supply route to China by invading Burma, but no troops were immediately available for the operation. The quick success in Malaya, however, freed units for the offensive in Burma.[4]

With China's vital supply route threatened, Bond and officials of China Defense Supplies drew up an expanded version of the air cargo project that had been presented to Currie in May 1941. The original proposal had envisioned freight service from Myitkyina to Yunanyi with 35 aircraft carrying a minumum of 2,100 tons and a maximum of 4,200 tons monthly from Burma to China. The new plan called for 100 aircraft to deliver a maximum of 12,000 tons monthly from Myitkyina to Kunming, 125 miles east of Yunanyi.

T. V. Soong presented the revised program at a meeting with President Roosevelt on January 30, 1942. The memorandum, which he left with the president, read:

> The Burma Road is placed in great jeopardy by Japanese successes in the South Pacific, and already Rangoon is closed. During the past four and a half years of war with Japan, the Chinese stock of war materials has never been so low. To supply the Chinese armies and to sustain civilian moral to enable China to keep on fighting it is necessary that a new life line to China be opened.
>
> Miraculously enough that life line is coveniently at hand. From Sadiya, the terminus of the India Railways, to Kunming or Suifu (the center of land and water communications in Szechuan) is only 550 or 700 miles respectively, flying over comparatively level stretches. These alternate routes have been surveyed for year round operations by Pan-American Airways which is ready to operate them, and the project has been declared feasible by the American military mission. All the necessary air bases are already established and in constant use.
>
> Studies by Pan-American Airways and by an expert of the Douglas Aircraft Company [Frank W. Sinclair] show that, carrying their own fuel, one hundred C-53 planes (the transport counterparts of the DC-3) will carry 12,000 net tons monthly, working under usual service conditions. Except for military tanks practically all articles carried over the Burma Road could be carried on those planes. This will nearly duplicate the present net capacity of the Burma Road. On the return trips these planes will carry all the necessary strategic materials from China, such as tungsten, tin, and wood oil.
>
> 35 of these planes have been allocated to China during this year, originally to supplement the Burma Road transport. If these are given at once, together with 65 more, the loss of the Burma Road could be offset.
>
> There are of course competing demands for transport planes, but we venture to submit that nowhere else in the world could 100 transport planes be placed to greater advantage for the cause of the United Nations.
>
> If 50 or more of these planes are provided, there will be enough carrying capacity to supply an additional 21 fighter squadrons and 45 Flying Fortresses in China with all necessary gasoline, lubricants, spare parts, ammunition, and bombs.

It is earnestly hoped that the President will approve the allocation, after which my staff and I will work out with the U.S. Army the details of the operation on which the necessary technical studies have already been made.[5]

Historians have cited Soong's memorandum as an example of the unrealistic attitude of the Chinese government regarding logistical matters. In particular, they note Soong's "memorable statement that only 700 miles of 'comparatively level' stretches lay between Sadiya, India, and Kunming, China. This was the famous Hump, as villainous and forbidding a stretch of terrain as there was in the world." But this is a misunderstanding of Soong's proposal. He assumed that the route from Sadiya to Kunming would be flown via Myitkyina, which was believed by most military authorities—Chinese, American, and British—to be secure from Japanese attacks. This route could be flown at 10,000 to 12,000 feet, a comfortable altitude for a DC-3. No one in January 1942 seriously considered operating the direct route from Sadiya to Kunming, which was "the famous Hump." If Soong is to be faulted for excessive optimism, his statement about the availability of suitable airports to handle 100 aircraft merits more attention.[6]

In any event, Soong reported the next day, January 31, that the president appeared to favor the scheme. Roosevelt told Soong to take the matter up with Harry Hopkins and other interested officials.[7]

American strategic planning, however, had already assigned to China the lowest priority of any theater of operations in the war. Germany was the most dangerous enemy, and the main Allied effort would be in Europe. China should be kept in the war in order to contain large numbers of Japanese troops that might be employed elsewhere in the Pacific and as an eventual base for operations against Japan.[8] As large numbers of American troops would not be sent to China in the immediate future, Roosevelt hoped to assist Chiang Kai-shek by providing limited amounts of supplies. In February 1942, the president wrote to General George C. Marshall, chief of staff, that "it is obviously of the utmost urgency . . . that the pathway to China be kept open." By early April, 25 DC-3s would be taken from domestic airlines and delivered to China for use by CNAC. An additional 75 aircraft, to be operated by the Army Air Forces, would arrive by June 15.[9]

The Air Force adopted the Bond-Soong air cargo scheme with some modification. Their 75 planes would carry a projected 7,500 tons a month from airfields in Upper Assam to Myitkyina. Instead of continuing on to Kunming, however, the Air Force planned to off-load the cargo at Myitkyina, from where it would be floated by barge down the Irrawaddy River some 80 miles to Bhamo, then loaded on motor transport for the trip over the Burma Road to China. Brigadier General Earl L. Naiden, chief of staff to General L. H. Brereton, commander of the 10th Air Force, surveyed this route in early March 1942. Operating on the premise that central and northern Burma could and would be defended, Naiden confirmed the feasibility of the line from Upper Assam to Myitkyina. He pointed out, however, that additional airfields would be required at both ends; as these could not be made ready until the close of year due to the monsoon season, he doubted that more than 25 aircraft could be operated along this route for the time being. General Joseph W. Stilwell, newly appointed commander for the China-India Theater, accepted Naiden's report and advised Washington not to send more than 25 aircraft.[10]

The Japanese offensive in Burma made such rapid progress during the early months of 1942 that Stilwell soon was looking for all the air support he could find. When the British evacuated Rangoon on March 7, Stilwell assigned two Army C-39s, the military version of a Douglas DC-2, to carry priority supplies from India to Burma, especially 200 tons of urgently needed medical supplies that were in Calcutta. The Army flew 12 tons of these goods to Lashio, while CNAC, operating the first two lend-lease aircraft that had arrived in late February, transported 27 tons. The C-39s, Arthur Young reported, were underpowered, the crews were inexperienced, and the planes did not have adequate direction-finding equipment. As a result, CNAC bore the brunt of air transport operations in the theater, flying 70 trips between Chittagong, in eastern Bengal, and Swebo, 250 miles to the east, in support of operations in Burma during March and April. Service between Dinjan in Upper Assam and Myitkyina opened on April 8; two aircraft moved 16 tons a day, mainly gasoline and ammunition.[11]

M. X. Quinn Shaughnessy, adviser to China Defense Supplies, criticized the lack of activity by the Air Force. In a message to Louis A. Johnson, President Roosevelt's personal representative to India, he pointed out that only three transports had arrived. "Believe this delay forwarding planes," he wired, "due primarily to discouraging reports by army on operations' feasibility. Understand army insist on new airports and has advised Washington that little freight can be carried until end of monsoon in October and is making the [current] limited freight movement only as token good faith." Shaughnessy reported that there were 1,300 tons of vital supplies in Karachi and another 700 tons in Upper Assam, all awaiting shipment. If Stilwell was to be supported and China assisted, this cargo had to be moved. "In the interest of getting the job done," Shaughnessy concluded, "I prefer to see Pan American and China National Airways [sic] handle the whole business."[12]

By late April 1942, the problem of supply became suddenly transformed into an almost disastrous problem of evacuation. The Japanese swept aside British forces and captured Lashio on April 29; Mandalay fell two days later, followed by Myitkyina. All transports were immediately diverted to salvaging men and equipment. CNAC evacuated 2,400 people and 50 tons of freight in face of the advancing Japanese. Indicative of the character of operations at this time was a flight on May 5 by Moon Chin, who made the dramatic night landing on the Yangtze River during the evacuation of Hankow in 1938. Chin had six passengers on board a DC-3 for the regular service from Chungking to Calcutta, including Colonel James H. Doolittle, who had crash-landed in China following his raid on Tokyo in April. "We had an emergency landing between Chung King and Kunming," Doolittle recalled, "because of reported Japanese fighters in the area. We were all hidden in a ditch—some distance from the airplane—until the alert was over. At Myitkyina we landed for

DC-2 (foreground) and Curtiss Condor, Hong Kong, 1941

After the first flight over the Hump:
plane #47 at Liang, Nov. 23, 1941
(C N A C Direcor Arthur N. Young in foreground)

After Japanese attack: DC-3 at Suifu, 1941

C N A C's "DC-2½"

fuel but the Japs were on the south side of the city, approaching the field, so we had to take off promptly—without refueling. We had six passengers when we landed and, if I remember correctly, seventy-two when we took off. Of course, many were children and the Burmese are small. Upon landing at Calcutta, well after dark, six of the 'passengers' were found in the rear baggage compartment."[13]

The airline was called upon to perform a variety of essential tasks during this hectic period. In early July, Chiang Kai-shek asked CNAC to assist some 10,000 troops that had been cut off in Burma by the Japanese. Three aircraft, under the supervision of Hugh Woods, dropped more than 70 tons of food and medicine to the soldiers between July 10 and 13. The Chinese government decorated the pilots for their efforts.[14]

With the fall of Lashio and Myitkyina, the Burmese railheads were gone, the low elevation airports were gone, and all the elaborate planning of late 1941 was wiped out in a stroke. The Japanese, Young telegraphed Soong in mid-May, could now intercept transports and attack bases in Assam. "Even more serious under the present conditions," Young continued, "is the weather which is already too bad for night flying. Monsoon end of May entails heavy storms lasting five months with strong up and down currents and high winds." The mountains were perilously high along the direct route between Upper Assam and Kunming; maps were not accurate; there were no emergency landing fields, no radio bearings, and no weather reports. DC-3s were not suited for the direct route. Young, in despair, recommended that alternate supply channels to China be developed, perhaps via Persia or Alaska.[15]

Officials in Washington were even more pessimistic about the air route to China. Louis Johnson and Colonel Arthur W. Herrington, members of the American mission to India, returned from the Far East in May and reported "that Burma is completely gone and that with the loss of Burma, particularly Lashio, all possible routes to China are closed." Construction of new roads would take at least two years. The air freight route "is no longer feasible as the planes must fly so high as to render attempts at ferrying freight into China almost useless. Personnel can still be flown in and out of China, but at great hazard." Coupled with the supply problem was Chiang Kai-shek's anger with the British, who had seemed reluctant to accept Chinese assistance during the defense of Burma. The effect of these developments on China, Johnson and Herrington concluded, "has been catastrophic." They did not believe that the Chinese intended to continue fighting in the war.[16]

Bond, who returned to the United States in early March, was very much alone when he argued that use of the direct route from Upper Assam to Kunming should not be ruled out. But his opinion did carry weight, at least in some quarters. Stanley K. Hornbeck, adviser on political relations, wrote to the Secretary of State on May 29, 1942, "that defeatist pronouncements . . . originate for the most part with people who sit in headquarters and make estimates, in contrast with which we have the opinion of Mr. Bond, who, on the basis of practical experience, firmly believes that the thing *can* be done and, while admitting that it may be proven impossible takes the position that he would not admit it to be impossible until it had been so proven by actual trial, trial for the making of which he has volunteered his own services, and those of the seasoned organization which he directs."[17]

"It is essential," President Roosevelt declared in early May, "that our route [to China] be kept open, no matter how difficult." This settled the matter. While officials in Washington may or may not have believed Bond, plans did go forward for the air cargo service between Upper Assam and Kunming. Both the Army and C N A C made a number of flights over the route during May and June. General Stilwell requested additional aircraft, and General Naiden pressed for new, expanded aerodrome facilities at Dinjan in Upper Assam and Kunming. The program received a severe blow, however, when General Brereton was ordered to the Middle East to assist the British. Brereton departed on June 26, 1942, taking the heavy bomber units of the 10th Air Force, several cargo 'planes, and the most experienced ferry pilots. General Naiden, who succeeded Brereton in command, "was left with a crippled air transport system, a skeleton staff, and virtually no combat strength." Stilwell wrote in his diary on June 25: "Bang! Brereton to go to Egypt with all the heavy bombers and all the transports he needs. Bang! The A-29s [for delivery to China] are to be held at Khartoum and diverted to the British. Now what can I say to the G-mo [Chiang Kai-shek]? We fail in *all* our commitments, and blithely tell him to just carry on, old top."[18]

The air cargo service between India and China could not have been launched under less auspicious circumstances. The Army, with 35 aircraft, 10 of which were out of service due to shortage of parts, delivered 73 tons of material to China in July. CNAC operated 10 aircraft and carried 129.3 tons. This disparity brought renewed consideration in Washington for the proposal that CNAC take charge of the freight service.[19]

When M. X. Quinn Shaughnessy of China Defense Supplies first advanced the idea for control by CNAC in mid-April, Louis Johnson had placed his considerable political influence behind the scheme. "After observing parallel operations [by] army ferry command and Pan American across Africa," Johnson had telegraphed the secretary of state, "I am convinced that expeditious and vital aid to China can most quickly be accomplished by Lend-Lease contract through army to Pan American and China National Airways [sic]. Recommend White House direct army make such arrangements." Although several officials, notably Stanley Hornbeck, also had favored the scheme, the question had been left open.[20]

The proposal came up again in July 1942. This time General Stilwell vigorously opposed the idea. While unhappy with the Air Force's performance and acknowledging CNAC's superior efficiency, Stilwell believed that military personnel should not be placed under civilian control in a combat area. Also, as the Ministry of Communications controlled CNAC, the air route would come under Chinese influence, and Stilwell would not accept such an arrangement. Operation of the air route by

CNAC, Stilwell argued, would undermine his position in the theater and hinder the war effort. Instead, he recommended that CNAC be placed under contract to the military authorities. If the Chinese opposed this plan, then the American government should deny additional aircraft to China. The War Department supported Stilwell, and the matter was decided in his favor.[21]

Brigadier General Clayton L. Bissell assumed command of the 10th Air Force in August 1942. Although not optimistic about the amount of cargo that could be flown to China, Bissell sought to improve operations over the Hump. Despite his efforts, progress remained slow. "Pilots cracked under the strain of long hours of hazardous flying without relief," an Air Force historian noted, "while the monotony of existence in Assam became almost unbearable to ground personnel. Living conditions, by far the worst in the theater, showed no signs of improvement. Inadequacy of quarters, rations, mail service, hospital care, and recreational facilities were sufficient cause for discontent, but, when it was learned that personnel and material intended for the 1st Ferrying Group were being diverted to combat units, the *esprit de corps* built up during the first weeks of ferrying operations died, morale dropping to a dangerous point."[22]

Bissell's lack of faith in the air transport operation further complicated the situation. Whiting Willauer, a representative of China Defense Supplies, discussed prospects for the freight service with Bissell in November 1942. Bissell, he reported, believed that only 50 aircraft could be handled on one airfield "with proper provision for dispersal and fast handling of concentrated traffic." In order to carry 5,000 tons monthly to China during the worst weather, 300 aircraft would be necessary. This meant, according to Bissell's calculations, five airfields in Assam and five in Kunming. On the other hand, Frank D. Sinclair, aviation technical adviser to China Defense Supplies, reported in September 1942 that 125 aircraft, properly supported, could carry 10,000 tons a month to China.[23]

Tonnage carried by the Army increased during the late summer and fall of 1942, but progress remained slow and painful. Disappointment in Washington led in October 1942 to acceptance of an offer by the Air Transport Command to operate the service. Transfer of responsibility took place on December 1, 1942.[24]

Washington's continued belief in the viability of the India-China aerial supply route was due in part to CNAC's outstanding performance during the last six months of 1942. The airline began full-time freight service in July with ten lend-lease aircraft. Maintenance, overhaul, and supply facilities were established at Calcutta's Dum Dum Airport, while Dinjan and Kunming became major operating bases. CNAC made good progress in meeting the critical need for additional pilots. Four Chinese captains—Hugh Chen, K. Y. Leung, Ed Chin, and Harold Chin—were checked out on the DC-3s in May. Donald Wong, M. K. Loh, and George Huang followed later in the year. Disbandment of the American Volunteer Group in July provided an unexpected windfall of pilots for the airline. General Bissell had sought to incorporate the AVG into the new 14th Air Force, but his arrogant and heavy-handed approach had alienated Chennault's individualistic fighter pilots. Only 5 pilots joined the Air Force, while 16 accepted positions with CNAC. "These men," Bond noted, "all turned out splendidly and were a great help." A comparably maladroit effort to induct into military service the civilian pilots of Pan American Air Ferries in Africa produced 11 new recruits for CNAC. By the end of 1942, CNAC had 43 qualified command pilots and another 10 men in training.[25]

CNAC flew 873 round trips over the Hump between August and December 1942, carrying 1,804.3 tons of material to China and 1,833.1 tons to India. The airline lifted to China more than 500 tons of bank notes, 300 tons of aircraft parts, 300 tons of brass and steel caps, 20 tons of medical supplies for the American Red Cross and another 30 tons for the American Medical Service. Nearly 1,500 tons of tungsten were flown out to India, together with lesser amounts of tin, wood oil, tea, bristles, mercury, and silk. In addition, CNAC airlifted more than 7,000 members of the Chinese Expeditionary Force to India during October, November, and December; these were Chinese soldiers who would be trained in India for the later campaign to drive the Japanese out of North Burma.[26]

CNAC suffered only two serious accidents during 1942 under contract operations. One aircraft crashed and burned during practice landings at Balijan airport, a small dirt strip near Dinjan, on October 10. The crew survived. On November 17, 'plane number 60, with Captain Dean, copilot Brown, and radio operator Young, disappeared on a flight between Kunming and Dinjan.[27]

Despite these accidents, CNAC had done extraordinarily well. "The year has been particularly gratifying," Bond wrote in his summary of operations for 1942, "not so much because of our actual accomplishments but because of our progress in things which we hope will lead to greater accomplishments." Bond took "real pride" in the fact that CNAC had flown at least one trip over the Hump every day since July 1. CNAC had averaged more than 150 round trips a month for the last six months of the year, and Bond looked forward to 500 round trips a month in the near future. Lack of spare parts and inadequate maintenance facilities had caused delays, but efforts were being made to improve the situation. He reported good progress in training new air crews. Fortunately, losses of aircraft and crews had been light. But, as Bond looked toward the future, he struck a note of caution: "Through the urgency of China's needs and the needs of the United Nations, CNAC has been forced to expand very rapidly. Every precaution possible under existing conditions has been taken, but we must recognize the fact that we are actually doing military flying and that we must take certain unavoidable risks. CNAC is actually fighting in this war and losses are unavoidable. We have experienced some and we can expect more."[28]

— II —

CNAC demonstrated in 1942 that China could be supplied by air. "We have set a pace which must be followed by others," Bond wrote to the managing director, "and I am sure this work will go on [and] that large amounts of freight will be flown into China, and I believe this is almost entirely due to the efforts that C N A C made and to the results which we accomplished at a time when it was uncertain as to whether such flying was possible." The airline assumed a different role in 1943: C N A C now became the yardstick of efficiency for the massive effort undertaken by the Air Transport Command (ATC).[29]

Colonel Edward H. Alexander brought a new spirit to the Army's freight service in 1943. Bissell—the essence of pessimism—had emphasized all the difficulties of the operation and had spoken in terms of 5,000 tons a month with 300 aircraft maybe. Alexander called for 11,250 tons a month with 100 aircraft, for a start. The Curtiss C-46 was on the way, and it could carry nearly twice the payload of a DC-3; and it was said that the "cream" of the graduating classes of Air Force Training Command would operate these new machines.[30]

Unfortunately, both equipment and personnel failed to meet expectations. The unproven C-46 turned out to be an engineering nightmare; most pilots considered the aircraft "a menace equal to the Hump terrain and weather." The new pilots were not much better. Rushed through flight training and with little practical experience thereafter, the green Army pilots had to learn everything the hard way. Their classroom was the most difficult and dangerous air route in the world, and the price for failure was death. "It would be untrue and unfair," writes the author of a semi-official account of the ATC, "to say that the 409 pilots and co-pilots furnished to the India-China Wing by the domestic Air Forces were personally in any way inferior. Their later achievements over the Hump refute any such suggestion completely. But they most certainly were not of the level of skill required. . . . The twin-engine men with 1,000 hours, 'cream of the graduating classes,' simply did not materialize."[31]

Alexander noted other problems in a lengthy jeremiad to headquarters in June 1943. Maintenance personnel were "inadequate," the supply situation was "critical," communications were "faulty and insufficient," the weather was terrible, the food was poor, and the native population of Assam was expected to riot in the summer. Cheering talks to the men by Edward V. Rickenbacker, head of Eastern Airlines and America's top ace in World War I, "were in most cases failures as a stimulant to morale simply because he said that personnel should be prepared to stay here and fight for a long, long time."[32]

The decline of Alexander's initial optimism matched only the rise of President Roosevelt's. Under constant pressure from the Chinese government and unable to furnish any significant assistance because of more demanding military commitments throughout the world, Roosevelt turned to increased lend-lease supplies as a palliative. In May, the president ordered ATC to raise tonnage over the Hump to 7,000 in July and 10,000 in September.[33]

ATC mounted a maximum effort to comply with the new objective, but results were disappointing. In July, ATC transported only 3,451 tons to China. "The overpromoted air corps is sunk when it comes to administration and management," a frustrated Stilwell wrote in his diary. "Just a bunch of aerial chauffeurs.... Alexander has 3,000 men and 750 pilots and still they can't get going. The C-46 is full of bugs, carburetor ices up. We have lost six over the Hump and the boys' morale is lower and lower ... June, about 3,400 tons. July, 4,500 tons. August .... ?? They were to hit 7,000 in July and 10,000 in September. The Air Transport Command record to date is pretty sad. The CNAC has made them look like a bunch of amateurs."[34]

ATC found its problems hard enough to bear, but the disparaging comparison to CNAC was the cruelest cut of all. But Stilwell was right. In June 1943, ATC carried 2,219 tons with 146 aircraft assigned, including nearly 100 C-46s and several four-engine C-87s (transport version of the B-24 Liberator). CNAC operated 20 aircraft, all DC-3s, and moved 734.7 tons. In other words, ATC, flying larger aircraft, transported 15 tons per plane to CNAC's 37 tons. "Regardless of the difficulties which ICW [India-China Wing] had with the C-46 and with diversion of planes to duties other than flying the Hump," an Air Force historian has commented, "ATC operations were obviously less efficient than those of CNAC."[35]

ATC's shortcomings led to a series of high-level investigations during the summer of 1943. Major General Harold L. George came out from ATC headquarters with Edward V. Rickenbacker, an experienced airline executive. President Roosevelt sent Major General George Stratemeyer. The experts reviewed all the problems of the India-China Wing: limited airport facilities, shortage of maintenance personnel and spare parts, inadequate radio aids to navigation, and so forth. Rickenbacker, with great accuracy, attributed CNAC's superior performance to the greater experience of the airline's pilots.[36]

The India-China Wing underwent extensive reorganization in the wake of these investigations. In September, Colonel Thomas O. Hardin, known as a hard driver, took command of the airlift. Sparing neither himself nor his men, and capitalizing on the groundwork that had been laid by Alexander, Hardin pushed tonnage over the Hump to above 7,000 in October. By the end of the year, ATC was carrying more than 12,000 tons a month to China.[37]

"We are paying for it in men and airplanes," Brigadier General Cyrus R. Smith observed in December. "The kids are flying over their head—at night and in daytime and they bust them up for reasons that sometimes seem silly. They are not silly, however, for we are asking boys to do what would be most difficult for men to accomplish; with the experience level here we are going to pay dearly for the tonnage moved across the Hump. . . . With the men available, there is nothing else to do." Between June and December 1943, the India-China Wing experienced 155 major accidents, 135 on the Hump route, with 168 crew fatalities.[38]

Flight between India and China over the high mountains could be hazardous even for the most experienced pilots. There are a number of descriptive accounts of the route, ranging from the death-lurks-in-the-sky romanticism of a young Theodore White to the philosophical ponderings of Lin Yutang.[39] One of the best pictures, however, comes from the prosaic pen of W. L. Bond.

In late January 1943, Bond boarded a DC-3 for a trip from

Chungking to Calcutta via Kunming and Dinjan. The flight to Kunming was uneventful, although a strong headwind resulted in a flying time of three hours and twenty minutes over the 400 miles. "About sixty miles out of Kunming," Bond wrote,

we ran into bad weather and started going up trying to get above it as ice began to form. I went into the control room partly to watch the flight carefully and partly because I knew it was going to be a tough flight at high altitude and I wanted to get up with the crew so I could get oxygen occasionally. I found recently that I could not take the high altitudes without oxygen like I used to. I acted as copilot for the flight.

We got into solid soup at about 14,000 feet and ice began to form. The temperature began to go down and although the alcohol spray on the front window was working, ice began slowly to form. It also began to form on the props and about every four or five minutes would let go and bang up against the cabin. It got a little rough but not too bad in that respect.

We continued to go higher and the thermometer went lower. The ice on the windows closed over completely until we had the most perfect hood you ever saw.

Then our heating system gave out. It was then 25 degrees below zero. I believe it got to 30 below at the lowest point. The engines were running perfectly. The Bendix radio compass had died. The Telefunken was perfect, except that the loops for our Telefunken are not housed and [radio operator] Joe Loh had to keep cranking the loop around to prevent it freezing up and sticking. We got as high as we could at about 20,800 and were just running in and out of the tops of clouds. The temperature inside the cabin got so low that the windows were frosted up on the inside. We could get bearings that told us we were on our course but no bearings to tell us where we were. We knew we were bucking a very stiff headwind. The icing condition outside got better and we had very little coming off the props and we could see the sun every now and then. Or rather you couldn't see it because the windows were still blanked out but you could tell every now and then the sun was there and that gave you a warm feeling—inside. Actually it was still cold as the deuce. We tried pumping up the window de-icer spray pump until the pressure got so high that the alcohol, which we use in it, worked out around the pump system. We could then catch this on our fingers and rub it on the inside of the window but it didn't help much and the rapid evaporation on our fingers plus the already cold conditions nearly took our fingers off. I found out, however, that I could press the palm of my bare hand against the side window and hold it there for awhile and I could thaw out a small part that would enable me to get a quick peep at the top of the engine and a part of the wing. This showed a little ice on top of the engine cowling and a little ice on the wings but not enough to cause any trouble, and most important, was not getting any worse. This lasted about 400 miles and four hours. Then we finally got safely over the Hump and now we could start down and the thermometer got up to zero and we felt like giving three cheers for the luxuries of life. The passengers stood it remarkable well. Really, it is amazing, almost pathetic, the licking CNAC passengers will take without complaint.

I think we stayed within the limits of safety but I admit we pushed those limits beyond normal boundaries. We had one of our older pilots [Sidney DeKantzow], our best radio operator, and a Telefunken. The instruments on the engines were all operating perfectly. We got to a point where we could safely figure the ice would get no worse, before it got dangerous. We are requiring the older pilots to set the pace and turn back or turn the younger pilots back if there is the least doubt. This condition has lasted a week now. We would have made over 240 flights last month easily if this condition had not arisen, and averaged nearly 140 hours per plane. That cannot be helped. We would not be helping to end the war by needlessly risking our crews and planes.[40]

In spite of CNAC's emphasis on safety, operations during 1943 were not without cost. Plane number 53, piloted by James Fox, disappeared on a flight over the Hump on March 11. (See Appendix for a list of wartime losses.) Two days later, Orin Welsh and crew were lost. C. J. Rosbert and his copilot miraculously survived a crash landing in the Naga Hills on April 7.[41]

In a letter to the managing director, Bond reflected on the cause of these accidents:

Some of the reasons are of course inherent in the work we are doing. These are: first, weather, which is nearly always bad and at times a great deal worse; second, extremely high terrain over which we are flying; and third, the urgency of our work. There is nothing we can do to correct these conditions. We simply have to accept them and endure them as best we can. There are also other reasons. These are: first, we have checked our new pilots out too quickly. Under normal conditions pilots should have from six to eight months experience as copilot over this route before he should be permitted to fly as captain. Secondly, we have greatly overloaded these planes. The standard gross load for these planes is approximately 24,400 pounds. We consistently carried a gross load of 27,000 pounds, sometimes more. Third, we have been pushing this flying too energetically. In other words, we have flown on many days when weather was such that we should have stayed on the ground. For all these things which fundamentally from a purely technical view are serious errors, I take my full share of responsibility.

I would like for you to believe that these errors have not been due to carelessness or indifference, but we have been faced with a serious problem. A problem of getting urgently needed supplies into China at a critical period, a period of serious uncertainty in the minds of the government and of the people as to whether it was possible to get supplies into China by air. This situation was in my opinion so serious that it justified CNAC making every effort to get supplies into China, and to completely demonstrate the fact that many more supplies could be brought in by air.

If we had waited six to eight months in checking our pilots out we would have been seriously delayed. If we were only to carry the standard load, the amount of cargo carried on each 'plane would be so small that the urgently needed cargo could never be flown into China. If we had stayed on the ground during bad weather we would have grounded our planes more than one-half the time. In saying these things I am afraid I am laying myself open to the criticism that I mentioned above, that is I am not giving reasons but excuses, but I sincerely do not intend all these things as excuses.

Measures were being taken to reduce accidents, but, as Bond concluded, "the only way we could really stop these accidents is to stop flying the Hump. This cannot be done and must not be considered."[42]

CNAC suffered its first confirmed loss to Japanese fighters on October 13, 1943, when Captain Schroeder was shot down. Fearing that this attack heralded the long-awaited Japanese aerial offensive against the Hump route, CNAC inaugurated night-time operations between India and China. "The night flying will no doubt reduce our total tonnage," Bond noted, "but not to any great degree after we get thoroughly organized for it."[43]

Although the Japanese aerial offensive failed to materialize, losses continued. Two aircraft crashed on November 19 on approach to Kunming. December 18 brought another double loss, when planes 83 and 79, loaded with cargoes of gasoline, crashed and burned at Suifu.[44]

CNAC also suffered from many of the same problems that plagued ATC. A threatened strike by ground personnel at CNAC's maintenance base in Calcutta resulted in an investigation of conditions by Managing Director Wang and Arthur

Young. "We found a very complicated situation," Young reported in September 1943.

The immediate cause of trouble was an unfortunate practical joke which had been magnified out of all proportion so as to become the occasion for the near strike. But the real causes of discontent lie deeper. CNAC's operations have expanded so rapidly, and it has been so hard to find proper personnel, that it has sometimes been found necessary to engage whatever technically qualified men that were available without being too "choosey." The mechanics here and at Dinjan often have had to work in improvised temporary shops and without adequate machinery or tools —merely because construction and procurement take time and require priorities. Also, it has not been possible to do as much as is desirable for the welfare of the men, in view of shortage of proper living quarters, lack of recreational facilities, etc. They are living in one of the worst climates in the world. Some of the men have been under considerable strain from bombing, etc. Some have individual grievances, which are unavoidable in any large group. To some extent the company has been at fault in not earlier taking up the causes of complaint. We are now busy rectifying matters.

CNAC's management raised the living allowance for Chinese staff, dismissed several individuals, transferred others, and sought additional personnel.[45]

Inauguration of night flying and maintenance difficulties resulted in lowered tonnage figures for the last three months of 1943. Nevertheless, CNAC's record during the year was outstanding. CNAC crossed the Hump from India to China 9,564 times in 1943, lifting 8,436.3 tons of goods. The airline made 8,742 westbound trips with 7,575.1 tons, mainly tungsten and tin, and carried 14,377 passengers, mostly members of the Chinese Expeditionary Force.[46]

Bond's original proposal of May 1941 had emphasized the need for careful selection of personnel for the air cargo service. "It will require pilots of experience and skill in handling multi-engine planes," he had written. The airline's record during the war years testifies to the fact that men of this caliber were found.[47]

CNAC's pilot group, one of their number has observed, "was probably one of the most unique in all aviation history, a wider assemblage of personalities, family and financial background, aviation experience, and nationalities could not be imagined." The men came from the United States, China, Australia, Canada, Great Britain, and Denmark; they had flown for the American Volunteer Group, the Eagle Squadron, the North Atlantic Ferry Command, the Royal Air Force, and the Royal Canadian Air Force. They had more than 1,000 flying hours to their credit, most had an instrument rating, and many had extensive multi-engine experience. "All were motivated by a thirst for either money or adventure or both, and it was impossible to gain much of the first without acquiring a considerable amount of the latter."[48]

A new pilot journeyed halfway around the world to join CNAC. Starting in New York, he might fly to Miami aboard a domestic airliner, and if he was lucky he would connect there with one of Pan American's Clippers for the flight to Natal on the bulge of Brazil. At Natal he might wait days or weeks for an Air Force B-24 or C-47 being ferried across the South Atlantic to Africa and the Middle East, or he might get a ride with a C-46 from Air Transport Command. A flight of 1,437 miles awaited him, halfway across the Atlantic, to the tiny volcanic island of Ascension for fuel. Another 1,357 miles over the water would bring him to Accra in the British colony of the Gold Coast. He would cross the width of Africa to Khartoum in Anglo-Egyptian Sudan, then follow the Nile northward to Cairo. Here he would most likely have to find new transportation, perhaps an aircraft on ferry to India via Iraq and Iran. Finally, he would arrive at Karachi, the aerial gateway to British India; but he would spend another two or three days flying across India to Calcutta via New Delhi. If his connections were the very best, he might have been able to fly from New York to Calcutta in ten days; otherwise the passage could take a month or more.

His first encounter with CNAC likely came in the person of William McDonald, former member of Claire Chennault's "Flying Trapeze" aerobatic group of the early 1930s, adviser to the Chinese Air Force, and now assistant to CNAC's chief pilot. McDonald told the new man in a salty Alabamian drawl what CNAC expected of him: be punctual when transportation calls, fill out your log books properly and legibly, read the bulletin board at least once a day, do not carry more passengers than there are seats on the aircraft. The new man would be warned against smuggling. Remember, McDonald would emphasize, "you are in a foreign country and you will contact Indians, Chinese, Burmese, English, and French; use tact and diplomacy in doing business with them. Above all, *Do Not Lose Your Temper.*" Dr. Richards would perform a physical examination; he would probably warn against excessive use of alcohol and describe some of the more esoteric venereal diseases. The new man would learn that the mailing address for Calcutta was APO 465; Kunming was APO 627.[49]

Following initial instruction in Calcutta on CNAC's aircraft and procedures, the new arrival would travel to Dinjan for advanced training as copilot on the Hump. He would learn that there were a number of routes over the Hump. The northern route, favored during good weather, called for take-off from Dinjan, direct to the local Army Direction Finding (DF) station, then a course of 098° for 112 miles to Fort Hertz DF Station; turn right to 107° for 208 miles to Lake Cheng Hai, then south to a course of 129° for 170 miles to the Army DF station at Kunming. Although this route required a cruising altitude of 19,000 feet to clear all obstacles, it could be flown much lower in good weather if one knew the terrain. The direct route from Dinjan to Kunming followed a course of 112° and could be flown at 16,000 feet. For the southern route, turn to a course of 143° from the Army DF station for 86 miles until reaching the fork of the Tanai River; then come to 105° for 497 miles to Kunming, using the CNAC DF station at Yunlung as a check point. This route could be flown at 14,000 feet, but beware of the Japanese.[50]

A new pilot would learn of the two routes used during instrument flying conditions: eastbound via Yunlung and westbound via Fort Hertz. He would come to know every mountain and every canyon on all the routes. Captain Robert W. Pottschmidt, the soft-spoken check pilot, would have him outline the routes, noting the elevations of the mountains. The new man would become proficient at instrument flying over the Hump. One day he might lose an engine in bad weather and be forced to descend to 10,000 feet. Maybe he could fly headings that would take him between the mountains—maybe.[51]

As he sat in the right seat over the Hump, his captain might tell him about the four distinct seasonal weather patterns that one could expect on the route. The monsoons came in the summer, bringing nearly constant instrument flying conditions. The seemingly endless light rain at flight altitudes was annoying, but there was not too much wind or turbulence, and the icing level was high enough so that heavy accumulations could be avoided; also, one did not have to worry about the Japanese because the bad weather kept them on the ground. The winter season generally brought clear weather, except for ground fog in the early morning. En route, high winds could be expected, invariably from a westerly direction, and reaching velocities of 100 to 150 miles an hour. The new man would be warned about the need for careful fuel management on the westbound trip. Watch the Chinese ground crews at Kunming: gasoline brought fantastic prices on the black market, and the crews were not adverse to siphoning off a few extra gallons. Spring and fall brought the worst flying weather, with unpredictable winds, frequent and violent thunderstorms, and severe icing conditions. Furthermore, the radio direction-finding equipment was unreliable in thunderstorms or during snow and icing conditions.[52]

The new pilot practiced the instrument approach to Kunming. Tune your Bendix to 375 kilocycles and identify the Army DF station. Approach at 12,000 feet from the northwest at an indicated airspeed of 120 miles per hour. Upon crossing the station, lower your landing gear, turn north for two minutes and descend to 10,500 feet. Make a procedure turn (15° of bank) to port, come to the reciprocal course of 180°, and cross the station again at 8,500 feet. Turn to course 195°, continue descent at 1,000 feet per minute until your altimeter registers 6,700 feet (approximately 500 feet above the field). If the airport is not in sight, pull up and follow the missed-approach procedure. If the new man was wise, he would practice this approach over and over again.[53]

An experienced pilot could be checked out in a few weeks, although the average was two to three months. If a new man did not make the grade within six months, he was sent home. As a CNAC captain, his base salary for 60 hours was $800 a month, or more than an Air Force colonel made; and the colonels, and others, would probably demonstrate their resentment of this fact. The CNAC captain made 20 rupees ($6) an hour for time between 60 and 70 hours; over 70 hours, he was "on gold," $20 an hour. If he was Chinese or of Chinese descent, however, he made 1,600 rupees ($485) for 60 hours and 20 rupees per hour for all time in excess of 60 hours; this kind of discrimination could rankle, especially if the new man was American- or Canadian-born.[54]

Most pilots flew 100 to 140 hours during a stay of from two to three weeks at Dinjan. Then a pilot would return to Calcutta. Part of his time was spent with refresher courses in radio operation and instrument flying. But mostly he relaxed. If he was so inclined, he read or visited the local scenic attractions, such as they were. He would pay at least one visit to the noisy labyrinthine passageways of Newmarket to buy some souvenirs of India for the folks at home. He might go to tea dances or dinner at the Great Eastern Hotel. He probably would spend some time at the British-American Club. Earthier pleasures could be found on Kariah Road.

In Dinjan, he stayed at the CNAC bungalow, located on a tea plantation about five miles from the airport. "The CNAC building," one pilot recalled,

like all others in the district, was set high on stilts to be well above the muddy floods of the monsoon season, but it was a giant, being a hundred feet wide and forty feet deep, with a huge porch covering the entire front and one side. The roof was steeply pitched and covered with a foot-thick layer of thatch to repel the heat of the sun as well as to shed the rain. The main floor of the building consisted of four large rooms, three of them in all containing about forty beds and double-decked bunks. The fourth room, which was the largest, was the lounge, and around its huge fireplace were grouped half a dozen comfortable leather chairs and an enormous couch. Elsewhere in the room were card tables, writing desks and bookcases, a radio and a phonograph. The favorite record of one of the native servants, Putlao, was an Andrew Sisters' rendition of "Down by the Ohio!" He played it every morning to wake the pilots.[55]

Miss Major, who later married Hugh Woods, ran the mess, and the food generally was excellent, especially compared with Army messes. Sweet-and-sour pork was a favorite dish. The pilots argued a good deal, usually about the performance characteristics of various aircraft and women. They played cards. And they probably drank too much, despite McDonald's plea "to drink more oxygen and less whiskey."[56]

The average CNAC pilot did not know very much about the relationship between CNAC and the Chinese government, and he did not really care. His attitude toward the natives, Chinese and Indian, ranged from affection to intolerance. He probably did some smuggling; surely, he believed that everyone else was doing some. He looked down upon the Army and took pride in the fact that CNAC flew when the Army remained on the ground. He was afraid, but he felt a bit heroic, and he was determined to get the job done.[57]

If he survived, he would come to look back on the war years with a good deal of nostalgia. The bad times would tend to blur in his memory, and the good times would stand out. The tales—Al Mah playing his saxophone at 18,000 feet, Hockswinder's landing in the Ganges River, Jimmy Scoff's escapades on Kariah Road—would grow taller with each passing year. Whether flying for the airlines, ranching, or running a gasoline station, he would remember his work—and his youth—with pride.

— III —

The Air Transport Command dominated the aerial supply route to China in 1944 and 1945. When Brigadier General William H. Tunner replaced Hardin in September 1944, ATC already had passed 20,000 tons a month. "As tonnage increased," writes an Air Force historian, "there was less talk about any figure to be regarded as the maximum possible achievement. General Tunner and his staff acted upon the thesis that virtually any amount could be delivered if only the requisite facilities and men were provided." Flying improved models of the C-46 and four-engined C-54s, ATC reached 30,000 tons a month by the end of 1944 and 40,000 tons monthly by early 1945. July 1945 was the record month: 71,042 tons were airlifted to China. Total tonnage over the Hump by ATC during the war years amounted to 650,000 with half this amount moving during the first nine months of 1945.[58]

Although relegated to a minor role, CNAC continued to airlift supplies between India and China in ever increasing amounts during 1944 and 1945. The airline flew more than 9,000 round trips over the Hump in 1944, flying over 10 million miles and carrying some 38 percent of all strategic cargoes on world routes, second only to the ATC. CNAC also performed a variety of other missions. Between October 22, 1944, and January 21, 1945, the airline made 224 trips with 540,719 pounds of equipment and 736 passengers to Paoshan and Myitkyina in support of the Ledo Road construction project. During the same period, CNAC flew 523 aerial supply missions, dropping 1,836,970 pounds of rice to Chinese road builders. The airline made several flights into Tibet, sometimes to purchase horses for the Chinese and American forces, once to return home two Tibetan princesses who had been attending finishing school at Darjeeling, India. CNAC frequently provided airlift for American Naval Intelligence units in China.[59]

One of CNAC's more important projects involved freight service from Dinjan to Suifu (Iping). By the end of 1943, ATC and CNAC were airlifting more than 10,000 tons a month to Kunming; however, the supply route east of Kunming to General Chennault's 14th Air Force and to units of the Chinese Army had a capacity of only 1,500 tons a month. In an attempt to relieve some of the pressure from the supply bottleneck at Kunming, CNAC inaugurated service from Dinjan to Suifu, a Yangtze River town some 140 miles west of Chungking, in October 1943. Between October and December, CNAC made 60 trips to Suifu, carrying 113.9 tons inbound, mainly gasoline and TNT for a large munitions factory in the area, and 112.2 tons of bristles outbound. The airline increased service in 1944, operating nearly 150 round trips monthly by the end of the year. Although CNAC facilitated movement of war materials to the Chungking area, carriage of supplies eastward from Kunming remained a vexing problem. Whiting Willauer, an official of China Defense Supplies who attempted to assist the Chinese government with this problem, termed the failure to solve the logistical tangle "the most glaring military error made in the prosecution of the war in China." The blame, he wrote, "is fairly equally divided between the United States leadership in China and the Chinese government."[60]

CNAC's airlift over the Hump reached 2,000 tons monthly by the fall of 1944. In November CNAC made 1,068 round trips between India and China, including 145 flights to Suifu. The airline flew 203 airdrop missions and 15 special charter flights. CNAC's 30 assigned aircraft averaged 8:56 hours of flying time daily, while pilots averaged 104:20 each for the month. Due to the success of the Allied offensive in Burma, the lower southern route via Myitkyina was now in use. CNAC's peak month came in July 1945, when it carried 2,648.4 tons to China.[61]

In all, CNAC flew the Hump more than 80,000 times between April 1942 and September 1945, carrying more than 50,000 tons of goods to China and bringing out nearly 25,000 tons. It cost the lives of 25 crews.[62]

The character of CNAC's operations during the latter stages of the war can be seen in the pages of a diary kept by one young pilot. Donald McBride joined the airline late in 1943, recruited from the War Training Service by Hugh Woods. In many ways typical of the pilots who flew the Hump during the war years, McBride had one special characteristic: he took the time to record his experiences in a diary. The entries, McBride later explained, "include incidents or conditions that tended to generate the emotions such as fear, anxiety, fatalism, curiosity and satisfaction that were our everyday mental companions and that undoubtedly influenced our attitudes toward CNAC and our job."[63] The following are excerpts from McBride's diary:

December 12 [1943]: Japs bombed our base at Dinjan—destroyed CNAC operations and supply warehouse—also Indian Customs building. The mountains were beautiful today, we passed around the base of Minya Konki (24,900 ft.). Cargo—gasoline to China & Chinese soldiers on return trips. Plane Captain was Al Wright.

December 18: Capt. Al Wright, Capt. "Cookie" Cook and a Chinese radio operator in Plane #83 and Capt. M. K. Loh along with his two Chinese crewmen in plane #79 were killed today when both ships hit mountains during instrument letdowns at Suifu. Both ships were carrying 100 octane gasoline as cargo. Wright was giving Cook a route check. I had flown three trips as copilot with Al this week. Japs bombed Kunming today.

December 21: Jap air raids on Kunming and Yunanyi today.

January 10 [1944]: Plane #88 lost an engine at Suifu today—gear folded on landing—not badly damaged. Pilot, Capt. G. A. Robertson.

January 17: Plane #75 caught fire and burned left engine at Kunming today. Pilot, Capt. Einar Mickelson. Casey Boyd and I hit a lot of ice over the Hump last night—scared me.

January 18: Japs shot down 3 A.F. transports over Irriwaddy River valley today.

January 19: Two more transports shot down near Ft. Hertz today.

January 20: Japs raided field at Ft. Hertz. I am scheduled for two trips over the Hump tonite—made three yesterday. Wish I had a clean shirt.

January 24: Last nite over the Hump was one of the worst in memory—snow, ice, rain and high winds. Today four ships went to Suifu—ours was the only one to make it back to Dinjan. We were forced to go to 21,000 feet to get over the ice and we ran into 100 mph headwinds. We haul TNT and copper to Suifu for a munitions factory.

February 21: One of my best friends, Mickelson, is 24 hours overdue. He left Dinjan for Kunming at 2 P.M.—Chinese copilot and no radio operator, Ship #75. Bob Prescott, flying nearby, lost radio contact with him about one hour out. We searched for him today but found no wreckage except that of Jim Fox's plane which crashed up earlier. It was almost completely covered with snow. "Micky" was a former Flying Tiger and one of the best liked fellows in CNAC. I hope he bailed out before it was too late or made a good crash landing. From all our calculations, he would have been east of the Irriwaddy River—all mountains, jungle, and Jap territory. I hope the plane is found soon because the suspense is causing a lot of unrest among the pilots. The weather is lousy, ice bad and wind strong. He probably hit a mountain or was shot down in a pass.

We live about fifteen miles from the new Ledo Road. It runs from the town of Ledo (Assam) into the Hukawng Valley in Burma. There is fierce ground fighting going on in there between Merrill's Marauders and Japanese jungle troops. There are also American-trained Chinese fighting in Burma. The Ledo Road will eventually join the old Burma Road. We use the road as a navigational check point at night because it can be seen for many miles due to the moving trucks. We also fly over about 150 miles of the Burma Road. It certainly looks rough. Often see Chinese soldiers marching over it to Burma.

It is 7:00 P.M. and we received a report from the Chinese Fifth Army that "an unidentified aircraft made a forced landing near Paochan. It contained one Chinese and a Foreigner." It must be Micky's ship and there is a possibility they are alive—we hope.

We have been losing lots of mail because the military pilots jettison it when they get into trouble, so I change APO, from China to India.

We had a slight earthquake here at Dinjan. It shook the building—knocked plaster off the walls and scared hell out of everyone in general. Some of the pilots asleep on the second floor mistook it for a Jap bombing raid and jumped overboard. One almost broke an ankle.

February 25: One of our planes was sent to Paochan to check on the downed aircraft rumor. It was found that the Chinese knew nothing of the affair. Since Paochan is the last point between us and the Japs in that region, it is now believed the Japs have Micky. He was over Jap territory when last contacted by radio. All of us hope he is dead rather than a captive.

Each time one of CNAC's planes goes down, I place an "X" on my map at the approximate location of the mishap. To date I have fourteen Xs. Three of the ships disappeared without any clues or traces. This time of year the snow is piled hundreds of feet deep on the Himalayas. Perhaps when it melts off during the monsoons, we will be able to find the lost ships.

February 26: Dr. Lin Yutang came through Dinjan today on one of our ships.

February 27: The scenery here is probably the finest anywhere, and undoubtedly the wildest and most isolated of any in the world. There are places in the Himalayas where we fly over dense tropical jungles and a few seconds later are over regions of eternal ice and snow. There are gorgeous waterfalls from the melting snow and beautiful sea-green rivers winding through canyons with vertical sides two and three miles high. I have seen mountains split in two by earthquakes, and freaks of nature like the "Devils Slide" in Nevada have been duplicated on a scale that make the original look like something in miniature. There are valleys in which the Creator could easily have lost the Grand Canyon. I found a valley west of Likiang that is an excellent replica of the "Garden of the Gods" in Colorado, only much larger. Between Likiang and Sichang there is a range of mountains that have tipped over on their side, completely revealing the layers deposited during the various geological ages. In a small valley on the west side of the Salween Range west of Paochan are three newly formed volcano craters, so recent that no vegetation has regrown. High up on the west bank of the Mekong River, west of Weishi, stands a tremendous natural stone arch. There are hundreds of crystal blue lakes hidden in watersheds slightly below the snow line. Sometimes there are native huts and villages on the shores of those lakes and I often think how peaceful their existence must be, surrounded as they are by an excellent climate, good hunting and fishing, plus plenty of pure cold water. I almost envy them.

March 12: Ship #86 was lost last nite. Capt. Glen Carroll and Chinese crew made radio contact long enough to tell they were lost and out of fuel. Visibility was almost zero.

March 14: Capt. Les Hall lost an engine over the middle of the Hump yesterday. He jettisoned a cargo of Chinese currency. Captains Carroll and Mickelson still missing.

March 15: We lost another ship and crew. It was a new plane being ferried over by Tutwieler. Lost an engine on takeoff.

Carroll's plane has been located. It crashed in a riverbed in the jungles 70 miles NW of Jorhat. Fate of the crew still unknown.

Two of our ships flew Mdme. Chiang, Mdme. and Dr. Kung, T. V. Soong and several other dignitaries from Kunming to Chungking today. Both ladies became ill in flight.

March 20: We are all on the ground for a few days due to a gasoline shortage. No relief in sight. One of our ships went from Dinjan to Calcutta today. It contained one of the highest valued loads ever flown, $9 billion in Chinese Government bonds headed for the U. S. for safekeeping until the war is over.

March 22: Last night we didn't get much sleep. Two leopards were seen about two hundred yards from the house at Dinjan, so seven of us went after them but it was very dark and they escaped into the jungle. When we returned to the hostel, we were warned to sleep with our guns. A group of natives had revolted and gone on the warpath. They burned a nearby house. Ghurka troops were called in to settle the trouble.

March 24: Last night we lost another plane, #51. Capt. Jim Scoff and crew were forced to bail out at 4 A.M. in the northern hills after being lost for ten hours and running out of fuel. They have been reported safe near Chengtu.[64]

March 28: Japs raided here today; 25 bombers and more Zeros than we could count. They dropped propaganda leaflets on Ledo.

March 29: Japs raided Kunming. One of the newly arrived pilots made one trip across the Hump as copilot. It scared him so badly that he resigned and is returning to the U. S. by boat.

April 1: The Japs have started an offensive designed to flank us and cut off our supply lines between Upper Assam and Bengal. They have captured a section of railroad at Kohima and the British airbase at Imphal. It is the first territory the Japs have taken in India.

We received an official report from Army G-2 that Mickelson and crew are prisoners-of-war somewhere in Burma. It was based on a Japanese radio report, so there is a possibility that they may still be free or dead. (Most likely dead.)

April 4: Four Jap prisoners escaped from the British near our base at Dinjan last nite.

May 6: The weather has been bad lately. During a 7 hour flight, usually 4 to 5 hours are on instruments. Ice has been bad. I was forced to turn back yesterday because I couldn't climb over 14,000 ft.

May 8: The mosquitoes are getting bad now. It is hot and wet all the time. We run into lots of thunderstorms and some hail. It makes flying very uncomfortable at times. Drift hasn't been over 8 to 12 degrees lately and is gradually getting less.

May 16: We lost another ship today. (#90) Leo Atwater took off from Dinjan [and] was cleared out over Roger Uncle to Kunming. He reported his position when 26 minutes out. That was his last message. The weather is all-instrument.

May 18: We lost another plane today. Jim Scoff landed #92 at Dinjan with one brake locked. He ground looped into General Olds' B-25 and wrecked both ships. No one seriously injured.

May 24: We lost another plane. (#96) Capt. 'Moose' Moss and crew are in the hospital. Power failure on takeoff, plane completely wrecked.

May 27: It appears as though we have lost another ship. #82 is twelve hours overdue. Capt. Dick Marchant left Calcutta at 4:00 PM. yesterday headed for Dinjan. The weather is PuHau [terrible]. We are having trouble with our fuel supply. Due to the monsoon rains, the fuel tanks condense too much water. We had two power failures yesterday. We are also picking up a lot of carburetor ice at present. Two ships were forced to return to Dinjan last nite because of severe external icing, both clear and rime.

June 1: Ship #82 still missing. It has turned into the worst disaster CNAC has suffered. There were at least 14 persons aboard and possibly more.

June 5: We had another air raid at Dinjan today. Saw three Jap bombers and three Zeros.

June 8: Tom Loomis and crew killed today when #85 blew apart in the air over Kunming during an instrument letdown. I was making a final approach when his burning plane fell past the nose of my ship. It was in several pieces. Ashes and burned parts fell all around us.

June 14: Nearly lost #86 today. One of the oxygen tanks in the rear end of the fuselage exploded and blew a large hole in the ship. Bob Hinkel flew it in O.K.

June 24: Lost another ship last nite. Pop Kessler left Kunming for Chungking. Five hours later he reported that he was lost, out of fuel and going down (on instruments)—didn't know what was below. They had no parachutes on board so couldn't bail out. (It is company policy not to carry chutes on planes regularly used exclusively for passengers.)

June 27: Wreckage of #71 (Pop Kessler) found, almost totally destroyed. Pop was slightly injured, copilot badly injured and one passenger (U. S. Navy officer) killed.

July 9: The Japs have been getting active again. Have been seeing their patrols out near Myitkyina and Paochan.

August 1: Lost another plane and crew today. Chinese Capt. K. L. Mah in #73. Hit a 3000-ft. cliff on the side of "Old Baldy" west of Kunming shortly before daylight this morning.

August 6: The U. S. Army made a little mistake several days ago and bombed our own field at Paochan. They mistook it for the Jap base at Tengchung a few miles west. Now all of us are restricted from flying over Paochan and the Burma Road bridges on the Salween and Mekong Rivers.

September 1: Tengchung now partially in allied hands—another hazard eliminated. We lost another ship yesterday (#97). It was the second newest ship in our fleet. I wish the boys would wreck the old ships instead of the new ones. Capt. Coulson and crew were returning from Suifu. They stopped at Yunanyi for fuel. Several hours later they radioed in saying that both engines were giving trouble. He thought there was water in the gasoline. His ETA put him in the Hukawng valley. The Army reported a burning plane sighted about 20 miles south of Shingbwyang about that time. I tried to search for them today, but the ceiling was only about a hundred feet over the trees and that was too low for comfort.

October 8: Jim Scoff is two days overdue on a flight to Suifu, so we have lost another ship, #101. I hope he bailed out. He is one of my closest friends. [Scoff was killed.]

November 13: Don Codrea crashed two miles from Dinjan (plane #80). He got out O.K. I located the wreckage of an old CNAC plane on a mountain peak near the Salween River about half-way between Paochan & Tengchung. The "Chung" (the Chinese CNAC symbol painted on our planes) was visible but not the number. There is little doubt that it is Mickelson's plane.

We recently have been given an additional job. That of dropping rice and supplies to surrounded Chinese soldiers and laborers. An effort was made to build a road from the Irriwaddy River at Myitkyina, Burma, to a point on the Salween River in China. However, the Japs intervened and are closing in on the Chinese. We were ordered to drop goods to them. Our first attempt was futile because our objective was captured by the Japs (unknown to us for several days) and all the food we dropped went to them. Now we are dropping supplies at a point several miles from there. The Japs are close on both sides. So far, no casualties.

November 16: Another plane wrecked. (#96) Capt. Julius Petach. Piled up on the runway at Yunanyi when the radio operator (he had no copilot) pulled the landing gear up before the ship was airborne.[65]

November 19: Several days ago the CNAC radio transmitter at Dinjan burned out a bunch of fuses. Upon investigation, they found a snake had crawled across the wires inside the transmitter box. He was well fried.

November 26: Last nite was a rough one for everyone. We lost one ship and the Army lost twelve. #106 with Pilot McClelland is missing.

December 16: The crew from #106 was found and are O. K. Bailed out near Kweilin. We lost another plane last week, #56. George Anderson, a new captain was pilot. All crew dead. Japs are busy again—they attacked three Army C-46s near Bhamo. Shot down one and damaged the other two. We are getting C-46s next month. Some of the pilots are starting their transition.

Christmas Eve 1944: [McBride was stranded on the former Japanese airstrip at Tengchung.] There was a brief church service conducted by a missionary flown in during the afternoon in an L-5. There were about a dozen American present (Burma Road Engineer Bat.) The boys don't get liquor rations there so they swiped two gallons of propeller deicer fluid from my plane (isopropol alcohol & glycerine). They prepared it for drinking by cutting the ends off a loaf of bread and pouring the fluid through it—they mixed the filtered liquid with canned grapefruit juice. There were a number of severe headaches the next morning.

December 28: We have been having air raids every nite the past week. Bombs have hit the runway twice. The bombings at Kunming have been very unusual. The Japs come into the traffic pattern at night, call the tower, make a regular approach, then blow up the runway. Christmas Eve the Japs called the control tower in perfect English & told the tower operator he had a Christmas present for him, then let the bombs go. Joe Kurzman, a CNAC pilot, was flying in the traffic pattern directly behind the Jap and saw the bombs hit.

January 23 [1945]: The moon is getting bright again and the Japs are starting nightly raids as usual. This has been one of the most trying months in CNAC history. We have lost five planes and all the crews on them.

February 3: The new Ledo-Burma (Stilwell) Road is officially opened. The opening ceremony took place on the Road near Mengshih (Burma). Several of the more important brass hats (including General Sultan) were present. The Japs were also there to help things along. During the ceremony they opened fire from the mountainside with cannons and mortars, so the General couldn't finish his speech until several days later after the Japs had been driven out.

July 27: The U. S. and Chinese governments are trying to stabilize Chinese currency by sending tons of gold bullion to the Chinese treasury. Today we flew nearly 30 tons of it over the Hump. Ten of us flew it from Calcutta to Chungking.

August 1: Home leaves have been cancelled again but I hope to go the latter part of September if nothing else interferes.

The war ended suddenly in August 1945, and McBride returned home. For a time, he operated an airport in his native Nebraska. Later, he purchased a ranch and fish hatchery near Orchard, Nebraska.[66]

— IV —

CNAC faced many problems during the war years—the debilitating heat and humidity of Assam, deadly ice over the Himalayas, threatened strikes in Calcutta, Japanese fighters, and so on; but at times it seemed that movement of cargo to China was less troublesome than dealing with the tangle of Chinese politics, the intransigence of the American military, and the tensions between the two.

Trouble began early in 1942, when General Ho Ying-chin, minister of war, resumed the bureaucracy's twelve-year-old struggle to place CNAC under the thumb of China's military faction. General Ho wanted to make the airline responsible to the National Commission on Aeronautical Affairs. Ostensibly an attempt to rationalize air transportation services, Ho's real purpose was to subordinate CNAC to military authority. Bond, who had fought similar attempts by the commission to gain control of CNAC, argued that military authority would not only result in marked inefficiency but would likely cause the departure of all American personnel.[67]

The Department of State, with the approval of the War and

Navy departments, rallied to the cause of CNAC's American management in this dispute. "The China National Aviation Corporation," Acting Secretary of State Sumner Welles wrote Ambassador Clarence E. Gauss, "has an outstanding record of efficiency over a long period and its operations afford a shining example of successful international cooperation in the field of communication and transportation. The pilots of CNAC have a notable record of loyalty and devotion to their present management, having performed at times almost impossible feats in maintaining communications under very difficult conditions. Any measure designed to change the set-up under which those pilots have been working might have highly adverse effects upon their morale." Welles suggested that Gauss convey these views "to appropriate, responsible Chinese authorities, expressing tactfully but clearly the earnest hope of this Government that nothing will be done to change at this time the administrative conditions under which the planes of CNAC are so effectively discharging their task of maintaining communications vital to the joint war effort of the United Nations." After Gauss raised the matter with the vice minister of foreign affairs, the proposal for Chinese military control of CNAC was dropped.[68]

Relations between CNAC and American military authorities were equally troublesome at times. General Stilwell objected to the presence of highly paid civilians in a combat theater, especially when those civilians were beyond his control. In September 1942, Stilwell spoke with Chiang Kai-shek about CNAC's use of lend-lease aircraft. "We nailed him to the statement," Stilwell noted after the interview, "that all transports must be used exclusively for the prosecution of the war." Major General Raymond A. Wheeler, commanding Services of Supply in the theater, set forth Stilwell's position in a letter to Bond on September 22. The United States Army, he wrote, would deliver cargo to CNAC and "utilize exclusively its entire capacity in each direction." CNAC would be compensated "on the basis of actual cost of operation."[69]

Contract negotiations in November between General Wheeler, Managing Director Wang, Bond, and Ho Mo-lin of the Ministry of

Communications brought out several fundamental points of difference on the nature of the proposed agreement. The aircraft would transport only war goods, the Chinese government said, but priorities would be controlled by Chiang Kai-shek rather than General Stilwell. CNAC, for its part, argued the case for "a reasonable management fee" in addition to the cost of operation. As the aircraft in question had been given to China under lend-lease, and as the Generalissimo had agreed that only war material would be carried, Wheeler reluctantly conceded both these points. The contract, effective February 17, 1943, specified that "the Chinese Government will determine all priorities for the movement into China of Chinese lend-lease and other Chinese government supplies." CNAC would carry a minimum payload of 4,200 pounds from Dinjan to Kunming and 5,600 pounds on the return trip, for which the airline would receive $600 per round trip.[70]

The contract satisfied neither the Chinese government nor the American authorities. The aircraft operated by CNAC, Stilwell noted, might have been given to China but they were really American aircraft and should be under the direct control of the American theater commander. Chinese officials pointed out that the theater commander was also chief of staff to Chiang Kai-shek; furthermore, China should have the same freedom to use lend-lease aircraft as that accorded other Allied governments. On several occasions during the war, the Army sought to conscript CNAC's lend-lease aircraft and their pilots into American military service, or, failing this, to return the aircraft to the Air Transport Command. The State Department and China Defense Supplies, lauding the airline's excellent performance, argued against such a move. In the end, nothing came of the matter except considerable ill will on both sides.[71]

The India-China freight service was only a part of CNAC's responsibility for maintaining China's vital communications links. The airline had four aircraft—one DC-2 and three DC-3s—for domestic and international passenger service in early 1942, one of which was out of commission awaiting repairs. CNAC flew three times a week between Chungking and Calcutta via

Kunming, and operated fortnightly schedules to Kweilin and Lanchow. Traffic was heavy on all routes, with frequent requests for extra service. The airline's ability to maintain this modest schedule suffered a severe blow when CNAC's last venerable DC-2 crashed shortly after take-off from Kunming on March 14, 1942. Three crew members and ten passengers died, including pilot Emil Scott, Major General Lancelot Dennys, chief of the British military mission to China, Lieutenant Colonel Frederick L. Kohler of the American military mission, and Fenimore B. Lynch, adviser to the Central Bank of China; four passengers survived.[72]

"Our greatest need at this moment," Bond wrote in his report on operations for 1942, "is more planes for CNAC's regular fleet which can be operated independently of the present freight service.... The importance of this can hardly be over emphasized. We are constantly having urgent requests for special flights which obviously are important and should be made. Also there is a great need for CNAC to increase its present passenger and mail schedule and this need will become even greater in the future."[73]

CNAC's board of directors asked the Ministry of Communications to make arrangements with the American authorities for five additional aircraft to supplement the airline's internal services. Although the Chinese request received the support of Ambassador Gauss and the State Department, the Munitions Assignment Board disapproved the allocation on February 3, 1943.[74]

Ten days later, on February 13, Captain Sidney DeKantzow took off from Chungking for Kunming with sixteen passengers. About a half-hour after take-off, he ran into severe icing and decided to return to Chungking. His starboard engine then caught fire; DeKantzow punched the feathering button, but the propeller kept turning. With the icing growing worse and the other engine running rough, the pilot made an emergency landing in the Yangtze River near Kiangtsing, southwest of Chungking. Fortunately, no one was injured, but the DC-3 suffered extensive damage. As a result of this accident, Ambassador Gauss reported, CNAC had to reduce service to Calcutta to two flights a week and curtail domestic operations. The ambassador urged "that prompt action be taken to supply planes to CNAC."[75]

Stanley Hornbeck passed Gauss's request to Acting Secretary Adolph E. Berle, Jr. "Now is the time, I think," Hornbeck wrote, "to throw our weight as heavily as possible behind the efforts of the Chinese National Aviation Corporation and the Chinese Government to obtain additional transport planes for CNAC." The airline, he noted, had a "superb record in China." It should be "kept alive ... for political reasons, for economic reasons and even for military reasons." Hornbeck concluded that the Chinese "should have some air service at their own command, independently of the U. S. Army and without the necessity of applying to the Army every time they want to send a pound of freight or passenger."[76]

Berle wrote to Harry Hopkins, chairman of the Munitions Assignment Board, on March 2, 1943. He pointed to CNAC's recent accident, Ambassador Gauss's support for additional aircraft, and President Roosevelt's statements pledging assistance to China. In view of all these factors, Berle expressed the hope of the State Department "that the Munitions Assignment Board may give this matter renewed and favorable consideration at an early date."[77]

"The Chinese requirement for five additional C-47 airplanes has been reviewed," Hopkins informed Berle in late March, "and I regret to inform you that it has been found necessary to adhere to the original decision. There is an acute shortage of this type of aircraft in all theaters of operation and the available supply must be distributed equitably. Consideration of all the factors involved indicates that China has been relatively as well provided for as any other theater of operations." Hopkins went on to observe that two aircraft per month were being delivered to CNAC for the India-China freight service. Although the original objective of 25 aircraft would be met by April 1943, the Munitions Assignment Board planned to continue deliveries through June. Use of these additional aircraft "is a matter which must be determined by other agencies." Hopkins understood, he said, that a contract had been concluded recently between Army authorities and the Chinese government for the use of lend-lease aircraft. "I think we must assume," Hopkins concluded, "that if General Stilwell's agreement results in undue restrictions upon the China National Aviation Corporation, the General will modify this contract if such action will best serve the common interest."[78]

Developments during the summer of 1943 were hardly calculated to arouse General Stilwell's sympathy for the plight of CNAC. General H. H. Arnold, commander of the Air Force, had visited China in February and, among other things, had promised five aircraft, independent of other allocations, to assist internal communications. Bond assumed that the aircraft were for CNAC; the National Commission on Aeronautical Affairs assumed that they would get the aircraft. When the five airplanes reached China in mid-July, the Air Transport Command advised CNAC that they could take delivery. There followed two weeks of uproar, intrigue, and confusion; finally, Chiang Kai-shek notified CNAC on August 2 that the Aviation Commission would operate the aircraft.[79]

This affair had unfortunate repercussions. The Army and the State Department had cause to doubt the depth of the Chinese government's attachment to CNAC. Furthermore, as Chargé George Atcheson pointed out, the Aviation Commission lacked qualified pilots to fly the aircraft. "It is doubtful," he commented, "whether it can operate them to capacity or to produce the benefit to the war effort which could be derived from operations by CNAC, not to mention greater risk of loss by accident." Events proved Atcheson correct: four of the commission's lend-lease aircraft crashed during the next six months. The Chinese government had once again cut its own throat, and China's need for airplanes to maintain internal communications was as desperate as ever.[80]

The State Department continued to support CNAC. In August 1943, the department went further than ever before on behalf of the airline. For most of the fourteen years since CNAC's founding in 1929, the State Department's attitude toward the enterprise had been hesitant and cautious. This began to change in 1942; in the summer of 1943 the change became pronounced.

C N A C's operations office, Calcutta, 1943

C N A C's operations office, Dinjan, 1943

C-46, 1945

William R. Langdon of the Division of Far Eastern Affairs drew up a memorandum on August 20, 1943, incorporating the ideas of Stanley Hornbeck and others, in an effort to sway the Munitions Assignment Board.[81]

Langdon reviewed the history of CNAC, emphasizing the airline's role in the present war, and he noted the fate of the airline's request for additional aircraft. The Army authorities in China, he observed, had objected to the expansion of "civilian" air service because of the critical fuel shortage. "From the immediate and strictly strategic point of view," Langdon went on, "the position taken by the Army authorities . . . with respect to the expansion at present of commercial air facilities within China has undeniable force. However, there are important reasons for taking a long-range view of the situation." Langdon argued that CNAC's presence in China "constitutes a political and economic asset valuable to the United States." This asset should be conserved and strenghtened. CNAC gave the United States a "ground-floor advantage in China." Should the airline collapse, European interests might move into the vacuum at the end of the war. "For political, diplomatic, and commercial reasons," Langdon concluded, "it thus seems to the Department that it is essential that American interests [in China] such as those represented by CNAC be given strong United States support within legitimate and appropriate limits."[82]

Secretary of State Cordell Hull sent Langdon's memorandum to Hopkins on September 1, 1943, and asked that the Munitions Board give "favorable consideration" to CNAC's request for five aircraft. Hull also wrote a personal letter to General Arnold and solicited his support for the request. The five planes, Secretary Hull pointed out, were necessary for vital communications service and to maintain the position which "an American interest has acquired in China and should continue to enjoy."[83]

Major General Barney M. Giles, chief of the air staff, replied to Hull's letter in the absence of General Arnold. A review of military developments in the Far East, Giles wrote, indicated that no major change has occurred since CNAC's original request in February 1942. Gasoline and other supplies being delivered to

China still fall "far short of meeting military requirements for essential operations." As long as it was necessary to fly aviation fuel to China, "we must regard civil air transport as a luxury which can be had only at the expense of curtailing military operations." The Air Force would not support CNAC's proposal until a sea port had been opened in China. The Munitions Board formally denied the request for additional aircraft on October 31.[84]

This episode revealed several things. First, it demonstrated the State Department's changed conception of the importance of American business interests in China and the lengths to which the department was prepared to go in support of those interests. The attitude of the department in 1943 was a far cry from the negative position that it had displayed in the past, most notably during CNAC's request for a postal subsidy in 1932 or when the Chinese military threatened to take over the airline in 1937. Second, the incident showed the unconcern of the military authorities with such matters; everything was to be subordinated to the war effort, and the war effort was defined in the narrowest possible terms. Finally, it illustrated the State Department's lack of influence during the war years. If the five aircraft were as important to American interests as the department believed, then the attitude of the American government was incredibly shortsighted. Admittedly, aircraft were scarce, but they were not *that* scarce. Granted, gasoline was in short supply, but use by CNAC of the fuel required to operate five aircraft would not really have impaired the war effort in China.

Aside from long-term considerations, CNAC did have a pressing need for the airplanes; and they were not "a luxury." As an official in the Far Eastern Division pointed out, CNAC afforded the only practical means of exit from or entry into China for civilians, and this service "in no small measure" contributed to the maintenance of morale in China. Also, the airline provided the sole means of fast transportation between Chungking and Kunming, Kweilin, and other cities. Early in 1944, there were 543 individuals on CNAC's waiting lists, including 180 military officers, 157 government officials, 39 bankers, 33 industrialists, and 34 educators. "The greater part of CNAC's work," Arthur

Young stressed, "is war work, as most of the passengers carried are military and Government officers, including a considerable number of American and other United Nations officers."[85]

The entire problem of additional aircraft could have been resolved without reference to Washington if only General Stilwell had permitted more flexible use of lend-lease aircraft. But the general generally remained unmoved by CNAC's repeated requests for assistance. "Stilwell never helped us, rather opposed us," Bond observed, "but it was evident that he wasn't opposing CNAC but the Chinese Government through CNAC." Bond remembered calling upon Stilwell to ask for his help in obtaining additional aircraft for the passenger service. The general responded with a brusque "No!"

"But surely, General, you see the urgency of this need in the war effort," Bond said.

Stilwell retorted, "Let them [the Chinese Government] show some cooperation."

"That's over my head, General," Bond said and got up to leave. "I am only trying to run my own little show."

As Stilwell walked to the door with Bond, the general's demeanor mellowed. "Always come in to see me, Bond, when you can."

"Why, General?" Bond replied, "I never get anywhere."

Stilwell smiled. Bond went away feeling that he had at least accomplished something: he had gotten a smile out of Vinegar Joe Stilwell.[86]

Stilwell eventually did make a small concession. He agreed in December 1943 to furnish replacements from CNAC's supply of lend-lease aircraft so that the airline could maintain three airplanes in passenger service at all times. As a result, the airline was able to operate twice weekly between Chungking and Lanchow (with occasional stops at Paoki), daily to Calcutta via Kunming, and six times a week to Chengtu.[87]

Despite the many problems, CNAC strengthened its financial position during the war years. The corporation received $600 per round trip between India and China under its contract of February 1943 with the Services of Supply. "It is my firm belief,"

Bond wrote to the managing director in March 1944, "that our US dollar and rupee costs now with proper reserves are equal to US$600 per trip." Following an audit of CNAC's books by the Army in the spring of 1944, compensation to the airline was reduced to $475 for the first 500 trips each month between Dinjan and Kunming, and $400 for each additional round trip. As the Army agreed to supply all fuel, and as CNAC operated more aircraft, total compensation remained virtually unchanged.[88]

CNAC's main financial problem was to earn sufficient revenue in Nationalist currency (CN$) to offset expenses within China. During the war, the Chinese government maintained an official exchange rate of US$1 = CN$20; but the blackmarket rate continued to rise, reaching US$1 = CN$500 in the latter part of 1944. As Bond noted, the problem of exchange "is an old controversy with the US Army and there is nothing at all that CNAC can do in such an argument. It goes all the way to the top of the US Army and government and I understand to the top of the Chinese government." CNAC, as a Chinese corporation, had to abide by the official rate. The airline was in good financial shape only as long as it could earn enough revenue in Nationalist currency to cover expenses in China. If it could not do this, then CNAC would have to convert American dollars at the disastrous official rate. "In this event," Arthur Young pointed out in March 1944, "US dollar assets could be dissipated very quickly. This is a very real danger, since of late prices in China have risen more rapidly."[89]

In order to generate sufficient revenue in Chinese currency, CNAC constantly sought approval from the government for increased passenger and freight rates. The average passenger rate per mile rose from CN$4.88 in December 1942 to CN$8.56 in March 1944 and CN$27.30 by the end of 1945. Freight charges were comparably increased. While increased rates did not keep pace with inflationary rise, they did enable CNAC to meet expenditures in Chinese currency without converting dollars.[90]

Available information does not reveal the extent of CNAC's profit from contract operations with the Army; however, the evidence suggests—a suggestion supported by the character of adjustments in rates following the Army's audit in the spring of 1944—that the financial returns were modest rather than excessive. The corporation's balance sheet in October 1943 showed total assets of CN$218,553,384, but this figure cannot be converted to American dollars because unspecified portions of the total represented American, Chinese, and Indian currency; also, the balance sheet carried flight and ground equipment at book value. Perhaps more indicative of the airline's financial status was CNAC's decision in January 1944 to set aside $2 million "for postwar readjustment and development." The funds were transferred to Pan American for investment in American government securities. Early in 1945, Pan American placed the net worth of CNAC at approximately $10 million.[91]

Pan American's contract with the Ministry of Communications was due to expire on July 8, 1945. Bond turned his attention to the future of CNAC in November 1943. Present American participation, he noted, "is a very substantial one." He pointed out that regulations in the United States specified that at least 75 percent of the capital stock of domestic airlines must be owned by American nationals in order for the company to be eligible to receive air mail contracts from the government. "We believe a similar regulation in China would be helpful," Bond stated. "The American partners would be willing to have their own interest reduced by purchase of say 25 percent or 20 percent in order to aid China to establish a practice in its own domestic airlines in keeping with the policy of the United States." The purchase of a portion of Pan American's 45 percent interest, he observed, could be effected out of the airline's assets and future earnings; there need not be any expense to the government. Bond continued:

So far the American partners, despite their large investment, and their services to China and to CNAC, which have largely contributed to the company's progress, have neither asked nor received any return on their investment. They are confident that a suitable financial arrangement can be worked out, which will be acceptable to them and which will also be in keeping with the government's policy of making business investment in China profitable to foreign investors. CNAC is widely viewed abroad as the outstanding example of Sino-foreign business cooperation; and the arrangements made in revising the contract with CNAC will afford an opportunity to show that such enterprises can be mutually satisfactory.[92]

Bond returned to the United States in December 1944 for consultation with Trippe, Bixby, and other officials. Bond found Bixby reluctant to reduce American participation in CNAC; however, he would defer to Bond's longer experience in China and closer contact with the situation. Trippe also appeared unenthusiastic about the proposal. Many years later, Bond recalled a dinner meeting with Trippe at the Pan Am House on F Street in Washington. Trippe optimistically predicted that China would be a strong, united country after the war with virtually limitless prospects. CNAC's future seemed assured, as the airline possessed a well-trained and proven staff and had substantial cash reserves for postwar expansion. Pan American deserved to share in the expected profits of CNAC.[93]

Bond took a more pessimistic view. He remembered that he answered Trippe substantially as follows:

I do not think China will have peace. The Communists are much stronger than we realize, and they will be very active when the war is over. China does not have a united country. There is much dissatisfaction. Chiang's government is weak and scattered and tired. Eight years of war is a demoralizing thing. The Generalissimo is getting old and is not well. The country is bankrupt. China has been fighting the war with printed money with nothing back of it. The U.S. dollar exchange rate that was three to one is now over five hundred to one. China will have to continue to operate on printed money and the exchange rate will be many times higher. Our present reserve will be dissipated. Our mission in China originally was to build up commercial aviation in China, get the Chinese air minded, make friends with the Chinese, and develop a feeder line for the Clippers when Pan Am [started] a route to China. We have accomplished our mission. I think Pan Am should reduce our interest to 10% using the cash CNAC has in New York to pay for it. If we do this, I think the Chinese will like it and it will be helpful to Pan Am on their trans-Pacific service.[94]

Trippe remained unconvinced. "I finally told him," Bond recalled, "that no doubt he was right and certainly his opinion should prevail but I still felt that I would be criminally disloyal to Pan Am if I did not oppose to the limit of my ability Pan Am's continuing its present interest in CNAC. And feeling that way I had no recourse but to offer my resignation effective at the end of the war." Trippe, Bond reported, "was very nice and said that if I felt that strongly of course he would agree." Trippe instructed Bond to return to China and negotiate on the basis of retaining 10 percent interest.[95]

Preliminary discussions with the Chinese began in April 1945. Bond offered to reduce Pan American's interest to 10 percent on a new five-year contract. The Ministry of Communications expressed appreciation for Pan American's past services and said that such a drastic reduction would be too harsh on the American partner. Instead, the Chinese suggested that Pan American retain 20 percent under a five-year contract that could be extended for an additional five years. Bond agreed. After some discussion over financial arrangements negotiations were concluded.[96]

For accounting purposes, the parties decided to terminate the old company and form a new one. Pan American sold its 45 percent interest in CNAC for $5,093,569 on December 20, 1945. The following day Pan American and the Ministry of Communications formed a new China National Aviation Corporation—the third in sixteen years. Pan American acquired 20 percent of the stock in the company for $1,554,857. The agreement would continue in force for five years with an automatic extension for another five years in the absence of termination notice by either party. In other words, Pan American actually received $3,538,712, which came from CNAC's cash surplus in New York (45 percent of these assets belonged to Pan American in any event, as Bond reminded Chinese officials during the negotiations).[97]

"CNAC and Bondie stand particularly well with T. V. Soong." Arthur Young wrote to Bixby in December 1945. "He [Soong] remarked to me recently that he agreed with the payment for sale of shares because of Bondie's good work, and that he would not have given as much to anyone else."[98]

— V —

Following the Japanese attack in December 1941, CNAC was left with a handful of aircraft and pilots, and faith in the feasibility of operating an aerial supply route between India and China. The insistence of President Roosevelt and the demonstrated ability of CNAC transformed this faith into reality. CNAC led the way over the Hump in 1942; thereafter, it served as the yardstick to measure performance by the Air Force.

CNAC inevitably became caught up in the acrimonious quarrel between General Stilwell and the Chinese government. Despite the obvious and pressing need for aircraft to maintain China's domestic air service, and despite the vigorous support of the State Department, the airline was unable to secure the necessary equipment. China's priority in the war effort simply was too low, and General Stilwell refused to help an agency of the uncooperative Chinese government.

Nevertheless, the summer of 1945 marked the apogee of CNAC's career. The airline boasted a large staff of trained personnel, it had substantial cash reserves for postwar expansion, and relations between the American and Chinese partners had never been better. But, as the past had demonstrated time and time again, CNAC's fortunes were tied to the fate of China. Most observers were optimistic about China's prospects in the postwar world; a few individuals, like W. L. Bond, took a less sanguine view.

August 1945 brought an end to the long and bloody war in the Far East. Whether this meant peace for China after years of struggle remained to be seen.

CHAPTER SIX

REVOLUTION, INFLATION AND COLLAPSE
1945-1949

— I —

EARLY in September 1945, shortly after the surrender of Japan, W. L. Bond headed a party of CNAC personnel that flew from Chungking to Shanghai. Not knowing what to expect, the group brought a jeep and trailer, 260 pounds of food, a radio station, and gasoline. "Everyone in our party was in the cocky CNAC uniform," Bond wrote to Bixby, "and with the Army jeep, you can imagine the wild enthusiasm with which we were received. It certainly was a triumphant procession through the town."

"Shanghai," Bond observed, "was certainly an interesting situation at that time. It was much more like an armed truce than it was an unconditional surrender. The Japanese were still responsible for peace and order and they had peace and order. However, I will say that they appeared to be far more friendlier than our past records indicate, but they were just as firm and for the first time in the eight years of this war, I had a certain slight, repeat slight, amount of respect for them. I still do not like them and I got great satisfaction from feeling that I had done all that I could to help lick them."

Despite the restraints, a holiday spirit filled Shanghai. Driving to the Park Hotel for dinner, Bond became caught up in the city's mood. He stood up in the jeep and waved and cheered to the crowd. Dozens of youngsters immediately jumped on board, and Bond had to push them off lest the group be crushed. "It was a wild scene," he wrote, "but it was a lot of fun." Finally, they reached the Park and went up to the dining room atop the hotel. "It was crowded and everyone was gay," he noted. "There was good music and plenty of drinks. They had good scotch. Goodness knows where it came from." Russian "princesses" abounded. Bond concluded: "Good old Shanghai—Wine, Women and Song."

The next day Bond turned to the business of examining facilities in preparation for reestablishment of air services from Shanghai. He inspected the former Japanese airfields at Tachang and Kiangwan, and found both in excellent condition. By comparison, CNAC's old airport at Lunghwa needed extensive renovation. Grass had grown over the runway, and many of the buildings had suffered bomb damage, although the airline's two hangars were in fairly good condition.

Upon returning to Chungking, Bond learned that all three airports had been reserved for military use. The Chinese Air Force wanted Tachang, the Air Transport Command needed Kiangwan, while the 14th Air Force desired Lunghwa. Arrangements were made for CNAC to begin services from Kiangwan until the 14th Air Force vacated Lunghwa. "Actually I think we are getting a very good break," Bond reported. "Lunghwa now needs a lot of work and a great deal of money will have to be spent on it which we do not have. The 14th Air Force will get it in reasonable shape far quicker than we can. . . . In the meantime, with only limited services, Kiangwan will be adequate for our needs and we will have the advantages of being close to the US Army where we will get supplies and gasoline very easily."[1]

CNAC made considerable progress in the reestablishment of services during the next few months. The airline moved more than 10,000 tons of equipment and some 1,000 employees from Calcutta to Shanghai. A maintenance base, capable of performing major overhauls of aircraft and engines, was established at Lunghwa. Runway improvements and construction of hangars and other ground facilities throughout China were undertaken by the airline when the government—as usual—proved reluctant to make expenditures for such purposes. A communications and weather reporting network, involving 48 radio stations and an investment of $1.5 million, covered the areas of operation. CNAC acquired approximately 50 C-47s and C-46s, in various states of repair and useful mainly for spare parts, from the

Army-Navy Liquidation Commission and the Surplus Property Administration; it also purchased six C-54s for $540,000 and had them converted to airline use at a total cost of $2.1 million. By May 1946, CNAC had 25 aircraft in operation.[2]

CNAC's initial task at the end of the war involved transportation of government employees from Chungking to Shanghai, Peking, Canton, and other points throughout China. Between September 1945 and January 1946, CNAC carried 20,857 passengers and 1,004 tons of freight, mostly government documents and property. CNAC next moved to reopen its prewar lines from Shanghai to Peking, Chungking, and Hong Kong. The airline reached 1,900 miles to the northwest to Hami in the Gobi Desert via Chengchow, Lanchow, and Suchow. New routes were opened to Haikow on Hainan Island and Taipei on Taiwan. International service extended to Bangkok, Rangoon, and Calcutta, while plans went forward for service to Manila and Tokyo, as well as a transpacific route to San Francisco. By the summer of 1946, CNAC was flying 400,000 miles a month. "China is not going to fold," Bond wrote to Bixby in July 1946. "Aviation in China is not going to fold. The field is unlimited."[3]

Bond's burst of optimism was not entirely warranted. Certainly, China's need for internal communications remained as great as ever, perhaps even more than ever, but air transportation depended upon imported equipment and fuel, and this meant a constant drain on the nation's depleted reserves of foreign exchange. As Arthur Young pointed out, one DC-3, flying 200 hours per month, cost approximately $500,000 a year in foreign exchange to operate. The estimated demand in 1946 for gasoline and lubricants for all forms of transportation amounted to $50 million. "Obviously," Young concluded, "such a rate of spending cannot be continued for many months without exhausting much more than China can afford to spend in foreign currency for such purposes."[4]

A partial solution to China's transportation dilemma lay in adoption of a comprehensive scheme for efficient air services, with major equipment purchases financed by long-term loans. Although several proposals were developed to that end, China's need for communications was too pressing and the will of the central government was too weak for the institution of such a program. In fact, the Nationalists allowed two additional airlines to emerge after the war: Central Air Transport Corporation and Civil Air Transport.[5]

The Central Air Transport Corporation (CATC) traced its lineage back to Eurasia, the prewar Sino-German airline. Eurasia had been taken over by the Chinese government in the summer of 1941, following the break in diplomatic relations between China and Germany. Only one airplane, a single-engine, six-passenger Junkers W-34, had survived the Japanese attack on Hong Kong in December 1941. The Ministry of Communications had operated sporadic service inside China with this single aircraft for more than a year, during which time it logged more than 150,000 miles. On March 1, 1943, Eurasia became CATC, and, by the end of the war, the airline had three Lockheed Hudson twin-engine transports in addition to the venerable Junkers, four pilots, ten copilots, and four radio operators.[6]

CATC entered a new era in August 1945, when the government sold 20 percent of its interest in the airline to private Chinese financial groups for $500,000. CATC purchased 12 C-47s from American Army surpluses in India at the end of 1945; it acquired some 150 surplus C-47s and C-46s in July 1946, most of which were cannibalized for spare parts. CATC averaged 15.4 planes in service during 1946. The airline served 26 cities in China, partly in competition with CNAC. In 1946, CATC carried more than 45,000 passengers and nearly 4,000 tons of freight; by comparison, CNAC carried 202,510 passengers and 8,826 tons of freight.[7]

A third airline appeared on the scene in October 1946, when the government signed a contract with Claire L. Chennault and Whiting Willauer for the operation of CNRAA Air Transport—later known as Civil Air Transport (CAT). A national hero in China, Chennault had led the Flying Tigers in 1941, a group of American volunteers who had challenged the Japanese for air supremacy over Burma and Kunming in their shark-nosed

P-40s; later, Chennault had commanded the 14th Air Force in China. Willauer was a younger man. A graduate of Princeton University and Harvard Law School, Willauer spend most of the war years in China on a variety of assignments for China Defense Supplies, mainly dealing with the logistical problems of the 14th Air Force.

Financed by a group of American businessmen, Chennault and Willauer hoped to operate a freight and passenger airline in postwar China. In early March 1946, Colonel Ralph W. Olmstead, director of operations for the United Nations Relief and Rehabilitation Administration (UNRRA), asked Chennault and Willauer to draft a proposal for the operation of an airline to carry UNRRA relief supplies—which were piling up in the ports—into the interior of China. The proposal was forthcoming and, after considerable political maneuvering on both sides of the Pacific, the contract was signed on October 25, 1946.

Under the terms of the agreement, UNRRA would allocate $2 million to its Chinese counterpart, Chinese National Relief and Rehabilitation Administration (CNRRA), for the purchase of aircraft and equipment and provide an additional $1.8 million in foreign exchange for payment of wages to foreign personnel and purchase of fuel and other necessary imports. CAT would operate the aircraft primarily to carry relief supplies into the interior of China; unused return space could be sold to the general public at prevailing commercial rates. Chennault and Willauer were obliged to furnish $250,000 for working capital and to absorb any losses in the conduct of the operation; they were also granted an option to purchase the aircraft at cost plus 10 percent interest, compounded annually.

Finding the $250,000 proved a difficult task. With their American backers no longer interested, Chennault and Willauer contacted Wang Wen-san, banking manager of the Kincheng Bank, a large commercial Chinese bank. Wang put together a syndicate of bankers, headed by the Kincheng interests, that offered a loan of $250,000. Terms were stiff: the loan would run for eighteen months at interest, and the Chinese financiers would obtain an equity of 42 percent in the airline. Chennault and

Willauer had no choice but to agree. As it turned out, the Americans made a good bargain; whenever they ran into difficulties with the government, the influential bankers would provide crucial support.

CAT established a main base at Canton (later moved to Shanghai), and weather and radio stations at the major operating points of Liuchow, Kweilin, Hengyang, Nanchang, and Hankow. Nineteen C-46s and C-47s were obtained from American government surpluses in Manila and Honolulu. Operations began on January 31, 1947, when CAT carried relief supplies from Shanghai to Canton.[8]

Increased competition from CATC and the threat of CAT on the horizon were only part of CNAC's problems in 1946. CNAC had entered the war as a small, compact organization, with a few highly trained and motivated pilots operating a limited number of aircraft. The postwar CNAC was a large, amorphous commercial company, marked by inefficient operations and unhappy personnel. "With the influx of new pilots and the enlargement of the establishment as a whole," one pilot has written, "some of the old camaradery faded away and there was a gap between labor and management that previously had not existed." Many of the newer pilots, and a few of the older ones, sought to unionize the flight crews; considerable ill will and several dismissals resulted. Employment of experienced Army-trained pilots to operate the four-engine C-54s instead of training personnel from within the ranks of the company also caused much resentment.[9]

Difficulty with the Chinese pilots proved an especially vexing problem. CNAC was hailed as a model of Sino-American cooperation, yet the company discriminated against Chinese flight personnel in the payment of wages. This practice had been tolerated in silence before the war. The Chinese pilots then had come from two major groups: native-born Chinese, who were content to receive higher wages than those paid to Air Force pilots, and foreign-born persons of Chinese descent, who deemed themselves fortunate to find a job during the depression. The war brought a new breed of man to the airline. As one Chinese-Canadian pilot pointed out: "Well trained pilots from the United

States and the different commonwealths, men who had rubbed shoulders and fought with groups of divers nationalities, joined the airlines in the Far East. These men were imbued with the Better World concept and were taught to fight for what they believed in." This type of person did not suffer in silence. "I had been a second-class citizen in Canada," writes another Chinese-Canadian pilot, "but at least I had received equal pay there, and I had shared other material things equally. Now in China, I never felt more discriminated against."[10]

There were two main stumbling blocks in according Chinese flight personnal equality of pay. Payment at the same rate as American pilots would have resulted in salaries higher than those paid to the airline's Chinese managers. Also, it would mean a further drain on foreign exchange. CNAC's Chinese management, therefore, opposed such a move, and they were supported to some extent by the American partner. As a result, many highly qualified Chinese pilots left CNAC after the war and joined CATC "where democracy was practiced"; the remainder agitated for equal pay.[11]

A more immediate problem in 1946 was a threatened strike by Chinese mechanics. Postwar inflation cut deeply into the wages of Chinese personnel. CNAC's chief mechanic in Nanking, for example, made CN$300,000 a month after sixteen years with the airline. At the unrealistic official exchange rate, this amounted to US$150; actually, the mechanic made a good deal less in terms of the open market rate. Also, pay raises failed to keep pace with the ever-increasing inflationary rises. American mechanics, on the other hand, were paid $600 to $1,200 a month in American funds, plus a living allowance, if married, of $300 a month. "No wonder there is anti-American feeling here," one observer commented.[12]

The Chinese Air Force used the threat of a strike to take over CNAC in June 1946. An Air Force colonel took charge, and military pilots and ground personnel ran the airline. "They made the most complete and beautiful mess you could imagine," Bond recalled. "In three weeks they were only flying one third of the schedules and none of them on schedule. The colonel then told me that he thought our mechanics had been taught a lesson and would be glad to return. I agreed and thanked him for his assistance." The military never again tried to operate CNAC, but, as Bond pointed out, "they never stopped harassing us whenever and wherever they could."[13]

Management problems also plagued the airline during the period of hectic expansion in 1946. Bond was no longer able to devote his full energies to CNAC; he had been promoted by Pan American to vice president for the Orient, responsible for the territory from Tokyo to Bangkok. In addition, Bond's health began to show the strain of his wartime duties. Charles Sharp, operations manager, had done an excellent job during the war years. Known as "strict but fair," Sharp lacked Bond's diplomatic talents. This had not been a problem during the war, when relations with the Chinese partner were largely separate from flight operations; after the war, the Chinese wanted a more amenable person and brought pressure to bear for Sharp's removal. "Each day," Bond wrote to Bixby in the summer of 1946, "I realize more and more how important it is to get new blood in Chuck's [Sharp] place and mine, particularly mine. CNAC is facing a situation today much like 1937. Anything can happen. It may take years to get back to normal. But the answer is the same as it was in 1937. We must be friendly and energetic. There must be someone in charge who completely believes in CNAC and in the future. Someone who likes the job and who is fresh." Bond suffered a heart attack in the fall of 1946 and returned to the United States; CNAC could not find a suitable replacement.[14]

The strain of rapid expansion and the lack of leadership became tragically apparent during the winter of 1946–1947, when CNAC experienced a series of major accidents. Lincoln Reynolds, former diplomat in China during the 1930s and now assistant to Harold Bixby in Pan American, was in Shanghai on Christmas Day, 1946, awaiting transportation to Nanking. He went out to the airport in the morning, but heavy fog caused all flights to be cancelled. He had lunch with Hugh Woods, who had replaced Sharp as operations manager, and spent the remainder of the day at Woods's house. At about 6:45 P.M., the airport called with news that a CATC plane had crashed on approach to Kiangwan field. What is more, three CNAC aircraft were circling above the murk waiting to land. "I immediately went outside to look at the weather," Reynolds wrote to his wife. "It was not possible to see across the compound, 100 feet or so away. While I was out there a plane flew overhead in the direction of Lunghwa. The ceiling was below the top of a low building just across the street. The condition was zero-zero."

Reynolds went out to the airport with Woods and Gordon Tweedy, who had replaced Bond as Pan American's chief representative in CNAC. Captain Greenwood was overhead in a DC-3, and was running low on fuel. Radar approaches (GCA) at Kiangwan had been unsuccessful because Greenwood had lost voice communication and had had to rely on morse code (CW). The aircraft did not have sufficient fuel to reach Tsingtao, the nearest alternate. Reynolds continued:

For something like forty-five minutes the plane flew around in the fog overhead. He made several attempts to "feel" his way down to a sight of the lights. Once he came in so low right overhead I was almost on the verge of diving into a mudhole. Instead of clearing, the weather seemed to get worse. By this time the drizzle was thick and without let-up. Finally Greenwood told Mac [William McDonald, the chief pilot] on the radio that he was so low on gas that he was coming in. I had been up on the hangar roof for the past few minutes, but with this news went down on the field with Gordon Tweedy. The fire engine was standing by near the runway, and ambulances were on their way to the field. The whole scene was tense to the breaking point. I recalled my own take-off from Lunghwa just twelve years before and the subsequent events at that time. It was certain that his plane would never get in whole except by the greatest good luck; the airport beacon seemed determined to reach out and help the pilot in; but at best its beams could only penetrate a small distance into the gray mass overhead and all around us. All was deathly silent on the field. The only sound was that of the plane in the distance, getting louder and louder as it approached the field from out of the southwest. As it came nearer I did my sincerest best to offer a silent prayer. I am sure everyone around me was doing the same thing at that moment. I am equally sure they were as scared as I—of what, I don't know because *we* were safe and sound on the ground. Never the less I was shaking so hard I could hardly conceal it from those around me.

The engines grew to a roar, and by now the whistling of the airfoils was clearly audible. It seemed long-since that he must have dropped below the field's level. Suddenly there was a dull red cone in the fog about two hundred yards away, followed in an instant by a muffled boom; then for an instant the silence was complete. Gordon turned to me in the rain and said in a hushed voice, "God, oh God" with what was unmistakably a reverent inspiration. In a matter of only seconds Woody picked us up in his car and we rushed down the runway to where there were several small fires burning. There was no large blaze for the reason that there had been no gas left in the plane to burn. Even though we were at the scene in less than a minute, the fire truck had already got there and men were dragging out extinguishers and hose. The rudder, which is covered with fabric, was burning, and odd pieces of fabric scattered about the ground were on fire, but the blaze was quickly put out.

Reynolds went back to the control tower and learned that the second CNAC plane had made a successful radar approach at Kiangwan. The third aircraft, a C-46 piloted by Rolf Preus, was unable to make contact with the radar unit. Preus decided to try Lunghwa. Reynolds wrote:

He flew back and forth over the field several times, coming down as low as he dared. The Lunghwa Pagoda and chimneys of a nearby cement plant were serious hazards in the soup that hid them. At one time at this stage, the fog seemed to break up a little and we got a glimpse of the plane as it roared overhead at about 500 or 600 feet. The pilot saw the runway lights and had a positive fix on his position. Four of the pilots who had come out to the field (Pottschmidt, Watson, Schilling and one other) had gone down to the south end of the runway over which the plane would come in to land. The plane, after getting his fix, made a dry run through his approach procedure and as he passed over these boys they fired Very Shells which the pilot saw clearly. He asked that they not be fired on his next approach as they would blanket out the runway lights, which, incidently, were only oil smudge pots. Next the pilot climbed up to the altitude called for in the standard approach procedure. Mac was talking to him all the time. He was calm and confident. We on the ground felt re-assured. I was back up on the hangar roof next to the Control Tower once again, listening for Mac as the plane went out for its final leg of the let down. As the pilot made his turn into the final leg, Mac asked him not to reply to Mac's transmission. Mac instructed him calmly to come on down the final leg at 110 miles an hour, and at 150 feet altitude as he passed over the inner marker—a radio beacon near the approach end of the runway.

REVOLUTION, INFLATION, AND COLLAPSE   203

I distinctly heard him coming in. His altitude sounded all right in the distance and fog. Mac all the time was talking to him. The fog had seemed to lighten a little. When it seemed he was nearing the inner marker there was a sudden dull thud-like sound and then again that awful silence. The wreckage and survivors were located a few hours later directly in line with the runway, but about two miles short of it. The heavy rain and the fact that that part of the country is cut criss-cross with canals delayed the search and rescue. It was finally necessary to use landing craft and crash-boats sent up by the Navy for this purpose even though the plane had crashed on the Lunghwa side of the river. It had hit a Chinese school which fortunately was empty at that hour of the night. The pilot and several others were removed to the hospital and are coming along well at the present time. The death toll for the three crashes stands at 71; and 16 survivors to date. I think this was the worst day in the history of commercial aviation.[15]

And CNAC's troubles were far from over. On January 5, 1947, Charles J. Sharkey crashed a C-46 into the side of a mountain near Tsingtao; 44 people perished. Three weeks later, on January 26, Jack Blackmore crashed outside of Chungking. On January 28, John Papajik went down about 100 miles west of Hankow; 25 of the 26 persons on board died. The Chinese government grounded all commercial passenger aircraft.[16]

In the wake of these accidents, a group of pilots from CNAC and CATC presented a petition to the government in which they outlined the "minimum requirements" for safe operations in China. The pilots demanded improved airport facilities, adequate lighting for night operations, equipment for instrument landings, expanded weather reporting, qualified dispatchers and air traffic control personnel, and additional ground and airborne radio facilities. "The recommendations," the pilots concluded, "are offered solely for the future safety of passengers and the sound development of China's airways."[17]

The pilots were no doubt right: inadequate facilities did contribute to the rash of accidents in December 1946–January 1947. Lincoln Reynolds, however, pointed to other factors. "CNAC," he noted,

is showing no sign of the initiative that won its leadership in the past. Instead, it is drifting from day to day with the tide of current events, without the direction of an agressive management or planning. This continued application of expedients can only lead eventually to serious consequences .... The organization's morale has been hard hit, as might well be expected, and is being reflected in decreasing efficiency. Too much blame is placed in a vague and general way upon the conditions that generally prevail in the country. There are many steps that can be taken and should be taken at once to pull the company out of its lethargy and get it back once more on the right road. Management must have the will to do it however, and will is what seems to be most lacking at the top level.[18]

Although he had not fully recovered from his heart attack, Bond returned to China in February 1947 in an effort to solve the airline's management problems. He had several conferences with the minister of communications. Bond promised greater safety of operations but demanded in return a freer hand to run the company. The minister promised to grant the necessary authority. Colonel C. Y. Liu replaced General T. H. Shen as managing director. Woods was pressured to resign, and Bond brought out Ernest Allison, chief pilot and operations manager in the prewar years, to take charge of operations. J. H. McDivitt succeeded McDonald as chief pilot. At the same time, Bixby sent out Quentin Roosevelt "to assist in the re-establishment of liaison between Pan American Airways and China National Aviation Corporation, and ... to obtain a first hand picture of the serious situation which had apparently developed with regard to the latter Corporation."[19]

Destined to play an important role in CNAC's future, Quentin Roosevelt was one of the bright young men of Pan American. Grandson of President Theodore Roosevelt, son of Theodore Roosevelt, Jr., and named after President Roosevelt's youngest son, who was killed while serving with the Air Service in France during World War I, Quentin Roosevelt had a proud and impressive heritage. The young man followed his grandfather and father along the path of adventure and service. In 1939, the Harvard undergraduate traveled to remote areas of Western China in search of scrolls and paintings to document a graduating essay on the spread of Buddhism from India to China and Tibet.

Roosevelt joined the Army in 1941 and served with the First Division under his father during the North African campaign. A forward artillery observer, Roosevelt was severely wounded in February 1943. He earned several decorations for gallantry in action, including the Silver Star and the Croix de Guerre. Following service with the OSS in China, he joined Pan American in 1946.[20]

Roosevelt arrived in China in mid-February 1947, just as the country underwent a violent financial upheaval. Prices had skyrocketed throughout 1946 at an average monthly rate of 12 percent, but there had been no panic. January 1947 saw yet a further climb in prices, followed by a dizzying rise in February. The exchange rate of the Chinese dollar (CN) went absolutely wild. The open or black market rate rose from US$1=CN$6,500 in December 1946 to US$1=CN$18,000 in February 1947. Meanwhile, the official exchange rate, set in August 1946, had remained a wildly unrealistic US$1=CN$3,350. CNAC's fare structure was based on the even older official exchange rate of US$1=CN$2,020. Using the black market rate, passengers could fly from Shanghai to Chungking for the equivalent of US$15. At this price, Roosevelt noted, each flight produced barely enough revenue to pay for fuel.[21]

But financial difficulties constituted only one of CNAC's major problems. Operating facilities were poor throughout China, Roosevelt reported. Adequate well-paved and lighted runways and modern navigational aids were "sadly lacking." Dispatching procedures were "unsatisfactory." The airline faced "critical shortages of vital spare parts and equipment." Relations with the Chinese management were poor. The extremely low level of morale was "one of the most serious single difficulties faced by CNAC." In part, loss of confidence in the company could be attributed to poor living conditions, shortage of housing, and unduly high prices. Another factor, Roosevelt continued, "is apparent when we consider that CNAC performed a brilliant wartime function during its Hump flying and that it has had to go through a re-adjustment to peacetime operations which had produced many of the morale problems which have become familiar in the case of American occupation troops in Europe and Asia. This let-down has had its effect in operations and maintenance since the small but important precautions which should be taken by each pilot are sometimes omitted under such circumstances, and the extra effort normally exerted by an average mechanic might be cut short with disastrous effects."[22]

Roosevelt was convinced that many of these problems were already on the way to solution. The runway at Lunghwa was being repaired and the Chinese government seemed prepared to renovate facilities throughout China. The government had granted an increase in rates, alleviating CNAC's immediate financial distress. A new managing director had been appointed. "Mr. Allison," Roosevelt noted, "coming in as he does with a good reputation and a fresh, vigorous approach, has gone far toward eliminating the general let-down which I have described earlier. It has been my impression of Mr. Allison that he has forcefully and methodically gone to the root of every problem facing him and has dealt with it summarily. A tightening-up in the organization will undoubtedly result." Good progress had been made, Roosevelt concluded, in overcoming the difficulties that had plagued CNAC. "It is important, however, to realize that many of the more difficult problems, particularly financial, still lie ahead of CNAC. I believe they will be solved, but I may be entirely wrong. In any case, the extremely poor economic and political situation in China will always affect CNAC adversely, so that we may only expect a temporary improvement in the company if the overall situation does not improve."[23]

Young Roosevelt evidently impressed Bond. Here was the vigor, intelligence, and tact that CNAC's management needed so badly. He asked Roosevelt to remain in China as Pan American's chief representative in CNAC. "The work so far as operations is concerned," Bond wrote, "will be easy. Allie [Allison] is doing a fine job and has that situation well in hand, but there is urgent need here for an American representative who would be steady under all circumstances, whom the Chinese know and respect, and who has a good knowledge of CNAC's background, present situation, and who has the necessary experience and ability. For all these reasons I would like to see you out here. It is a tough job and I think a swell one and I think the opportunities it offers for establishing a name are unsurpassed."[24]

The proposition flattered and tempted Roosevelt. His salary would be doubled, and the job would mean opportunity for advancement with Pan American. "Ordinarily," he wrote to his wife, Frances,

and at any other time, it would have been hard to refuse. I said no, however, because I have become convinced that this is not a safe place to bring a family right now. Not only is CNAC's future clouded (to say the least), but I have grave doubts for the first time about the future of China. It's really very simple: 1) A full-scale civil war is going on, 2) this necessitates tremendous expenditures on Army, etc., 3) this in turn allows no government money for peacetime development, 4) which in turn adds fuel to the fire of inflation, 5) the only way to lick this inflation and get for China much-needed dollar exchange would be to develop China's exports and create a favorable foreign trade balance, which can not be done as long as civil war continues. And there is no prospect of ending the civil war, in my opinion. Meantime the Chinese require urgently an airline and air-communications throughout the country, since very few other communications exist. They do not, however, provide even the most basic facilities and airway aids, nor do they allow said airline to import vital spares and equipment without interminable delays. As a corellary [sic] to the above, living conditions here are terrible. Some one with friends and connections can get a place to live, but the average person cannot do this. I really think there may be serious collapse out here within the next few months, possibly accompanied by bloodshed.[25]

Roosevelt's assessment of China's future was accurate if a bit premature. The Nationalist government took drastic action in the spring of 1947 to deal with the financial crisis. It prohibited speculative activity in gold and foreign exchange, and adopted a new exchange rate of US$1 = CN$12,000. Relief, however, proved temporary. By August 1947, the open market rate had shot up to US$1 = CN$45,000, a decline of almost 200 percent in the Chinese dollar. Meanwhile, the civil war increased in fury, with the situation favoring the Communists. The Red Army mounted its first major offensive in Manchuria early in 1947, and by mid-year most Nationalist garrisons in the north were under seige.[26]

Demand for CNAC's services increased as the situation in China worsened. Flying hours for CNAC's 6 DC-4s, 17 DC-3s, and 18 C-46s rose from 2,900 in March to 5,000 in December. During 1947 the airline logged 5,654,831 revenue miles and carried 173,317 passengers, 16,166 tons of freight, and 2,696 tons of mail. On October 7, 1947, CNAC inaugurated 40-hour, bi-weekly, transpacific service from Shanghai to San Francisco via Guam, Wake, and Honolulu. Thanks in large part to its international routes, CNAC made good progress in meeting obligations in foreign exchange. Early in 1947, CNAC's indebtedness to Pan American for purchases of equipment and supplies had stood at $1.5 million, and the parent company had had no choice but to cut off all shipments to China. CNAC effected various economies, including reduction of the foreign payroll and payment of a portion of salaries in Nationalist currency. As a result, the airline paid Pan American $1.5 million by the end of the year and pledged $100,000 monthly to meet current expenses.[27]

CNAC's competitors also had a good year. CATC operated 32 DC-3s and C-46s and carried 116,080 passengers, 14,050 tons of freight, and 1,377 tons of mail. CAT flew over 2 million miles in 19,000 hours and carried nearly 7,000,000 ton/miles of cargo, all without a fatality. Chennault and Willauer paid off the funds advanced by UNRRA. They and their partners owned an airline with 18 operational aircraft and 800 employees, an airline with a reputation for efficiency and flexibility. On January 2, 1948, the government granted CAT a one-year extension of its contract.[28]

Despite CNAC's progress, Bond and Bixby remained dissatisfied with Pan American's representation in China. Gordon Tweedy, who had borne the brunt of CNAC's problem since the war, wanted relief. Bond did not feel that his health could stand the strain of full-time activity in China. Roosevelt finally gave in to considerable pressure and agreed to go to China as vice president and director of CNAC, effective April 1, 1948.[29]

— II —

Quentin Roosevelt arrived in China in the spring of 1948 to find that the outlook for the Nationalist government had not improved since his last visit. The inflationary spiral continued at an accelerating rate, and the military picture remained bleak. Although no one could predict it with certainty, Chiang Kai-shek's regime was on the verge of collapse. Roosevelt learned that the demand for CNAC's services was greater than ever, as surface transportation became disrupted. The airline flew nearly 5,000 hours in February, and the Chinese management called for 10,000 hours by the end of the summer.[30]

The first problem to require immediate attention involved a festering dispute over salaries for American personnel. In order to conserve foreign exchange, CNAC had instituted a program in September 1947 whereby one-third of the basic salary of Americans was paid in Nationalist currency. Payment had been made on the first and fifteenth of each month, based on the open market rate for the preceding fifteen days; the company had guaranteed that personnel would not suffer a financial loss under this arrangement. The system had worked reasonably well for the first six months because the weekly fluctuation in exchange rate had not been great. Beginning in March, however, the exchange rate skyrocketed so fast that the average received by employees was substantially less than the rate prevailing on the date of payment. Seething discontent had resulted.[31]

Fortunately, CNAC had a reserve of Hong Kong funds, derived from air services operated out of the British colony. Upon his arrival in China, Roosevelt arranged to pay one-third of salary in the more stable Hong Kong currency instead of Nationalist money, thus averting a serious morale problem.[32]

Roosevelt also came under pressure from the Chinese managers to eliminate living allowances paid to American employees. "It is their contention," Gordon Tweedy advised Roosevelt, "that this causes trouble among the Chinese personnel and also with CATC and the maintenance of comparable wage scales in the two companies." Tweedy argued that the allowance—$200 monthly for married employees and $150 for bachelors—"is justifiable in view of the fact that American pilots have only a limited period of service in China during which they must save sufficient to compensate them for the fact that they in all probability will not be able to take over flying jobs when they return to the states."[33]

Prior to Roosevelt's arrival, the managing director had ordered Allison to abolish the living allowance. Allison had not acted, fearing the resignation of the airline's experienced American pilots. Roosevelt, Allison, and Managing Director Liu met on May 7 "to fight out the first potential crisis that has developed." Roosevelt agreed to end living allowances. In return, Liu permitted increases in base pay, higher maximum limits for base salaries, and increased flying pay. "All in all ok," Roosevelt noted, "and just about what they got before, in some cases a little more, in others a little less."[34]

These adjustments forestalled a crisis with the airline's personnel, but the problem of spiraling costs remained unsolved. In early June 1948, the price of aviation gasoline increased by 80 percent. Working in astronomical figures, Roosevelt tried to project expenses for June:

Disbursements

Payroll for Chinese personnel	CN$350,000,000,000
Gasoline and oil	600,000,000,000
Purchase of US$200,000	240,000,000,000
Miscellaneous expenses	200,000,000,000
Total	CN$1,390,000,000,000

Receipts

Revenue	CN$1,340,000,000,000

"You will see," Roosevelt observed, "that based on the above figures CNAC will come at the end of June to have a deficit of 50 billion CNC$." The only way to reduce losses was to secure further rate increases, although the government had already granted increases of 286 percent since February 1, 1948. If increases could not be obtained at once, Roosevelt concluded, then flying hours would have to be curtailed "even though there is a continuous demand from the government and from the public for increased air service at almost every point in China."[35]

During the remainder of June, the government granted increases in rates as gasoline prices soared. The airline managed to survive the month: revenue amounted to CN$1,386,000,-000,000, while expenses were CN$1,333,000,000,000. July brought no relief; by the middle of the month, daily revenue reached CN$500,000,000,000. Depreciation of Nationalist currency was so rapid, however, that it was possible to fly from Shanghai to Nanking for the equivalent of one American dollar.[36]

With its currency nearly worthless as a medium of exchange, the central government instituted drastic fiscal reforms. Effective August 19, 1948, a new gold yuan (GY) replaced the old currency at a ratio of GY1 = CN$3,000,000. Exchange with American currency was at the rate of US$1 = GY4. Market prices were fixed by the government, and black market dealings brought severe penalties. The public was required to sell gold, silver, and foreign exchange to the government at fixed prices. In return, Nanking promised to limit the new note issue to GY2,000,000,000. Although not convertible, the new currency would be backed by gold, silver, foreign exchange holdings, and the securities of certain government-owned enterprises.[37]

"The Cabinet is staking its life on the success of its currency and economic measures," Ambassador John Leighton Stuart reported. "If we assume vigorous, ruthless and effective Government action against hoarders, black marketeers and cheaters (in whose hands control of the wealth of the country largely lies), it would still seem that the most this program can accomplish is three or four months surcease from the upward flight of prices."[38]

Fiscal reform, as Stuart predicted, did produce temporary economic stability. Introduction of the new currency, Roosevelt observed in November 1948, "did us good rather than harm, at least as long as the scheme was moderately successful. The main salutory effect was the tight control it imposed on the gasoline price which eliminated what had been almost our major single worry for the last months of the old [currency]. We were also fortunate in that we had received a substantial fare increase very shortly before the new currency regulations were promulgated so that our revenue position during August and September was extremely good."[39]

When Roosevelt arrived in China in April, CNAC derived approximately half its revenue from regular passenger service and half from contract freight operations. Increases in passenger fares required the government's approval, whereas charges for freight service were negotiated between the airline and the shipper. Because even a brief delay in obtaining approval for fare increases meant that inflation would wipe out any real gain, passenger service usually operated at a loss. "It is only because of the C-46 freight runs," Tweedy reported in March 1948, "that we have kept out of bankruptcy."[40]

Roosevelt ordered ten additional C-46s at a cost of $400,000 in late April to expand freight operations. As CNAC had $350,000 on deposit in New York, Bixby believed that "Pan American will be fully protected in the event additional funds are not made available by CNAC." He therefore sought and obtained Trippe's approval to make the necessary purchases.[41]

While awaiting delivery of the new aircraft, CNAC's cargo fleet undertook a major airlift operation into besieged Mukden under contract to the Nationalist government. The airline established bases at Peking and Chinchow under Captain C. C. Parrish. Flights began in late April, reached 12 a day in early June, and rose to 20 by the end of the month. CNAC averaged 30 flights daily in July. Between April 21 and July 23, the airline carried 3,418 tons of supplies, mainly food, into the isolated northern city.[42]

Roosevelt made a trip to Peking, Mukden, and Taiyuan in August to promote the freight service. As a result, CNAC obtained contracts to transport 8,000 tons of salt and 5,000 tons of foodstuffs into Taiyuan and large quantities of raw cotton from Sian to Shanghai. In addition, CNAC agreed to carry a further 1,000 tons of flour into Mukden for the Economic Corporation Administration. Freight operations now accounted for 75 percent of CNAC's revenue.[43]

CNAC's increased business during the summer of 1948 paralleled the declining fortunes of the Nationalists. On September 23-24, the strategic city of Tsinan, key to the Nationalist position in northeastern China, fell to the Communists. "Business in Shanghai has become very jittery," Bond reported a few weeks later, "and there is much uncertainty as to the future. The Government is attempting to stabilize prices and to hold the official exchange rate of 4 to 1 by strong-arm methods. A few people have been shot and a number have been put in jail. As a result, practically all the stores have simply withdrawn their commodities from sale and you cannot buy anything over the counter. It is not exaggerated to say that prices of many things have increased from 30 per cent to 60 per cent within the last two weeks, and they are becoming increasingly scarce, which means that prices will undoubtedly go higher."[44]

Roosevelt shifted CNAC's northern base of operations from Peking to Tientsin following the surrender of Chinchow on October 15. The airline continued to operate into Taiyuan and Mukden, as Communist forces drew their ring tighter around the Nationalist strongholds. By the end of the month, however, Mukden capitulated and Taiyuan could be supplied only by airdrops. "The situation," one of the pilots observed, "looks rather gloomy as far as flying is concerned in N. China. All our 46's are practically at a standstill up here. They are at Tientsin sitting on the ground."[45]

Late November 1948 brought the crucial battle of Hsuchow. Chiang Kai-shek committed the last of his troops in a vain effort to stop the advancing Communists. CNAC, CATC, and CAT provided para-military support for the Nationalists at this critical time. CNAC carried rice into Hsuchow and wounded Nationalist soldiers from Hsuchow to Nanking; at one point, the airline made 33 flights with 46 to 60 casualties per trip in a single day. CAT went even further: between late November and early January, Chennault's airline airlifted or airdropped 37,136 troops, 135 tons of ammunition, and 1,500 tons of food to Hsuchow.[46]

Roosevelt defended CNAC's participation in the Chinese civil war. Although the airline did not go as far as CAT in support of the Nationalists, CNAC did carry military cargoes on occasion. "At a time when the American government is rushing huge quantities of such materials to China by all available transport," he explained to Bixby, "and at a time when a large staff of US Army officers is stationed in China training and advising Chinese troops, it seems that this minimum participation is justified and strictly in line with US government policy."[47]

While the battle of Hsuchow was in progress, the minister of communications ordered CNAC to begin preparations for movement of the airline's main base to Hong Kong. Roosevelt needed little urging; CNAC had been making such plans for three months. "It seemed to me an excellent thing," Roosevelt noted, "from the standpoint both of the American interest in CNAC and the US Government, that these shops and their equipment be transferred (at the request of the Minister) to Hong Kong territory; we would be in a position . . . of not having to worry about possible seizure by any government which might have the opportunity to interfere, and not having to worry about possible damages to equipment in the event of civil disturbances or sabotage."[48]

The physical transfer of the airline's equipment would take place in December. Roosevelt expected problems during the transitional period, but he was confident that they could be overcome. He planned to reduce the staff of the operations department by about 50 percent in order to conserve Hong Kong funds, and he hoped to increase schedules from the Colony in order to generate additional revenue. Roosevelt, in fact, was "quite optimistic" about the future. CNAC now operated twice-weekly transpacific service and carried full loads both ways. Preparations were underway to inaugurate a route to Tokyo. Also, Roosevelt continued, "there appears to be a lot of lucrative business in the area South China—Siam—Indo-China—Philippines, etc., and I believe if we reduce our staff realistically at the outset and use discretion in making commitments regarding the construction of our new base, that we can continue a sound operation."[49]

Roosevelt had met all of Bond's high expectations during the difficult period April–November 1948. "It is especially gratifying to me," Bixby wrote to Roosevelt in October, "that Bondie is so pleased with your work with CNAC. As you know, we all have the greatest respect for his opinion and judgment, and then, too, everyone around here feels that we owe our position in China to Bondie's unfailing loyalty and resourcefulness. As a result, his recommendations carry a lot of weight."[50]

Like Bond before him, Roosevelt had kept the airline going during a time of great stress. He had in abundance that quality of common sense so appreciated by his predecessor; he had the common courtesy and tact necessary to work in reasonable harmony with the sometimes irascible—but able—Allison and the beleagured Chinese officials. And he won the respect of his pilots. Roosevelt, one aviator wrote, took "an active interest in the affairs of the pilots and the problems of the different routes, the airplanes, etc., in addition to his main job of trying to coordinate business matters. Whenever a new route or contract was taken over he was first to ride along and see how it was going, and that I really admired him for, as it meant a certain amount of personal risk of late. Such as, when we were flying into Hsuchow . . . we took him in the first morning on the first shuttle. Just a few days after that the town was taken over by the Communist Forces. Roosevelt may have gotten his job through connections, but I think he was really proving his worth around here."[51]

On December 21, 1948, Roosevelt boarded one of CNAC's plush DC-4s for a flight from Shanghai to Hong Kong. As the aircraft neared its destination, pilot Charles Sundby received reports of fog and low ceilings along the coast. Kai Tak airport is bounded on three sides by mountains and is one of the most difficult airports in the world to approach, even in the best of weather. CNAC's instrument procedure called for a let-down out to sea; after breaking out in the clear, the pilot would reverse course and proceed to the field while maintaining visual contact with the ground. Sundby did not follow the procedure. He came down through a hole in the overcast to an altitude of 200 feet. He became trapped as the weather closed in; he reversed course and tried to make it out to sea through the lowering overcast. Sundby probably never saw the top of the small mountain which the aircraft struck. Roosevelt and all aboard were killed.[52]

Allison, for one, could not understand the causes of the accident. CNAC's approach procedure was specifically designed to keep aircraft away from the area where the DC-4 crashed. Ten days prior to the accident, Allison had been in the cockpit and observed Sundby conduct a perfect let-down to Hong Kong through a low overcast. "For some reason we will never know," Allison wrote of the accident, "he disregarded the established procedure entirely and let-down at sea in this area that causes difficulties even in sea navigation."[53]

A younger pilot offered an explanation: "His mistake was to try and come in contact when the conditions were not good enough for it. . . . There may have also been a sense of the wrong kind of pride involved in which the pilot thinks he is showing his ability by always getting in regardless of the weather. Also, perhaps when you fly a long time and get really complete confidence in your abilities you may tend to let yourself get into predicaments in which a greater degree of skill is required."[54]

Roosevelt was thirty years old at the time of his death. Handsome, intelligent, and ambitious, he had the brightest future before him. He left an attractive and courageous young wife and three charming little girls. Roosevelt's body was cremated, and his ashes were buried on the island of Basalt where he had crashed. "As you know," his wife wrote, "I have always believed in soldiers staying where they fall and Quentin very strongly did."[55]

CNAC accomplished the move to Hong Kong without incident following Roosevelt's death. The airline erected two buildings to house stores and maintenance facilities at a cost of $500,000. CNAC continued to fly international passenger service and cargo operations to the areas of the mainland controlled

C. L. Sharp, "steady as a rock," 1944

Quentin Roosevelt, vice-president and director when killed in 1948
(Fabian Bachrach)

REVOLUTION, INFLATION, AND COLLAPSE 217

by the Nationalists. By mid-1949, CNAC had cash assets in American and Hong Kong currency of $2 million. Pan American placed the value of the airline at approximately $15 million.[56]

Meanwhile, the struggle in China reached its denouement. Tientsin fell to the Communists on January 15, 1949. Chiang Kai-shek "retired" the next week, transferring the government's gold, silver, and foreign exchange to Taiwan. The Communists occupied the old Imperial capital of Peking on January 31. Taiyuan surrendered on March 24. The Red Army crossed the Yangtze River on April 20; Hankow and Shanghai fell in May.[57]

Harold Bixby visited the Far East in June to assess the situation. One thing, he wrote, was clear: "The corrupt Nationalist Government of China, disunited, inefficient, wholly lacking in any support from the people is on the way out. It is only a matter of time." The new Communist regime had so far adopted a "conciliatory attitude" toward CNAC. Bixby learned that the Communists welcomed the American interest in the airline and wished to continue operations. Above all, the new Peking regime wanted Pan American to preserve the assets of the company against possible looting by the Nationalists. Bixby was suspicious of these professions of friendship. "When they get control," he predicted, "it will be a different story. They have already—for example—banned the use of the English language without which, as a practical matter, CNAC cannot operate. In short, I see no way in which PAA can live with the new regime and certainly no method by which we can ever realize a profit out of CNAC operations."

After weighing the alternatives, Bixby strongly recommended "that we sell out as soon as possible for as much as we can get." The main problem, he thought, would be the policy of the American government. In Bixby's view, the United States faced two choices:

First, our own Government may wish to use CNAC as a means of turning the Chinese Reds toward our way of thinking. In this the American partners may be very useful—though they will have to possess the patience of Job and will certainly lose their total investment. Therefore, if our Government wishes us to stay, we should be guaranteed—one way or another—the present value of our investment. The second alternative is that our Government may not wish the 56 airplanes owned by CNAC to fall into Communist hands. This should not be considered too seriously as the airplanes are all commercial types and if withheld by us would be perhaps replaced by some other power. Certainly PAA would be in a very undesirable position with respect to our international services if we confiscated the CNAC fleet and flew it to Manila—even if we could do so."[58]

Shortly after Bixby returned to the United States in late July, Pan American's representative in Communist-occupied Shanghai called over the transpacific telephone and reported that the Communists had offered to permit Pan American to operate commercial services into Shanghai. There were two strings attached to the offer. As the Nationalists were blockading Shanghai, the State Department would have to guarantee safe conduct for American aircraft—and thus be a party to breaking Chiang's blockade. Also, Pan American would have to exert its best efforts to preserve CNAC's assets. Colonel C. H. Wang, former finance manager for CNAC who had joined the Communists, had assured Pan American's representative "that the new regime considers the CNAC contract as fair and equitable and would like to see it continued." The Communists also indicated that negotiations were in progress with Northwest Airlines, Pan American's competitor on the Pacific route, and with the British firm of Jardine Matheson looking toward reestablishment of domestic air services.[59]

Bixby and Bond went to Washington on August 3 to discuss the offer with Livingston Merchant of the State Department. Merchant, Bixby reported, stated that the American government took the position "that unless and until the Chinese Communists were willing to regularize relations with foreign carriers, especially the two American lines, more particularly a validation by the Communists of the existing bilateral agreements, the Department would prefer that the American carriers should not service Shanghai." The department, Merchant continued, had requested Northwest Airlines not to enter Peking or Shanghai and to desist from attempts to organize a domestic company in

Communist territory. Similar representations had been made to the British government.[60]

At the conclusion of the interview, Bixby wired Shanghai: "Unable at this time [to] make arrangements suggested. However, will use best efforts to preserve CNAC assets."[61]

The British authorities in Hong Kong grew apprehensive about the fate of the Colony as Communist armies reached southern China. In June, the government ordered CNAC to remove its facilities from Kai Tak. "Their principal fear," Bixby reported after an interview with the governor, "is that once the Communists have taken over complete control, the British do not want to run the risk of a large Communist 'cell' in the middle of their airport." When the British authorities sought to execute the order in August, CNAC obtained an injunction from the local courts on the grounds that the government could not issue such instructions without declaring a state of emergency. The government promptly proclaimed a state of emergency and requisitioned CNAC's facilities under emergency defense regulations. CNAC suspended all flights.[62]

Although only partially recovered from a second heart attack suffered the previous January, Bond returned to Hong Kong in the late summer of 1949 to represent Pan American's interest in CNAC. He managed to obtain permission for limited operations from the Colony. CNAC could utilize half of its warehouse space on the airport and perform maintenance work in facilities adjacent to Kai Tak.[63]

Otherwise, Bond was no more impressed than Bixby had been with the situation in China. Canton had fallen without a struggle. "Each day," he wrote, "it seems to become more and more clear that China will have, in fact now has, a Communist government and our government may as well face up to it now as later." The Nationalists, both on the mainland and on Taiwan, had lost the will to fight. "The Generalissimo apparently hopes that World War III will break out soon and that through the following world-wide confusion he will regain power. A very pious hope. Failing in this, he apparently hopes to imitate Herr Hitler and bring all China crashing down with him. In this he is already failing very rapidly.

His people are more realistic. They prefer Straus to Wagner."[64]

Bond noted that the Chinese staff of CNAC had become convinced that their future depended upon holding the airline together for the new government. They would refuse to move to Taiwan, if ordered, and they wanted Bond's support. He pointed out that Pan American held only 20 percent interest in the company and therefore could not set policy. Furthermore, Pan American had to be guided by the policy of the American government. He urged caution lest they jeopardize their own lives and the lives of their families on the mainland. "All I can do now," Bond reported to New York, "is to prevent silly actions and overly zealous people who would like to lead the rush to the bandwagon. And also be prepared to do whatever is possible when the bottom falls out of the present situation. That exciting event is coming, I believe. I wish I knew what the U. S. government intends to do."[65]

The bottom fell out sooner than Bond expected. On November 9, Colonel C. Y. Liu, CNAC's managing director, and Colonel C. L. Chen, general manager of CATC, declared for the Communists and left Hong Kong for Peking with eleven aircraft and crews. "I had not the least suspicion that this defection was planned," Bond wrote, "but I dislike to be even close to such a doublecross. As you know, I am convinced that the Nationalist government is finished and should be. I have served them to the best of my ability and I owe them nothing. But I would not have been a party to this defection. C. Y. Liu owed much loyalty to the Central Government. He had been one of the fair-haired boys in the government for thirty years. However, for thirty years he has been the kind of Chinese official that caused the collapse of China, so I guess little else could be expected of him."[66]

A week of moves and countermoves by the Nationalists, Communists, CNAC's employees, Pan American, and the government of Hong Kong ensued—at times it seemed that Eric Ambler was writing the script. CNAC's Chinese staff, largely sympathetic to the de facto government in Peking, took physical possession of the remaining aircraft and announced that the aircraft belonged to the new regime and warned that "this sacred property should be respected by the Hongkong authorities." The

Nationalist government appointed a new managing director and withdrew the airworthiness certificates of the aircraft. The authorities in Hong Kong stated that the aircraft would not be permitted to depart without proper registration and placed guards around the CNAC employees guarding the aircraft. Pan American froze the airline's assets held by American banks.[67]

CNAC's Chinese staff again sought Bond's support. He told them that "it was impossible for PAA to recognize in any such way any government that the United States has not recognized." Bond concluded in his report to New York: "I am convinced that an absolute stalemate has been reached and that there is no possibility of getting around this. I hope we can maintain our position that it is a purely Chinese political matter and that PAA will take no part until they settle it."[68]

Chennault and Willauer, operators of CAT, sought to assist the Nationalist government. Willauer flew from Hong Kong to Taipei on November 10 for discussions with Chiang Kai-shek. He offered the Generalissimo a scheme which would involve transfer of ownership of CNAC and CATC from the Nationalist government to an American company to be incorporated by Chennault and Willauer. The aircraft then would be registered under American law. In this way, they believed, the aircraft could be recovered; at a minimum, litigation would keep the planes out of Communist hands for a long time. Chiang Kai-shek welcomed this proposal. Before the plan could be put into effect, however, the government would have to acquire Pan American's interest in CNAC.[69]

Preliminary discussions between the Chinese Embassy in Washington and Pan American began on November 20. Negotiations continued in to December, with T. V. Soong representing the Chinese government while Bond and Vice President Henry J. Friendly spoke for Pan American. As the two sides neared a settlement, Bixby and Bond called on Livingston Merchant in the State Department to seek the American government's sanction for any agreement that might be made. Three days later, on December 19, Bixby was shown in draft form the department's reply. Although phrased in the usual legalistic jargon, one part of the letter was clear: "The Department would prefer to see Pan American disassociate itself from any connection with CNAC ... as rapidly and as completely as its contractual obligations and its responsibilities to its stockholders would permit."[70]

The following day, December 20, Pan American sold its interest in CNAC to the Chinese government for $1,250,000, which was covered by the airline's assets in American banks. Shortly thereafter, the Nationalist authorities transferred ownership to Chennault's and Willauer's new American company.[71]

Only the formalities remained. Bond flew to Hong Kong for the last meeting of CNAC's Board of Directors. The board assembled in Room 231 of the Hong Kong and Shanghai Bank Building on December 31 and confirmed the terms of purchase. Later that evening, Bond, representing the American shareholders, and C. S. Nibson, acting for the Chinese owners, ratified the board's action on behalf of the airline's stockholders. Shortly after 8 P.M., Saturday, December 31, 1949, the China National Aviation Corporation passed out of existence.[72]

— III —

CNAC's fate had always been tied to that of the Nationalist government, and the demise of Chiang's regime—except for the remnants on Taiwan—inevitably meant an end for CNAC. The American personnel were given a month's salary for every year of service, and they soon scattered to the four winds. A few stayed in the Far East; most returned to the United States. W. L. Bond retired to his farm in Warrenton, Virginia, at the end of 1950. Harold Bixby died in the mid-1950s. E. M. Allison remained active in aviation for a few years, then retired to Arcadia, California. Periodically, some of the airline's former personnel hold reunions, where the drinks and the talk flow freely.

Chennault and Willauer staged a three-year legal battle for possession of CNAC's assets. The case involved politics at the highest level, and finally reached the Privy Council in London. The Americans won the case, and the aircraft were shipped by sea to the United States for disposal.[73]

REVOLUTION, INFLATION, AND COLLAPSE   223

The Chinese, of course, endured. Their need for internal transportation remained as great as ever. Once again, they sought foreign technical assistance: for a time Russians sat in the cockpits of commercial airliners in the People's Republic.[74] It would not be surprising if they experienced the same frustrations and rewards as their predecessors.

CONCLUSION

COMMERCIAL aviation in China, when all is said and done, depended upon a combination of factors. China required air transportation for purposes of economic communication and political centralization. Western nations were prepared to lend assistance in hopes of finding profit. China and the West were thus tied together by bonds of mutual self-interest.

Initial attempts by the British to establish air services after World War I came too early. At a time when commercial aviation had barely got off the ground in the more advanced industrial nations of the world, it would have been too much to expect success in an underdeveloped area like China. The immediate causes of failure were lack of long-term financing and political instability; yet, it is difficult to see how the venture could have worked under the best conditions, given the technical state of aviation in the years immediately following World War I.

Curtiss-Wright's efforts in the late 1920s came at a more promising time. The main problems, then and later, were on the ground rather than in the air—as Clement Keys so aptly pointed out. Adequate financial support was crucial. In light of the economics of aviation at this time, airlines throughout the world required financial support. Curtiss-Wright realized this, and the American company initially planned for long-term financing. The Great Depression shattered any such scheme; the airline was expected to pay its own way, and of course it could not. The attitude of the Chinese government was hardly enlightened. They wanted the benefits of aviation without having to pay the cost. Furthermore, the factional disputes that plagued the Nationalists during their quarter-century of power in China frequently spilled over into the area of commercial aviation. Whether the Ministry of

Railways battled the Ministry of Communications for control of civil aviation, or the Ministry of Communications fought the military, commercial aviation inevitably suffered.

The Sino-American partnership endured during the early 1930s largely because Curtiss-Wright managed to tap the military aviation market and could afford to carry the commercial company as a gesture of goodwill. Pan American Airways acquired Curtiss-Wright's unwanted stepchild in 1933, and CNAC became a part of Juan Trippe's worldwide aviation empire. The company prospered under Pan American's guidance, and it appeared likely that the Chinese would take over the enterprise by the end of the decade.

The outbreak of the Sino-Japanese war in 1937 dramatically altered the situation. CNAC—and to a lesser extent, Eurasia—became essential to the survival of an independent China. Airlines furnished the sole means of speedy communication with the outside world for the beleaguered Nationalists. Under the leadership of William L. Bond, CNAC operated the most unique and hazardous air service imaginable. The airline went on to pioneer the Hump route between India and China, the main supply line to Chiang Kai-shek's forces during 1942–1945.

Commercial air service underwent rapid expansion in the postwar years. CNAC grew to ten times its prewar size, while CATC and CAT provided additional services. But this came at a time of rampant inflation and civil war. The collapse of the Nationalist government in 1949 doomed Sino-Western economic partnerships.

CNAC experienced mixed success in its twenty years of existence. Juan Trippe has termed the airline "the most successful venture [of its kind] that Pan American got into." He believes that the company generated tremendous goodwill and would have been a major permanent factor on the Chinese scene if civil war had not intervened. Dr. C. Y. W. Meng of the Central Bank of China agreed: "To many Chinese observers, the CNAC stands as a symbol of Sino-American cooperation, financial as well as technical, governmental as well as commercial."[1]

There are also negative views. C. C. Liang, longtime chief

secretary of CNAC, observes that the Chinese had "mixed feelings" about the partnership. Dissatisfaction centered on the failure to train adequate numbers of Chinese pilots and the fact that "certain junior American personnel did not behave properly." E. M. Allison concurred that the inadequate training program was a great failing of the airline. As far as the abrasive aspects of Sino-American relations were concerned—and there were complaints on both sides—these were inevitable given the existence of a superior-inferior relationship. Those who extend the helping hand, for whatever reason, are rarely loved—nor should they expect to be. It should be enough to derive satisfaction from being a part of one of the great pioneering ventures in the history of commercial aviation.[2]

APPENDICES

A. CHRONOLOGY OF COMMERCIAL AVIATION IN CHINA

1919

February 24	Contract signed between Peking government and Handley Page for commercial air service
October	Colonel F. V. Holt appointed air adviser to Chinese government

1921

July 1	Commercial air service inaugurated between Peking and Tsinan
August 15	Peking-Tsinan service suspended indefinitely
September	Holt leaves China

1929

February	Curtiss-Wright mission arrives in China
April 20	Contract signed between Curtiss-Wright and Chinese government for commercial air service
May	Contract signed between Chinese government and Stinson Company for commercial air service
July 8	Shanghai-Chengtu Line (Stinson Company) inaugurates service between Shanghai and Nanking
October 21	China Airways (Curtiss-Wright) inaugurates service between Shanghai and Hankow

1930

July 8	Curtiss-Wright and Chinese government renegotiate contract; China National Aviation Corporation formed (55 percent Chinese and 45 percent Curtiss-Wright)
August	Contract signed between German Lufthansa and Chinese government for commercial air service;

	Eurasia Aviation Corporation formed (two-thirds Chinese and one-third German)
1931	
March 17	W. L. Bond, new operations manager of CNAC, arrives in China
April 15	CNAC inaugurates service between Shanghai/Nanking and Peking
May 30	Eurasia inaugurates Shanghai-Berlin air service; suspended following inaugural flight
June	Eurasia inaugurates Shanghai-Manchuli service; suspended in July
October 31	CNAC extends service along Yangtze River to Chungking
1933	
April 1	Pan American Airways acquires American interest in CNAC
June 4	CNAC extends Yangtze route from Chungking to Chengtu
October 24	CNAC inaugurates service between Shanghai and Canton
1935	
March	CNAC acquires first Douglas DC-2
April	CNAC inaugurates service to Kweiyang
July	CNAC extends Shanghai-Kweiyang service to Kunming
September	Eurasia acquires first Junkers JU-52.
1937	
August 22	CNAC suspends all service at outbreak of Sino-Japanese war
December	Agreement between W. L. Bond and Chiang Kai-shek to resume American participation in CNAC; main base of operations transferred to Chungking
December 16	CNAC inaugurates service between Chungking and Hong Kong
1938	
August 24	CNAC DC-2 *Kweilin* shot down by Japanese aircraft
October 22–25	CNAC evacuates Chinese officials from Hankow

APPENDICES

1939

March 15	CNAC inaugurates Chungking-Hanoi service via Kunming
October 30	CNAC inaugurates service between Chungking and Rangoon

1940

November	Bond surveys route from India to China via Hump

1941

March-July	CNAC operates Hong Kong–Nanshiung freight service
August 1	Eurasia taken over by Chinese government following break in diplomatic relations with Germany.
December 8–10	CNAC evacuates Hong Kong
December 18	CNAC inaugurates service between Chungking and Calcutta

1942

July	CNAC inaugurates India-China service via Hump

1943

March 1	Central Air Transport Corporation formed out of remnants of Eurasia

1945

September	CNAC resumes service from Shanghai
December 21	Chinese government and Pan American Airways sign new five-year contract; Pan American share in CNAC reduced to 20 percent

1946

October 25	Civil Air Transport (CAT) signs contract with Chinese government for freight service

1947

January 31	CAT begins operations
October 7	CNAC inaugurates Shanghai–San Francisco transpacific service

1948

January 2	Chinese government extends contract with CAT

230   APPENDICES

December   CNAC transfers base of operations from Shanghai to Hong Kong

1949

December 31   Pan American sells interest in CNAC to Chinese government

B. CNAC TRAFFIC STATISTICS, 1929–1941

	Miles Flown	Passengers	Mail (lbs.)	Freight (lbs.)
1929	57,305	354	8,650	
1930	329,385	2,654	39,365	
1931	444,238	2,296	75,742	
1932	430,368	3,153	111,872	
1933	666,448	3,132	110,403	
1934	889,615	5,223	139,115	
1935	1,182,000	11,004	162,899	84,277
1936	1,539,615	18,588	190,225	57,011
1937	1,277,878	14,896	188,034	111,665
1938	810,910	14,505	265,148	212,671
1939	733,000	16,546	225,000	258,800
1940	1,005,000	16,432	182,400	1,094,600
1941	1,322,000	21,292	199,000	7,847,600

C. CNAC CONTRACT OPERATIONS INDIA–CHINA, 1942–1945

	India–China cargo (tons)	China–India cargo (tons)	Passengers	Round trips
1942				
May–July	129.3	198.7		110
August	317.0	461.7		179

APPENDICES

	India–China cargo (tons)	China–India cargo (tons)	Passengers	Round trips
September	340.4	480.2		170
October	379.0	340.9	1,688	181
November	358.7	127.0	4,304	155
December	409.2	423.3	1,602	188
Total	1,933.6	2,031.8		

1943

	India–China cargo (tons)	China–India cargo (tons)	Passengers	Round trips
January	487.6	470.1	1,062	225
February	641.0	694.0	1,450	317
March	706.8	711.9	573	335
April	635.8	627.6	603	335
May	734.4	725.2	312	372
June	734.7	698.7	1,386	364
July	998.7	794.1	635	497
August	1,160.9	944.1	1,239	551
September	1,125.7	818.9	3,075	561
October	979.2	897.9	2,749	504
November	624.5	644.4	1,696	319
December	735.4	715.2	2,206	417
Total	9,564.7	8,742.1		

1944

	India–China cargo (tons)	China–India cargo (tons)	Passengers	Round trips
January	1,068.3	606.2	1,590	421
February	1,397.2	735.5	3,579	645
March	1,125.1	590.8	1,301	498
April	1,201.4	632.9	739	544
May	1,475.0	520.6	404	632
June	996.7	468.8	1,200	351
July	1,649.3	676.8	634	652
August	1,749.1	754.2	220	629
September	2,245.4	937.0	838	859
October	2,352.3	999.0	652	942
November	2,349.1	961.4	1,669	910
December	1,979.5	879.6	71	690
Total	19,588.4	8,762.9		

1945

	India–China cargo (tons)	China–India cargo (tons)	Passengers	Round trips
January	1,993.8	698.0		
February	1,699.3	328.2		
March	2,072.6	625.0		

APPENDICES

	India–China cargo (tons)	China–India cargo (tons)	Passengers	Round trips
April	1,981.9	647.4		
May	2,001.0	590.3	Not Available	
June	2,377.2	410.1		
July	2,648.4	515.9		
August	2,072.2	729.3		
September	2,156.5	639.0		
Total	19,002.9	5,183.2		
Grand Total	50,089.6	24,720		

D. MAJOR ACCIDENTS & LOSSES FROM APRIL 1942 TO SEPTEMBER 1945

Aircraft	Captain	Date	Location	Crew	Remarks
52	Bartling	Oct. 10, 1942	Balijan	OK	Crashed on landing during training flight
60	Dean	Nov. 17, 1942	Hump	Lost	
46	DeKantzow	Feb. 13, 1943	Chungking	OK	
53	Fox	March 11, 1943	Hump	Lost	
49	Welch	March 13, 1943	Hump	Lost	
58	Rosbert	April 7, 1943	Hump	OK	Crashed into side of mountain; radio operator killed
48	Anglin	Aug. 11, 1943	Hump	Lost	
69	Robertson	Oct. 6, 1943	Kunming	OK	Landing
72	Schroeder	Oct. 13, 1943	Hump	Lost	Shot down by Japanese fighters
84	Petach	Oct. 17, 1943	Kunming	OK	Take-off
61	Kirkpatrick	Oct. 23, 1943	Dinjan	OK	Take-off
78	Hockswinder	Oct. 26, 1943	Calcutta	OK	Landing
59	Privensal	Nov. 19, 1943	Kunming	Lost	Let-down
63	Charville	Nov. 19, 1943	Kunming	Lost	Let-down
79	Wright/Cook	Dec. 18, 1943	Suifu	Lost	Let-down
83	M. K. Loh	Dec. 18, 1943	Suifu	Lost	Let-down
88	Robertson	Jan. 10, 1944	Suifu	OK	Gear collapsed on landing; aircraft repaired
57	Loux	Feb. 18, 1944	Dinjan	OK	Take-off
75	Mickelson	Feb. 20, 1944	Hump	Lost	
86	Carroll	March 11, 1944	Hump	OK	Lost and out of fuel; aircraft rebuilt

Aircraft	Captain	Date	Location	Crew	Remarks
91	Tutwiler	March 13, 1944	Cuba	Lost	Ferry flight from Miami to Calcutta
51	Scoff	March 23, 1944	Chengtu	OK	Crew bailed out
90	Atwater	May 16, 1944	Hump	Lost	
92	Scoff	May 18, 1944	Dinjan	OK	Brake located on landing; ground-looped into B-25
96	Moss	May 24, 1944	Kunming	OK	Power failure on take-off
85	Loomis	Jun. 8, 1944	Kunming	Lost	Exploded on mid-air
71	Kessler	Jun. 23, 1944	Kunming-Chungking	OK	One passenger killed
73	K. L. Mah	Aug. 1, 1944	Kunming	Lost	Take-off
97	Coulson	Aug. 31, 1944	Hump	–	Crew bailed out; pilot survived but two other crew members were killed
101	Scoff	Oct. 7, 1944	Hump	Lost	Wing torn off in turbulence
80	Codrea	Nov. 13, 1944	Dinjan	OK	Landing
98	Petach	Nov. 16, 1944	Yunanyi	OK	Gear retracted before airborne
106	McClellan	Nov. 25, 1944	Hump	OK	Crew bailed out
56	R. E. Anderson	Dec. 12, 1944	Hump	Lost	
74	Warren	Jan. 6, 1945	Hump	Lost	Aircraft drifted north of course in severe crosswinds
77	Coldren	Jan. 6, 1945	Hump	Lost	Aircraft drifted north of course in severe crosswinds
102	Ball	Jan. 7, 1945	Hump	Lost	

Aircraft	Captain	Date	Location	Crew	Remarks
70	Thorwaldson	Jan. 14, 1945	Ledo Road	Lost	Rice dropping mission
93	Huang	Jan. 16, 1945	Hump	Lost	
105	H.E. Anderson	Feb. 1945	Hump	OK	Crew bailed out
96	Mulloy	March 1945	Kunming	OK	Gear collapsed on landing
88	Smith	April 9, 1945	Hump	Lost	
55	Mart	May 1945	?	?	
94	Hammel	May 1945	Dinjan	Lost	
87	H.E. Anderson	June 1945	Dinjan	OK	Crashed on runway
114	Sullivan	Aug. 1945	Dinjan	OK	Take-off

NOTES

CHAPTER 1

1. H. G. W. Woodhead, "Aviation in China," *Oriental Affairs*, 1 (May 1934), 14–19; *Far Eastern Review*, 25 (1929), 269.
2. For the political history of China during this period, see Li Chien-nung, *The Political History of China, 1840–1928*, trans. Ssu-Yu Teng and Jeremy Ingalls (Princeton, 1956), and O. Edmund Clubb, *Twentieth Century China* (New York, 1964).
3. Loh Han-chin, "Commercial Aviation," *The Chinese Year Book, 1937* (Shanghai, 1937), pp. 935–46; *Far Eastern Review*, 15 (1919), 493.
4. Harald Penrose, *British Aviation: The Great War and Armistice, 1915–1919* (London, 1969), p. 470.
5. *Far Eastern Review*, 15 (1919), 493; Lincoln C. Reynolds, "Aviation in China," May 1935, State Department File 839. 796, National Archives, Washington, D.C. (hereafter cited simply by SD File number).
6. The agreement with Vickers was finances by a loan of £1,803,200, involving the issuance of Chinese Treasury notes, paying 8 percent interest annually and maturing during 1925–1929. Lloyd's Bank, with the approval of the British government, sold the notes on the London market at £98. *Far Eastern Quarterly*, 15 (1919), 723; Ambassador John W. Davis to Secretary of State Robert Lansing, Nov. 22, 1919, *Papers Relating to the Foreign Relations of the United States, 1919*, 2 vols. (Washington, D.C., 1934), p. 673 (hereafter all references to this series will be by the abbreviated title *FRUS* and year).
7. Jordan to Earl Curzon, Oct. 15, 1919, *Documents on British Foreign Policy, 1919–1939*, 1st Ser., vol. 6 (London, 1956), p. 1004n.
8. Air Chief Marshal Sir Philip Joubert de la Ferté, *The Third Service* (London, 1955), pp. 45, 52–53.
9. *Far Eastern Review*, 16 (1920), 55–56.
10. Loh Han-chin, "Commercial Aviation."
11. Woodhead, "Aviation in China," R. L. Craigie, Secretary of the British Embassy [Washington, D.C.], to J. V. A. MacMurray, Chief of the Division of Far Eastern Affairs, March 1, 1921, *FRUS, 1921*, 2 vols. (Washington, D.C., 1936), 1: 548–50.
12. *The Third Service*, p. 45.
13. Reynolds, "Aviation in China."
14. *Millard's Review*, March 19, 1921.

NOTES

15. A. R. Ruddock, American Chargé d'Affairs, Peking, to Secretary of State C. H. Hughes, Aug. 14, 1921, SD File 893. 796. For an account of the operation by one of the British pilots, see Cecil Lewis, *Sagittarius Rising* (London, 1936), pp. 277ff. The Mexican dollar was used widely in China at this time and is not readily convertible to other currency.

16. Reynolds, "Aviation in China." Holt in April 1931 was placed in charge of Fighting Area, Royal Air Force, becoming one of the youngest formation commanders in the service. He was killed three weeks later in a mid-air collision. Joubert, *The Third Service*, p. 53.

17. For political developments in China during this period, see C. Martin Wilbur, "Military Separatism and the Process of Reunification under the Nationalist Regime, 1922–1937," in P. T. Ho and Tang Tsou (eds.), *China in Crisis*, vol. 1 (Chicago, 1968), pp. 203–63.

18. Earl D. Osborn, "The Industry's Progress during 1928," *Aviation*, XXVI (Jan. 1929), 24–25, 64; Elsbeth E. Freudenthal, *The Aviation Business* (New York, 1940), p. 88; John B. Rae, *Climb to Greatness: The American Aircraft Industry, 1920–1960* (Cambridge, Mass., 1968), p. 49.

19. Little has been written about the career of this remarkable pioneer in aeronautical financing. One of the few articles of substance is Earl Reeves, "Why Aviation's Future is 'Strictly Business,'" *Forbes*, 23 (April 1929), 13, 48, 50. See also Key's obituary in the *New York Times*, Jan. 13, 1952. The Keys Papers, a fragmentary collection, is deposited in the Firestone Library, Princeton University.

20. Keys to William B. Robertson, Jan. 18, 1929, copy in the Papers of Ernest B. Price, in the possession of the Price Family, Los Gatos, Cal. See also Keys to Richard Hoyt, Dec. 20, 1928, Keys Papers.

21. Hayward memorandum, "Chinese Aviation," March 26, 1929, Price Papers. See also Edwin S. Cunningham, Consul General Shanghai, to Minister J. V. A. MacMurray, Feb. 14, 1929, SD File 893. 796.

22. Memorandum, Division of Far Eastern Affairs, Jan. 7, 1929, SD File 893. 796.

23. Keys to Kellogg, with copy to President Coolidge, Jan. 8, 1929, SD File 893. 796.

24. Memorandum Office of the Assistant Secretary, "Commercial Aviation Projects of Mr. C. M. Keys," Jan. 10, 1929, SD File 893. 796.

25. Hornbeck Memorandum, Jan. 16, 1929, SD File 893. 796. Assistant Secretary of State Nelson T. Johnson noted on the top of the memorandum: "Please tell Captain Furlong [of the Navy Department] that we would prefer that they discourage this contemplated action. I told the Secretary that we would disapprove. He assented."

26. Keys to Robertson, Jan. 18, 1929, Price Papers.

27. *China Weekly Review*, March 30 and April 6, 1929; Frank S. Williams, Trade Commissioner, Shanghai, "Weekly Report to the De-

partment of Commerce," March 2, 1929, Papers of Julean Arnold, Hoover Institution, Stanford University.

28. Hayward memorandum, "Chinese Aviation," March 26, 1929, Price Papers; Williams to Leighton W. Rogers, April 25, 1929, Arnold Papers. The Nationalist government undertook measures to rehabilitate the credit reputation of China, but foreign investors had suffered so badly from earlier defaults that they understandably were slow to trust the new regime.

29. Hayward memorandum, March 26, 1929; Keys to Hornbeck, April 9, 1929, and F. P. Lockhart, Consul General, Hankow, to the Secretary of State, June 15, 1929, SD File 893. 796.

30. Price memorandum, "Possibilities for the operation of Air Transport Lines in China," May 12, 1930, Price Papers.

31. Air mail receipts were understood to include receipts for carriage of passengers and freight as well as mail. Sun Fo to Aviation Exploration, Inc., April 24, 1929, Price Papers. The contracts were published in full by the *China Weekly Review*, April 27, 1929.

32. Arnold to O. P. Hopkins, Assistant Director, Bureau of Foreign and Domestic Commerce, May 25, 1929, and Williams to Rogers, April 25, 1929, Arnold Papers; Cunningham to MacMurray, April 26, 1929, SD File 893. 796.

33. Keys to Hornbeck, May 3, 1929, SD File 893. 796.

34. *China Weekly Review*, May 4, 1929.

35. Williams to Rogers, May 10, 1929, Arnold Papers; "Airport Six percent Gold Loan Agreement," July 16, 1929, Price Papers. Expenditure of funds under this agreement was to be carefully supervised by the lender. Each request for land purchases or improvement would be carefully scrutinized. Title to the land would be conveyed to the lender and held as security for the loan. Promissory notes bearing 6 percent interest would mature in 1938.

36. For a discussion of the structure of the Nationalist government, see Paul M. A. Linebarger, Djang Chu, and Ardath W. Burks, *Far Eastern Governments and Politics*, rev. ed. (New York, 1956), pp. 151–68.

37. *China Weekly Review*, July 13, 1929.

38. *New York Times*, June 20, 1929. On the powers of the Central Executive Committee of the Kuomintang, see Linebarger, Chu, and Burks, *Far Eastern Governments*, p. 160.

39. Keys to the editor, June 24, 1929, *New York Times*, June 29, 1929.

40. Partial transcript of E. L. Sloniger's memoirs, taped c. 1968, supplied to the author by Jerry Sloniger, May 12, 1968.

41. K. Reid Campbell, "Aircraft Finance during 1929," *Aviation*, 28 (Feb. 1930), 315–17.

42. Smith's salary of $10,000 per year equalled that of the president

of the airline. China Airways, "Pay Roll List," Nov. 1, 1929, Price Papers.

43. Biographical information of Smith taken from newspaper clipping, *circa* 1929, supplied to the author by E. M. Allison.

44. Radio, Keysko (New York) to Aviexplor (Shanghai), June 18, 1929; Price to Sun Fo, Nov. 2, 1929; both in Price Papers. Radio messages between New York and Shanghai were sent in code. On the Loening amphibian, see Grover Loening, *Amphibian: The Story of the Loening Biplane* (Greenwich, Conn., 1973).

45. Randall Gould, "China Spreads Her Wings," *China Weekly Review*, Aug. 31, 1929; China Airways, "Pay Roll List," Nov. 1, 1929, Price Papers. Annual salaries were as follows: Allison and Kaufman, $7,200; Johnsen, $6,000; Wilke and St. Louis, $5,400.

46. "Articles of Incorporation of China Airways Federal Inc. U.S.A.," Aug. 29, 1929, Price Papers; Price to MacMurray, Sept. 8, 1929, Papers of John Van Antwerp MacMurray, Firestone Library, Princeton University.

47. *Who's Who on the Pacific Coast* (Chigaco, 1949).

48. Price memorandum, "Suggested Program for the Enterprise in China," Aug. 13, 1929, Price Papers; Price to MacMurray, Sept. 8, 1929, MacMurray Papers.

49. Price memorandum, "Suggested Program," Aug. 13, 1929, Price Papers.

50. Price to MacMurray, Sept. 8, 1929, MacMurray Papers.

51. "Contract between the China National Aviation Corporation and Aviation Exploration, Inc." April 17, 1929, published in *China Weekly Review*, April 27, 1929. Also, Price memorandum, "Suggestions for Development of Civil Aviation in China," n.d., and Price to Sun Fo, Nov. 2, 1929, Price Papers; Allison to the author, Nov. 27, 1967; photographs supplied to the author by Ralph W. Mitchell.

52. Edgar Snow, "The 'Middle Kingdom' from the Clouds," *China Weekly Review*, Oct. 19, 1929. Snow's prediction proved not quite as far-fetched as it might seem. Air transportation did play a small but noteworthy part in flying mediators from Nanking to Sian to resolve the Sian Incident of December 1936, when Chiang Kai-shek was kidnapped by dissidents.

53. Radio, Aviexplor to Keysko, Oct. 17, 1929, and Price memorandum, "Possibilities for the operation of Air Transport Lines in China," May 12, 1930, Price Papers; *China Weekly Review*, Oct. 26, 1929.

54. Price to MacMurray, Nov. 3, 1929, Price Papers; James F. Starr and Samuel J. Mills, "The Chinese Air Post, 1920–1935," *Collectors Club Philatelist*, XV (July 1936), 157; and Birger Johnsen, "War Birds of the Far East," *New York Herald Tribune Magazine*, Feb. 28, 1932. Johnsen's highly imaginative article was the first in what was to prove a

long line of improbable, romantic, misleading, and inaccurate stories about the operation of the airline in China.

55. Campbell, "Aircraft Finance."
56. Radios, Aviexplor to Keysko, Oct. 29, 1929, and Keysko to Aviexplor, Nov. 1, 1929, Price Papers.
57. Price to Sun Fo, Nov. 9, 1929; Price untitled memorandum, Nov. 9, 1929; both in Price Papers.
58. Radios, Aviexplor to Keysko, Nov. 4, 16, and 18, 1929; Keysko to Aviexplor, Nov. 19, 1929; all in Price Papers.
59. Price memorandum, "Possibilities," May 12, 1930, Price Papers.
60. Keys to Price, Dec. 2, 1929, Price Papers.
61. Price to Sun Fo, Dec. 5, 1929, and Sun Fo to China Air-Ways, Dec. 6, 1929, Price Papers.
62. Price memorandum, "Possibilities," May 12, 1930, Price Papers.
63. Soong to Price, Dec. 13, 1929, and Radio, Aviexplor to Keysko, Dec. 16, 1929, Price Papers.
64. Translation from the *Shun Pao*, Price Papers.
65. *Shanghai Evening Post*, Dec. 19, 1929.
66. Hamilton to Keys, Dec. 23, 1929, Keys Papers.
67. Radio, Keysko to Aviexplor, Jan. 10, 1930, Price Papers.
68. Radio, Aviexplor to Keysko, Jan. 14, 1930, and Price Memorandum, "Possiblities," May 12, 1930, Price Papers.
69. Price to the President and members of the State Council, Jan. 24, 1930; published in the *Far Eastern Review*, XXVI (Feb. 1930), 59–62.
70. Price memorandum, "Possibilities," May 12, 1930, Price Papers; Price to MacMurray, May 24, 1930, MacMurray Papers.
71. *Finance & Commerce*, Feb. 12, 1930. See also comments in *China Weekly Review*, Feb. 8, and 15, 1930; *North-China Daily News*, Feb. 7, 1930; and *North-China Herald*, Feb. 11, 1930.
72. Young to Soong, Feb. 7, 1930, the Papers of Arthur N. Young, Hoover Institution, Stanford University.
73. Price memorandum, "Possibilities," May 12, 1930, Price Papers. In an attempt to save face, the council publicly denied that it had ever approved the original proposal to cancel the contract. *China Weekly Review*, Feb. 12, 1930.
74. Radio, Keysko to Price, March 26, 1930, Price Papers; Price to MacMurray, May 24, 1930, MacMurray Papers.
75. Price to MacMurray, May 24, 1930, MacMurray Papers; *Who's Who on the Pacific Coast*.
76. Bureau of Economic Information, "Commercial Aviation in China," *Chinese Economic Monthly*, Dec. 1923.

77. China Airways, "Financial Statement for the Period October 21, 1929 to March 31, 1930," Price Papers.

78. For statistics on governmental subsidies and discussion of the value of air transportation, see Oliver James Lissitzyn, *International Air Transport and National Policy* (New York, 1942). Arthur N. Young, *China's Nation-Building Effort, 1927–1937* (Stanford, 1971), is best for the economic situation in China during the 1930s.

CHAPTER 2

1. Interview with George J. Schlenker, an associate and close friend of Polin's, June 28, 1969. Polin died in Hong Kong in the late 1940s.

2. New York had ordered Price to maintain friendly contact with the government while awaiting Polin's arrival. Radio, Keysko to Aviexplor, Feb. 26, 1930, and Price to Keys, March 12, 1930, Price Papers.

3. "Contract between Ministry of Communications, National Government, Republic of China, and China Airways Federal Inc. U.S.A.," July 8, 1930, Young Papers. The contract was summarized in H. G. W. Woodhead (ed.), *The China Year Book, 1931* (Shanghai, 1931), pp. 253–54.

4. C. Y. W. Meng, "Development of Airways in the 'Middle Kingdom,'" *China Weekly Review*, Aug. 6, 1932; Chi-ming Hou, *Foreign Investment and Economic Development in China, 1840–1937* (Cambridge, Mass., 1965), pp. 109–11.

5. *China Weekly Review*, July 19, 1930.

6. For a summary of the contract, see Woodhead (ed.), *China Year Book, 1931*, pp. 252–54.

7. Little information is available on Eurasia's operations and even less about the nature of its relationship with the Chinese government. A sketchy account of the airline's activities can be found in Chang Kai-ngau, "Development of Civil Aviation in China," *China Quarterly*, 4 (1939), 601–13; and Lincoln C. Reynolds, "Aviation in China," May 1935, SD File 893.796.

8. *China Weekly Review*, July 19, Aug. 23, Sept. 10, and Nov. 1, 1930.

9. *Survey of International Affairs, 1931* (London, 1932), p. 406.

10. Westervelt memorandum, "Shanghai to Chungking and Return," April 29, 1931, Papers of George Conrad Westervelt, University of Virginia Library.

11. Ibid.

12. Federal Reserve Board, *Banking and Monetary Statistics* (Washington, D.C., 1943), p. 667; Westervelt to Keys, Dec. 31, 1930, Westervelt Papers.

13. Frank J. Taylor, *High Horizons* (New York, 1951), pp. 25–26. See also Harold Mansfield, *Vision: A Sage of the Sky* (New York, 1956), pp. 8–14.

14. Westervelt to Soong, March 28, 1932, Young Papers; Ralph S. Barnaby to the author, March 6, 1968; Rieta Westervelt du Manoir to the author, Nov. 15, 1967.

15. Rieta Westervelt du Manoir to the author, Nov. 15, 1967; Barnaby to the author, March 6, 1968.

16. Ibid.

17. James J. Hudon, *Hostile Skies: A Combat History of the American Air Service in World War I* (Syracuse, N.Y., 1968), pp. 68, 124, 308. On the incident between Smith and Allison, see Westervelt to John Sanderson, April 21, 1931, Westervelt Papers. Sanderson was Keys's "right hand man on all his operations." J. S. Allard, vice president, Curtiss-Wright Export Corporation, to J. Leighton Rogers, Chief of the Aeronautics Trade Division, Department of Commerce, Feb. 10, 1931, Archives of the Department of Commerce, File 560, National Archives, Washington, D.C.

18. Vaughn to the author, June 27, 1969; Westervelt to Keys, Dec. 31, 1930, Westervelt Papers; *China Weekly Review*, Dec. 13 and 20, 1930.

19. F. P. Lockhart, Consul, Hankow, to the Department of State, Jan. 6, 1931, SD File 893.796; Westervelt to Keys, Dec. 31, 1930, Westervelt Papers.

20. Westervelt to Keys, Dec. 31, 1930, Westervelt Papers.

21. Ibid.

22. Westervelt to Sanderson, May 19, 1931, and Westervelt memorandum, "Shanghai to Chungking and Return," April 29, 1931, Westervelt Papers.

23. Westervelt memorandum, "Shanghai to Chungking and Return," April 29, 1931, Westervelt Papers.

24. Westervelt to Sanderson, April 27 and Nov. 10, 1931, Westervelt Papers.

25. Westervelt to Sanderson, May 19, 1931, Westervelt Papers; Allison to the author, June 25, 1969; W. L. Bond to the author, June 28, 1969.

26. Westervelt to Sanderson, April 21 and May 19, 1931, Westervelt Papers.

27. Ibid.

28. Westervelt to Sanderson, March 17 and May 19, 1931, Westervelt Papers; Allison to the author, June 25, 1969; Vaughn to the author, June 27, 1969.

29. Westervelt to Sanderson, March 25, April 21, and May 1, 1931, Westervelt Papers.

30. Saint-Exupéry dedicated *Vol de Nuit* to Daurat. Marcel Migeo, *Saint-Exupéry* (London, 1961), pp. 71, 157–58.
31. Bond to the author, March 29, 1969.
32. Interview with Bond, Aug. 24, 1967.
33. Ibid.; Bond to the author, March 20, 1969.
34. Ibid.
35. Ibid.
36. Interview with Bond, Aug. 24, 1967; Bond to the author, March 20, 1969; Westervelt to Sanderson, Nov. 10, 1931, Westervelt Papers.
37. Westervelt to Sanderson, Nov. 10, 1931, and Jan. 12, 1932, Westervelt Papers.
38. Toynbee, *Survey of International Affairs, 1931*, pp. 397–415.
39. Westervelt to Sanderson, May 22, Nov. 10, 1931, and Jan. 12, 1932, Westervelt Papers.
40. Westervelt to Sanderson, Nov. 10, 1931, Westervelt Papers.
41. *China Weekly Review*, Jan. 2, 1932; Kenneth E. Folson, "The China National Aviation Corporation," unpublished senior thesis, Princeton University, 1943.
42. Toynbee, *Survey of International Affairs, 1931*, pp. 415–18; Arthur N. Young to the author, July 22, 1970.
43. Westervelt to Rieta Westervelt, Dec. 8, 1931, Westervelt Papers.
44. Westervelt to Keys, Dec. 7, 1931, Westervelt Papers.
45. Westervelt to Keys, Dec. 15, 1931, Westervelt to Sanderson, Jan. 12 and Feb. 4, 1932, Westervelt Papers.
46. Westervelt to Sanderson, n.d. [Jan. 26, 1932], Westervelt Papers.
47. Westervelt to Rieta Westervelt, Jan. 28, 1932, Westervelt Papers.
48. Westervelt to Rieta Westervelt, Jan. 30, 1932, Westervelt Papers, quoting Bond's wire.
49. Westervelt to Sanderson, Feb. 4, 1932, Westervelt to Rieta Westervelt, Feb. 8, 1932, Westervelt Papers.
50. R. C. Mackay memorandum, "Re China National Aviation Corporation," Feb. 4, 1932, SD File 393.115.
51. Westervelt to Rieta Westervelt, Feb. 15, 1932, Westervelt Papers. The details of the proposal were related in Nelson T. Johnson to William R. Castle, April 14, 1932, SD File 393.115.
52. 72nd Cong., 1st Sess., April 23, 1932, pp. 8746–47.
53. Cunningham to the Secretary of State, April 15, 1932, SD File 393.115.
54. Johnson to Castle, April 14, 1932, SD File 393.115.
55. R. C. Mackay memorandum, "China Airways Federal Inc.—Shanghai's Recommendation of a Postal Subsidy," April 25, 1932, SD File 393.115.

56. Westervelt to Soong, March 10, 1932, Young Papers.
57. Young memorandum, April 2, 1932, Young Papers.
58. Howard memoranda, April 6 and May 17, 1932, Young Papers.
59. *Blue Book of Aviation* (Los Angeles, 1932), p. 18; Soong to Howard, May 24, 1932, Young Papers.
60. Rogers to Thomas H. McConnell, May 26, 1932, Commerce Department File 560—Aeronautics (China).
61. Hamilton memorandum, "American Aviation Training Mission in China," June 1, 1932, SD File 893.20.
62. John H. Jouett, "War Planes Over China," *Asia*, 37 (1937), 827–30. The pilots were G. B. Clark, Harry T. Rowland, L. R. Holbrook, Jr., W. C. Kent, M. R. Knight, Christopher Mathewson, Jr., R. L. Sansbury, E. D. Shannon, and T. L. Taylor.
63. Jouett memorandum, July 14, 1932, Jouett to Soong, Aug. 14, 1932, Young Papers.
64. Jouett to Major Ralph Royce, Jan. 27, 1933; Howard memorandum, "Progress of American Mission—Hangchow Flying School," Dec. 16, 1932, enclosed in Rogers to Stanley K. Hornbeck, Feb. 2, 1933, both in SD File 893.20.
65. Lincoln C. Reynolds, "Aviation in China," May 1935, SD File 893.796.
66. Jouett memorandum, Sept. 15, 1934, Young Papers; Jouett to Royce, Jan. 27, 1933, SD File 893.20; Jouett, "War Planes Over China," p. 828.
67. Howard memorandum, "Progress of American Mission," Dec. 16, 1932, SD File 893.20; Jouett, "War Planes Over China," p. 828.
68. Howard memorandum, Dec. 16, 1932; Jouett, "War Planes Over China," p. 828.
69. Reynolds memorandum, March 18, 1933, SD File 893.20; Reynolds, "Aviation in China," May 1935, SD File 839.796; Jouett memorandum, Sept. 15, 1934, Young Papers.
70. Consul General Cunningham to Secretary of State Cordell Hull, April 22, 1933, *FRUS, 1933*, 5 vols. (Washington, D.C., 1949), III, 285, 300–301. See also Wilbur Burton, "'Mandate from Heaven,'" *Asia*, XXXV (Aug. 1935), 458–65.
71. Jouett to Young, Sept. 18, 1933, Young Papers.
72. Jouett to Young, Oct. 14, 1933, Young Papers.
73. Consul General W. R. Peck to Hull, Nov. 14, 1933, *FRUS, 1933*, III, 455–56.
74. *China Weekly Review*, Jan. 13, 1934; Burton, "Mandate From Heaven," p. 462.
75. On this point and on all other aspects of Sino-American diplomatic relations during the 1930s, see Dorothy Borg's masterful study

The United States and the Far Eastern Crisis of 1933-1938 (Cambridge, Mass., 1964), pp. 55-92.

76. Reynolds memorandum, May 6, 1934, SD File 893.20.

77. Borg, *The United States and the Far Eastern Crisis*, p. 576, n.114.

78. Ibid., pp. 55-92; Raymond C. Mackay, "Italian Aviation Interests in China—Conduct of Central Aviation School, Hangchow, by Colonel John H. Jouett and Associates," Sept. 12, 1934, SD File 893.20.

79. Consul General Cunningham to Hull, June 10, 1935, *FRUS, 1935*, 4 vols. (Washington, D.C., 1953), 3: 224-25.

80. Reynolds, "Aviation in China," May 1935, SD File 893.796; Evans Fordyce Carlson, *The Chinese Army: Its Organization and Military Efficiency* (New York, 1940), pp. 46-47. See also Claire Lee Chennault, *Way of a Fighter* (New York, 1949), pp. 37-38.

81. Reynolds, "Aviation in China," May 1935, SD File 893.796.

82. Ibid.; Young memorandum, "Aviation Factory Proposal," Aug. 17, 1932, and William D. Pawley to H. H. Kung, May 15, 1933, Young Papers.

CHAPTER 3

1. Memorandum, "CNAC," Aug. 7, 1942, the Records of Pan American Airways, Pan Am Building, New York (hereafter cited as PAA Records); Folson, "China National Aviation Corporation."

2. Arnold J. Toynbee, *Survey of International Affairs, 1933* (London, 1934), p. 461.

3. Foreign Air Transport Division, Civil Aeronautics Board, "China National Aviation Corporation," Jan. 31, 1946, copy in PAA Records.

4. *China Weekly Review*, Jan. 21 and Feb. 25, 1933; Allison to the author, June 25, 1969.

5. *China Weekly Review*, Oct. 7, 1933.

6. *World Airline Record*, 6th ed. (Chicago, 1968). For the history of Pan American, see Henry Ladd Smith, *Airways Abroad* (Madison, Wisc., 1950), and Matthew Josephson, *Empire of the Air* (New York, 1944).

7. Clarence M. Young to the author, Feb. 14, 1969.

8. See William A. M. Burden, *The Struggle for Airways in Latin America* (New York, 1943).

9. Interview with Pawley, July 5, 1969. Pan American, Bixby noted, preferred March 31 to April 1 as the date of acquisition "for obvious reasons." Bixby, "Top Side Ricksha," n.d. [c. 1938]. Bixby wrote "Top Side Ricksha" apparently as the first draft of a book intended for publication. He put aside the uncorrected manuscript and never

resumed work on it. Mrs. Harold M. Bixby graciously permitted the author to copy the original manuscript.

10. Memorandum, "Acquisition of China Airways Federal, Inc., U.S.A. by Pan American Airways," n.d. [c. 1942]; Foreign Air Transport Division, CAB, "China National Aviation Corporation," Jan. 31, 1946; memorandum, "CNAC," Aug. 7, 1942; all in PAA records.

11. Lindbergh to the author, July 21, 1968.

12. Lindbergh, *The Spirit of St. Louis* (New York, 1953), pp. 58–67; Lindbergh to the author, Aug. 17, 1969.

13. The preceding paragraphs are based on Bixby's "Top Side Ricksha."

14. Ibid.

15. "Brief of Pan American Airways, Inc., before the Civil Aeronautics Board," Docket No. 1499, Feb. 17, 1947, copy in PAA Records. The Civil Aeronautics Authority was to rule against Pan American. "The mere intention of the petitioner," said the CAA, "to connect this service with the trans-Pacific service when it would be inaugurated is not sufficient to warrant the inclusion of the expense so incurred as an item to developmental cost of the trans-Pacific service. . . ." Civil Aeronautics Authority, *Decisions of the Civil Aeronautics Authority, February 1939 to July 1940* (Washington, D. C., 1941), pp. 385–411.

16. "Brief of Pan American Airways," Feb. 17, 1947, PAA Records.

17. Division of Far Eastern Affairs, "Memorandum of Conversation with Mr. Stokely W. Morgan, Pan American, Mr. Hamilton and Mr. Mackay," June 6, 1933, SD File 893.796.

18. William S. Grooch, *Winged Highway* (New York, 1938), pp. 164–69. On the S-38, see Frank J. Delear, *Igor Sikorsky* (New York, 1969).

19. Grooch, *Winged Highway*, pp. 164–69.

20. Bixby, "Top Side Ricksha"; interview with Z. Soldinsky, June 27, 1969.

21. Bixby, "Top Side Ricksha"; Grooch, *Winged Highway*, p. 189.

22. Bixby, "Top Side Ricksha"; Grooch, *Winged Highway*, p. 189; Josephson, *Empire of the Air*, p. 101; *China Weekly Review*, July 15, 1933.

23. Bixby, "Top Side Ricksha;" *China Weekly Review*, Aug. 19, 26, and Sept. 2, 9, 1933.

24. Division of Far Eastern Affairs, "Memorandum of Conversation with Mr. Stokely W. Morgan, Pan American, Mr. Hamilton and Mr. Mackay," June 6, 1933; Willys R. Peck to Ambassador Nelson T. Johnson, July 26, 1933, reporting a conversation with Bixby; Bixby to Julean Arnold, Aug. 8, 1933; all in SD File 893.796.

25. "Summary of Provisional Operating Contract between CNAC and Pacific American Airways," Oct. 8, 1933, PAA Records.

26. Bixby to Morgan, Oct. 12, 1933, PAA Records.
27. "Memorandum of Conversation between Mr. W. R. Peck and Dr. Chu Chia-hua," Nov. 4, 1933, SD File 893.796. On Dr. Chu, see Harold L. Boorman and Richard C. Howard (eds.), *Biographical Dictionary of Republican China* (4 vols., New York, 1967-1971), I, 437-40.
28. Grooch, *Winged Highway*, pp. 207-14; *North-China Herald*, Nov. 29, 1933; *China Weekly Review*, Dec. 2, 1933; Reynolds to Starr and Mills, April 16, 1936, printed in "The Chinese Air Post," p. 168.
29. Grooch, *Winged Highway*, pp. 205-27; interview with Z. Soldinsky, June 27, 1969; *China Weekly Review*, Jan. 27, 1934.
30. Grooch, *Winged Highway*, pp. 230-42; *China Weekly Review*, April 14, 1934; Reynolds to Starr and Mills, April 16, 1936.
31. *Slide Rule* (New York, 1964), p. 111.
32. Bixby to Morgan, Oct. 4 and 14, 1934, PAA Records.
33. *China Weekly Review*, Oct. 20, 27, and Nov. 10, 1934; memorandum, "CNAC," Aug. 7, 1942, PAA Records.
34. Second Secretary of the Legation in China to the Secretary of State, April 29, 1935, *FRUS, 1935*, III, 800-1; *Far Eastern Survey*, VI (Dec. 1935), 206-7.
35. Nelson T. Johnson to the Secretary of State, Feb. 29, 1936, *FRUS, 1936*, 5 vols. (Washington, D.C., 1954), 4: 639-40; Bixby to Arthur N. Young, Jan. 22, 1936, Young Papers.
36. The British Ambassador to the Secretary of State, July 11, 1936; memorandum by the Assistant Chief of the Division of Protocol and Conferences, Aug. 24, 1936; Johnson to the Secretary of State, June 15, 1936; all printed in *FRUS, 1936*, 4: 641-44.
37. Bixby to Morgan, March 2, 1935, PAA Records.
38. Bixby, "Top Side Ricksha."
39. *China Weekly Review*, May 1, 1937.
40. "Memorandum of Conversation between Mr. W. R. Peck and Dr. Chu Chia-hua," Nov. 4, 1933, SD File 893.796; interview with Bond, Aug. 24, 1967; Westervelt to Sanderson, May 19 and 22, 1931, Westervelt Papers; Bixby, "Top Side Ricksha."
41. Memorandum, "CNAC," Aug. 7, 1942, PAA Records; Hewitt F. Mitchell to Louise Mitchell, Apr. 7, 1933, Papers of Hewitt F. Mitchell in the possession of Ralph F. Mitchell, Los Gatos, Cal.
42. Bixby to Young, April 18, 1933, Young Papers.
43. Bixby, "Top Side Ricksha."
44. Ibid.
45. Ibid. Allison to the author, Sept. 18, 1970.
46. Bixby, "Top Side Ricksha"; Allison to the author, Sept. 18, 1970; Allison, "Landing in a Walled City—1933," Jan. 22, 1961, the Papers of Ernest M. Allison, in the possession of Mr. Allison, Arcadia, Cal.
47. Bixby, "Top Side Ricksha."
48. *China Weekly Review*, Dec. 2, 1933, and Jan. 6, 1934.

49. The author is indebted to Ralph F. Mitchell for permission to use his brother's letters and diary. Ralph Mitchell followed in Hewitt's footsteps and joined CNAC after World War II. He is presently a captain with Flying Tiger Line.

50. Radio, J. Leighton Rogers, Department of Commerce, to Howard, April 11, 1933, Commerce File 560; Bixby, "Top Side Ricksha."

51. Interview with Allison, Nov. 18, 1968; Ralph F. Mitchell to the author, Sept. 8, 1969.

52. Mitchell to Ralph F. Mitchell, Sr., March 23, 1933, and Mitchell to Louise Mitchell, April 7, 1933, Mitchell Papers.

53. McCleskey to the author, Aug. 25, 1970; Mitchell Diary, June 1, 6, 7, 10, 13, 15, and 16, 1933.

54. Diary, June 7, 10, and 16, 1933.

55. Ibid., Dec. 22, 1933.

56. Ibid., Jan. 17, 1934.

57. Ibid., March 22 and April 27, 1934.

58. Ibid., March 21, 1934.

59. Ibid., April 25, 1934.

60. Ibid., April 7, 1934.

61. Ibid., April 18, 1934.

62. Ibid., Feb. 22, and May 13, 1934.

63. Ibid., May 12, 1934.

64. Mitchell to Ralph F. Mitchell, Sr., March 20, 1935.

65. Ibid.

66. Mitchell to his parents, May 11, 1935.

67. R. F. Mitchell to the author, Sept. 8, 1969.

68. Mitchell, "Shanghai-Peiping via CNAC," June 1933.

69. Bixby, "Top Side Ricksha;" *China Weekly Review*, June 30, 1934.

70. Bixby, "Top Side Ricksha."

71. Dai Enki, "The First Five Years of Commercial Aviation Activity in China," *China Weekly Review*, Dec. 22, 1934; interview with Allison, Nov. 18, 1968.

72. Bixby, "Top Side Ricksha."

73. Ibid.

74. Report by L. H. Gourley, consul, Shanghai, "Commercial Aviation in China before and after Hostilities," Feb. 28, 1938, SD File 893.796; memorandum, "CNAC," Aug. 7, 1942, PAA Records; Harrison Forman, "China Spreads Her Wings," *Aviation*, 35 (May 1936), 11–14. The author is indebted to Walter Quinn for a copy of China National Aviation Corporation, *Pilots Manual*, n.d. [c. 1934].

75. Bixby, "Top Side Ricksha," T'ang Leang-li (ed.), *Reconstruction in China* (Shanghai, 1935), p. 239; Dai Enki, "Aviation in China," *Far Eastern Review*, 33 (May 1937), 199–201, 205.

76. George K. T. Wang, "Tibet and America to be Linked Up by Air," *China Weekly Review*, Feb. 24, 1934.

77. Arnold J. Toynbee, *Survey of International Affairs, 1935* (London, 1936), pp. 306–7; Foreign Air Transport Division, CAB, "China National Aviation Corporation," Jan. 31, 1946, PAA Records.

78. Bixby, "Top Side Ricksha."

79. *China Weekly Review*, March 14, 1936; *North-China Daily News*, April 25, 1936; Sydney Bernard Smith, *Air Transport in the Pacific Area* (New York, 1941), p. 36.

80. *China Weekly Review*, Nov. 23, 1935; Chang Kia-ngau, "Development of Civil Aviation in China," *China Quarterly*, IV (Autumn 1939), 601–13.

81. *Far Eastern Survey*, 6 (Jan. 29, 1936), 29–30.

82. *China Weekly Review*, May 5, 1934; Reynolds, "Aviation in China," May 1935, SD File 893.796.

83. Bixby, "Top Side Ricksha."

84. Ibid.; *China Weekly Review*, April 4, 1936; Toynbee, *Survey of International Affairs, 1936* (London, 1937), pp. 885–86.

85. Foreign Air Transport Division, CAB, "China National Aviation Corporation," Jan. 31, 1946, PAA Records; W. R. Peck memorandum, "Relations between the Chinese Government and the China National Aviation Corporation," reporting a conversation with W. L. Bond, June 11, 1936, SD File 811.79690; statement by Dai Enki, *Far Eastern Review*, XXXIII (June 1937), 250.

86. Bond to the author, June 28, 1969.

87. Bixby, "Top Side Ricksha."

88. Ibid.

89. Ibid.; *New York Times*, Dec. 13, 1935; Peck memorandum, reporting a conversation with Bond, June 11, 1936, SD File 811.79690; Bond to Morgan, July 13, 1936, PAA Records.

90. Johnson to the Secretary of State, March 11, 1937, SD File 893.796.

91. *Far Eastern Survey*, 33 (June 1937), 250; Gourley report, Feb. 28, 1938, SD File 893.796.

CHAPTER 4

1. Toynbee, *Survey of International Affairs, 1936*, p. 889.

2. Arthur N. Young, *China and the Helping Hand, 1937–1945* (Cambridge, Mass., 1963), p. 11.

3. "Brief of Pan American Airways," Feb. 17, 1947, PAA Records.

4. Toynbee, *Survey of International Affairs, 1937* (London, 1938), pp. 145–323, contains an excellent contemporary account of the Sino-Japanese war in 1937.

5. Walter C. Kent to his family, Aug. 18, 1937, published in *Atlantic Monthly*, 160 (Nov. 1937), 644–48.
6. Ibid.
7. Memorandum, "CNAC," Aug. 7, 1942, PAA Records; Robert W. Pottschmidt to the author, March 28, 1968.
8. Bixby to Lem, Aug. 15, 1937, Allison Papers.
9. Interview with Pottschmidt, July 4, 1969; memorandum, "CNAC," Aug. 7, 1942, PAA Records.
10. *New York Times*, Aug. 22, 1937; *North-China Herald*, Aug. 25, 1937; *China Weekly Review*, Aug. 28, 1937.
11. Bond to the author, June 3, 1969.
12. Ibid. Allison's recollection of the incident differs substantially from Bond's. "I do not recall that Bond was dissatisfied with my performance," he has written to the author, Sept. 18, 1970, "or that I got 'angry as hell' at the time of his arrival in Hong Kong."
13. Bond to the author, June 3, 1969.
14. Ibid.
15. Ibid.; Bond to the author, June 28, 1969; interview with Bond, Aug. 24, 1967; memorandum, "CNAC," Aug. 7, 1942, PAA Records.
16. Bond to the author, June 3 and June 28, 1969; interview with Bond, Aug. 24, 1967; memorandum, "CNAC," Aug. 7, 1942, PAA Records.
17. Bond to the author, June 3 and June 28, 1969; interview with Bond, Aug. 24, 1967; memorandum, "CNAC," Aug. 7, 1942, PAA Records.
18. Woods to the author, Aug. 30, 1967, and July 19, 1968; interview with Pottschmidt, July 4, 1969.
19. *New Horizons*, 11 (Dec. 1940), 10–11. Pan American published *New Horizons* primarily for the airline's employees.
20. Woods, "Pilot Report," Aug. 26, 1938; copy supplied to the author by Captain Woods.
21. *China Weekly Review*, Sept. 3 and 10, 1938.
22. Hull to Grew, Aug. 25, 1938, *FRUS, 1938*, 5 vols. (Washington, D.C., 1955), 4: 451–52.
23. Kazushige Ugaki, Minister of Foreign Affairs, to Grew, Aug. 31, 1938, ibid., 460–62.
24. Hull to Grew, Sept. 14, 1938, ibid., 473–74.
25. Minutes of the 37th Meeting of the Board of Directors, China National Aviation Corporation, Nov. 17, 1938, Young Papers.
26. Arnold J. Toynbee, *Survey of International Affairs, 1938*, 2 vols. (London, 1941), 1: 493–517.
27. Bond to Morgan, Oct. 29, 1938, Young Papers.
28. Ibid.
29. Ibid.

30. Saburo Hayashi and Alvin D. Coox, *Kōgun: The Japanese Army in the Pacific War* (Quantico, Va., 1959), pp. 12–14.
31. Young, *China and the Helping Hand*, pp. 49–51.
32. Royal Leonard, *I Flew for China* (New York, 1942), p. 220; Martha Gellhorn, "Flight Into Peril," *Collier's*, 105 (May 31, 1941), 21, 85–87; Irving S. Friedman, "Air Lines Preserve China's Outside Contacts," *Far Eastern Survey*, 8 (Dec. 1939), 284–86.
33. Theodore H. White, "China's Last Lifeline," *Fortune*, 27 (May 1943), 106–10ff.; Chang Kai-ngau, "Development of Civil Aviation in China"; Minutes of the 40th Meeting of the Board of Directors, China National Aviation Corporation, June 22, 1940, Young Papers; Bond to Bixby, March 20, 1941, Young Papers.
34. Leonard, *I Flew for China*, p. 196.
35. Ibid., p. 197.
36. Randall Gould to the author, June 19, 1968.
37. Charles S. Reed, II, consul, Hanoi, to the Secretary of State, March 12, 1940, SD File 893.796.
38. *North-China Herald*, Feb. 1, 1939; *New York Times*, March 1, 1939; W. Leonard Parker, vice consul, Rangoon, to the Secretary of State, Aug. 17, 1939, SD File 893.796; Minutes of the 40th Meeting of the Board of Directors, China National Aviation Corporation, June 22, 1940, Young Papers.
39. *China Weekly Review*, Nov. 2 and 23, 1940; *North-China Herald*, Nov. 6, 1940; Ambassador Grew to Yosuke Matsuoka, Minister for Foreign Affairs, Nov. 8, 1940, and Matsuoka to Grew, Dec. 8, 1940, *FRUS, Japan, 1931–1941*, 2 vols. (Washington, D.C., 1943), 1: 700–2, 705–6.
40. Bond to Allison, Dec. 1, 1940, Allison Papers.
41. *North-China Herald*, Feb. 5 and March 19, 1941.
42. *New Horizons*, XI (Aug. 1941), 11–12.
43. Chang Kia-ngau, "Development of Civil Aviation in China"; Foreign Air Transport Division, CAB, "China National Aviation Corporation," Jan. 31, 1946, PAA Records; China National Aviation Corporation, "Financial Report for the year 1940," n.d., and Bond to Bixby, June 27, 1940, Young Papers.
44. Woods to the author, July 19, 1969; Bond to Sharp, Dec. 9, 1938, Young Papers.
45. Bond to Bixby, June 27 and Sept. 24, 1940, Young Papers.
46. Young, *China and the Helping Hand*, pp. 107–24; Allison to Kung, Feb. 21, 1940, and Bond to Kung, May 29, 1940, Young Papers.
47. Young memorandum, "Recommendations Re Air Transport of Freight," March 16, 1940, Young Papers.
48. Minutes of the 40th Meeting of the Board of Directors, China National Aviation Corporation, June 22, 1940, and Bond to Bixby, Jan.

3, 1941, Young Papers. As it worked out, CNAC operated three aircraft and Eurasia operated two.

49. Memorandum, "Hong Kong–Nanshiung Freight Service," n.d., and Bond to Bixby, Feb. 22, 1941, Young Papers.

50. Morgenthau memorandum for the President, "Preliminary Report on the Possibility of Financial Assistance to China," July 15, 1940, enclosing Soong memorandum, "Aid to China," July 12, 1940; printed in United States Senate, Committee on the Judiciary, *Morgenthau Diary (China)* (Washington, D.C., 1965), pp. 177–79.

51. Bond to Bixby, Dec. 2, 1940, Young Papers.

52. Woods to the author, Aug. 30, 1967.

53. Bond to Bixby, Dec. 2, 1940, and April 19, 1944, Young Papers.

54. Young memorandum, "Non-military Aviation Equipment for China," March 26, 1941, Young Papers.

55. Bond to Bixby, March 30, 1941, Young Papers.

56. Young memorandum, "Conversation at New York between Messrs. Trippe, Bixby, Cooper and Reynolds of Pan American, and Dr. T. V. Soong and Dr. Arthur Young," Nov. 6, 1940, Young Papers.

57. Currie to the author, Sept. 16, 1970.

58. Bond memorandum, "Air Freight Service Into China," May 8, 1941, Young Papers.

59. Young memorandum, "Conversation between Currie, Bond, Bixby, Reynolds, Corcoran, and Young," May 22, 1941, Young Papers; Currie to the author, Sept. 16, 1970.

60. Charles F. Romanus and Riley Sunderland, *Stilwell's Mission to China* (Washington, D.C., 1953), pp. 20–21; Young to Bixby, Aug. 28, 1941, Young Papers.

61. Bond to Chang Kia-ngau, Minister of Communications, July 5, 1941, Young Papers.

62. Ibid.

63. Bond to Bixby, April 19, 1944, Young Papers; Young memorandum, "First Flight India-China, via the Tibetan border," Nov. 30, 1941, copy supplied to the author by Dr. Young.

CHAPTER 5

1. Bond to Bixby, Dec. 17, 1941, Young Papers.

2. *New Horizons*, XII (Dec. 1942), 13; Harold Sweet, "Whistling Willie," *Douglas Airview*, April 1943, pp. 4–7; Bond memorandum, "Report on Operations during 1942," Feb. 24, 1943, Young Papers.

3. Bond to Bixby, Dec. 17, 1941, Young Papers; Paul Frillman and Graham Peck, *China—The Remembered Life* (Boston, 1968), pp. 36–39.

NOTES 253

4. Hayaski and Coox, *Kōgun*, pp. 36-39.
5. Soong memorandum, Jan. 30, 1942, copy supplied to the author by the Hoover Institution, Stanford University.
6. Romanus and Sunderland, *Stilwell's Mission to China*, p. 165. See also Barbara W. Tuchman, *Stilwell and the American Experience in China, 1911-45* (New York, 1970), pp. 240-41.
7. Harry Dexter White memorandum, "Conference in Mr. White's office [with T. V. Soong]," Jan. 31, 1942, *Morgenthau Diary (China)*, I, 661-62.
8. For wartime strategic planning, see Louis Morton, "Germany First: The Basic Concept of Allied Strategy in World War II," in Kent Roberts Greenfield (ed.), *Command Decisions* (New York, 1959), pp. 3-38.
9. Wesley Frank Craven and James Lea Cate (eds.), *The Army Air Forces in World War II*, 7 vols. (Chicago, 1948-1958), 1: 134; 7: 114-15.
10. Ibid., 1: 497-98; 7: 114-15; Gen. H. H. Arnold, Commanding General, Army Air Forces, to the Acting Secretary of State, April 18, 1942, *FRUS, 1942: China* (Washington, D.C., 1956), pp. 677-78.
11. M. X. Quinn Shaughnessy, adviser to China Defense Supplies, to Louis A. Johnson, President Roosevelt's personal representative in India, n.d., enclosed in Johnson to the Secretary of State, April 16, 1942, ibid., pp. 675-77; Young to Soong, March 11, 1942, and Minutes of the 42nd Meeting of the Board of Directors, China National Aviation Corporation, July 1942, Young Papers.
12. Shaughnessy to Johnson, *FRUS, 1942: China*, pp. 675-77.
13. Doolittle to the author, July 18, 1969.
14. Agenda of the 42nd Meeting of the Board of Directors, China National Aviation Corporation, July 1942, Young Papers; "Brief of Pan American Airways, Inc., before the Civil Aeronautics Board," Docket No. 1499, Feb. 17, 1947, PAA Records.
15. Young to Soong, May 13, 1942, Young Papers.
16. Calvin H. Oakes, Division of Near Eastern Affairs, memorandum of meeting with Johnson, Herrington, et al., May 26, 1942, *FRUS, 1942: China*, pp. 56-57.
17. Bond memorandum, "Report on Operations during 1942," Feb. 24, 1943, Young Papers; Hornbeck memorandum, May 29, 1942, *FRUS, 1942: China*, pp. 59-60.
18. Roosevelt to Arnold, May 4, 1942, quoted in Romanus and Sunderland, *Stilwell's Mission to China*, p. 164; Smyth, Division of Far Eastern Affairs, memorandum, Aug. 19, 1942, SD File 893.24; American Chargé in India to the Secretary of State, June 21, 1942, *FRUS, 1942: China*, pp. 580-82; Craven and Cate (eds.), *The Army Air Forces*, I, 512-13; *The Stilwell Papers* (New York, 1948), p. 119.

19. Romanus and Sunderland, *Stilwell's Mission to China*, p. 167; China National Aviation Corporation, "Special Shipments during May, June and July 1942," n.d., Young Papers.

20. Johnson to Hull, May 12, 1942, *FRUS, 1942: China*, pp. 677–78; Hornbeck memorandum for the Under Secretary of State, April 17, 1942, ibid., p. 677.

21. Romanus and Sunderland, *Stilwell's Mission to China*, p. 167; Craven and Cate (eds.), *The Army Air Forces*, 4: 413.

22. Craven and Cate (eds.), *The Army Air Forces*, 4: 411–13.

23. Willauer memorandum, "Conference with General Bissell," Nov. 20, 1942, the Papers of Whiting Willauer, Firestone Library, Princeton University; Craven and Cate (eds.), *The Army Air Forces*, 4: 120. The debate over capacity of the India-China airlift continued throughout the war and into later historical accounts. Basically, tonnage estimates depended upon definition of terms: type of aircraft, allowable take-off weight, route, availability of spare parts, experience of crews, maintenance facilities, and the extent of enemy opposition, among other things. Bissell tended to use the most adverse set of variables, while Sinclair was more optimistic. As time passed, circumstances favored Sinclair's estimates.

24. Craven and Cate (eds.), *The Army Air Forces*, 7: 120–21.

25. Agenda of the 42nd Meeting of the Board of Directors, China National Aviation Corporation, July 1942, Young Papers; Agenda of the 43rd Meeting of the Board of Directors, China National Aviation Corporation, Feb. 24, 1943, Young Papers; Craven and Cate (eds.), *The Army Air Forces*, 1: 506; Bond memorandum, "Report on Operations during 1942," Feb. 24, 1943, Young Papers; Oliver La Farge, *The Eagle in the Egg* (Boston, 1949), pp. 92–93; memorandum, "Report of CNAC," March 15, 1943, PAA Records.

26. China National Aviation Corporation, "Operating Report for the Year 1943," n.d.; "Special Shipments during May, June and July 1942," n.d.; "Report of the Business Department," Feb. 15, 1943; "Tonnage Carried by Our Freight Service for the Chinese Government and Allied Nations Organizations during the year 1942," n.d.; all in Young Papers.

27. Agenda of the 43rd Meeting of the Board of Directors, China National Aviation Corporation, Feb. 24, 1943, Young Papers.

28. Bond memorandum, "Report on Operations during 1942," Feb. 24, 1943, Young Papers.

29. Bond to Colonel Cheng Fu Wang, April 15, 1943, Young Papers.

30. Craven and Cate (eds.), *The Army Air Forces*, 7: 122–24; La Farge, *Eagle in the Egg*, p. 114.

31. Craven and Cate (eds.), *The Army Air Forces*, 7: 124; *Eagle in the Egg*, pp. 116–17.

32. Quoted in La Farge, *Eagle in the Egg*, pp. 116–17.

NOTES   255

33. Craven and Cate (eds.), *The Army Air Forces*, 7: 125.
34. *The Stilwell Papers*, pp. 217-18. Stilwell's preliminary tonnage figures for June and July proved optimistic.
35. Craven and Cate (eds.), *The Army Air Forces*, 4: 446.
36. Ibid., 446-48.
37. Ibid., VII, 129.
38. Ibid., 131-32. Hugh Woods, CNAC's chief pilot, recalled a meeting he had before the war with Gen. H. H. Arnold, commander of the Air Force, during which Woods explained the advanced techniques of instrument flying that had been developed by CNAC. "General Arnold," writes Woods, "seemed genuinely interested in the description I gave him of our procedures although there is little indication he made use of my information. Had he done so and incorporated the experience and technology that we had developed into Air Force training, hundred and hundreds of pilots' lives would have been saved in World War II. It was absolutely cruel and inhuman to send those boys out in hazardous weather conditions on the 'Hump' run with their lack of background training, and it wasn't until sometime after the war that the Air Force High Command realized this." Woods to the author, July 19, 1969. An Air Force historian has commented: "The nature and extent of the instrument indoctrination given to pilots of basic schools were insufficient until late in 1943, partly because of the traditional peace-time attitude of training officers who subordinated instrument work to conventional visual maneuvers." Craven and Cate (eds.), *The Army Air Forces*, 6: 570-71.
39. White, "China's Last Lifeline"; Lin Yutang, "Flying over the Hump," *Asia*, 44 (Dec. 1944), 555-57.
40. Bond to Bixby, Feb. 2, 1943, PAA Records.
41. Colonel Cheng Fu Wang to Bond, April 30, 1943, Young Papers. On Rosbert's adventure, see C. J. Rosbert, "Only God Knew The Way," *Saturday Evening Post*, Feb. 12, 1944, pp. 11ff.
42. Bond to Wang, April 15, 1943, Young Papers.
43. Bond to K. C. Lee, Oct. 18, 1943, Young Papers.
44. Minutes of a Special Meeting of the Board of Directors, China National Aviation Corporation, Dec. 30, 1943, Young Papers.
45. Young to H. H. Kung, Sept. 21, 1943; Bond to Bixby, Sept. 2, 1943, and Nov. 6, 1943, SD File 893.796.
46. China National Aviation Corporation, "Operating Report for the Year 1943," n.d., Young Papers.
47. Bond memorandum, "Air Freight Service Into China," May 8, 1941, Young Papers.
48. Donald McBride to the author, March 15 and April 14, 1969.
49. McDonald's talk was recalled many years later by a number of pilots. The specifics are taken from a memorandum, "McDonald to All

Flight Crews," June 24, 1943, copy in China National Aviation Corporation, *Route Manual*, 1943. The author is indebted to Al Mah for a copy of the *Manual*.

50. *Route Manual*.

51. Interview with Pottschmidt, July 4, 1969; interview with Al Mah, July 3, 1969.

52. McBride to the author, March 15, 1969.

53. *Route Manual*.

54. Al Mah, with more than 4,000 hours, a good part of it command time in multi-engine equipment, checked out in two weeks. James Dalby arrived with 1,600 hours and no multi-engine experience; he flew 33 round trips over the Hump in two months before being checked out. Interview with Mah, July 3, 1969; interview with Dalby, Jan. 15, 1969. Also, Bixby to Mah, May 20, 1943, and collection of letters and newspaper clippings supplied to the author by Mr. Mah.

55. J. Gen Genovese, *We Flew Without Guns* (Philadelphia, 1945), pp. 155-56.

56. Interview with Al Mah, July 3, 1969; McDonald memorandum to All Flight Crews, July 20, 1943, *Route Manual*.

57. Arthur Young noted with respect to smuggling: "Smuggling has been a serious problem for CNAC to control, in view of the shortage of goods in China and the ease of making big profits by irregularly bringing in currency, gold, or goods of small bulk and high value. The constant movement of company personnel in and out of China provides constant opportunity and temptation. The U. S. Army faces a similar situation, which has been a serious problem to them also. CNAC has issued many orders and warning to personnel about smuggling. A considerable number of employees, including several foreigners, have been discharged for smuggling offenses." Young memorandum, "CNAC Action Re Smuggling," Aug. 12, 1943, Young Papers. See also Hugh L. Woods, "Organizing the Assam Airlift into China," *Wings Over Asia: A Brief History of China National Aviation Corporation* (privately printed for the China National Aviation Association Corporation, 1971), pp. 22-26.

58. Craven and Cate (eds.), *The Army Air Forces*, 7: 140, 142-43.

59. Foreign Air Transport Division, CAB , "China National Aviation Corporation," Jan. 31, 1946, PAA Records; *New Horizons*, XV (Oct.-Dec. 1945), 16; interview with Pottschmidt, July 4, 1969; newspaper clipping supplied by Al Mah; Milton E. Miles, *A Different Kind of War* (New York, 1967), pp. 414, 570.

60. Charles F. Romanus and Riley Sunderland, *Stilwell's Command Problems* (Washington, D.C., 1956), pp. 19-20, 289-90; China National Aviation Corporation, "Operating Report for the Year 1943," n.d., Young Papers; Gordon Tweedy to Bixby, Dec. 19, 1944, SD File

893.796; Willauer memorandum, "United States Military and Lend-Lease Relations with China from 1941 through September 1944," n.d. [c. 1945], Willauer Papers.

61. Tweedy to Bixby, Dec. 19, 1944, SD File 893.796; China National Aviation Corporation, "Inward and Outward Shipments Carried by CNAC Planes, January 1944-September 1945," n.d., Young Papers.

62. Interview with Pottschmidt, July 4, 1969.

63. McBride to the author, April 4, 1968. The diary is in the possession of Mr. McBride, Orchard, Nebraska.

64. Bond writes of this incident: "They bailed out over the Chengtu Plains. Scoff did a wonderful job. He knew he was over the Chengtu Plains when he realized he was in trouble, that he had gone past Kunming owing to an incorrect bearing given him by the ground control in Kunming, which was due to an 180° ambiguity in the system. If you passed the loop while they were tracking other planes, but did not know that this had happened, then the bearing they gave you could be 180° off. If the traffic was not too heavy this would be detected by the signals becoming weaker, but if reception was bad this could effect the 'readings' given you. Scoff, when he knew he had to bail out, put the plane on automatic pilot, got parachutes on his crew and himself, and one by one forced the side door open and shoved them out. He then forced the door open and squirmed out only to find that his parachute harness had hung on the door handle on the inside and he was hanging on the outside of the plane. He managed to pull himself up by the outside door handle, get his knees against the side of the plane, pull the door open, reach inside, unhook himself and drop. Damn!! what an experience. The co-pilot and radio operator, both Chinese, got to Chengtu two days later. Scoff got in the next day." Bond to the author, Sept. 20, 1970.

65. James Dalby recalls that during the winter of 1944-45 CNAC could not find sufficient Chinese copilots and radio operators. As a result, he writes, "we were given a choice of a radio operator *or* a co-pilot. We almost always wanted the radio operator, if possible, because they were usually good and almost always spoke English. Some of the co-pilots were so new that they hadn't even been in an airplane as a passenger before. I believe that I am the only one that ever flew over the Hump without anyone else in the airplane. In the winter of 1945 I made two round trips across the Hump by myself. Both these trips were on the same day. Between apprehension and fatigue it wasn't much fun." Dalby to the author, Sept. 15, 1970.

66. McBride to the author, Sept. 20, 1970.

67. Ambassador Gauss to the Secretary of State, March 26, 1942, *FRUS, 1942: China*, pp. 673-74; Division of Far Eastern Affairs memorandum, "Placing CNAC under National Commission on Aeronautical Affairs," April 1, 1942, SD File 893.796.

68. Welles to Gauss, April 4, 1942, and Gauss to the Secretary of State, April 10, 1942, *FRUS, 1942: China*, pp. 674–75.

69. *The Stilwell Papers*, p. 148; Wheeler to Bond, Sept. 22, 1942, Young Papers.

70. Agenda of the 43rd Meeting of the Board of Directors, China National Aviation Corporation, Feb. 24, 1943, and Young memorandum, "Operation of CNAC Lend Lease Aircraft," n.d. [c. Nov. 1942], Young Papers; Contract W–1002–S.O.S.–4, "Air Transportation Service of Personnel, Supplies and Other Material," approved Feb. 17, 1943, PAA Records.

71. Young, *China and the Helping Hand*, p. 248; Romanus and Sunderland, *Stilwell's Command Problems*, p. 312; Willauer memorandum for T. V. Soong, Jan. 1, 1944, Willauer Papers.

72. China National Aviation Corporation, "Report of the Business Department for 1942," Feb. 15, 1943, Young Papers; *New York Times*, March 16, 1942; Sharp to the Managing Director, March 28, 1942, Young Papers.

73. "Report on Operations during 1942," Feb. 24, 1943, Young Papers.

74. Agenda of the 43rd Meeting of the Board of Directors, China National Aviation Corporation, Feb. 24, 1943, Young Papers; Secretary Hull to Ambassador Gauss, Jan. 23, 1943, and Acting Secretary Adolph E. Berle, Jr., to Hopkins, March 2, 1943, *FRUS, 1943: China* (Washington, D.C., 1957), pp. 662, 664–65.

75. Agenda of the 43rd Meeting of the Board of Directors, China National Aviation Corporation, Feb. 24, 1943, Young Papers; Gauss to Hull, Feb. 26, 1943, *FRUS, 1943: China*, p. 662.

76. Hornbeck memorandum to Berle, Feb. 27, 1943, *FRUS, 1943: China*, pp. 662–63.

77. Berle to Hopkins, March 2, 1943, ibid., pp. 664–65.

78. Hopkins to Berle, March 26, 1943, ibid., pp. 668–69.

79. State Department memorandum, "China Commercial Aviation," June 19, 1943, SD File 893.796; Young memorandum, Aug. 6, 1943, Young Papers; Chargé Atcheson to the Secretary of State, Aug. 9, 1943; *FRUS, 1943: China*, pp. 676–77.

80. Atcheson to the Secretary of State, Aug. 9, 1943, *FRUS, 1943: China*, pp. 676–77; Young memorandum, "Need for Planes for the Service of the China National Aviation Corporation," Feb. 1, 1944, Young Papers. See also Young's *China and the Helping Hand*, p. 249.

81. On Hornbeck's role in the development of policy, see his notes in SD File 893.796, especially for Aug. 14 and 25, 1943.

82. Langdon memorandum, "Position of China National Aviation Corporation in Chinese Internal Air Transport," Aug. 20, 1943, *FRUS, 1943: China*, pp. 678–81.

83. Hull to Hopkins, Sept. 1, 1943, ibid., pp. 681-82; Hull to Arnold, Sept. 1, 1943, SD File 893.24.
84. Giles to Hull, Sept. 5, 1943, SD File 893.24; Lt. G. E. Bennett, assistant secretary, Munitions Assignment Committee (Air), to the Secretary of State, Oct. 13, 1943, ibid.
85. John Carter Vincent to Hull, September 16, 1943, ibid.; Young memorandum, "Need for Planes," Feb. 1, 1944, Young Papers.
86. Bond to the author, Sept. 20, 1970.
87. Minutes of a Special Meeting of the Board of Directors, China National Aviation Corporation, Dec. 30, 1943, Young Papers; "Articles of Agreement for Air Transportation," June 1, 1944, and Foreign Air Transport Division, CAB, "China National Aviation Corporation," Jan. 31, 1946, PAA Records.
88. Bond to K. C. Lee, March 26, 1944, Young Papers; "Articles of Agreement," June 1, 1944, PAA Records.
89. Bond to Lee, March 26, 1944, and Young to Bond, March 22, 1944, Young Papers.
90. Foreign Air Transport Division, CAB, "China National Aviation Corporation," Jan. 31, 1946, PAA Records.
91. Ibid.; Young memorandum, Jan. 7, 1944, Young Papers; "Brief of Pan American Airways," Feb. 17, 1947, PAA Records.
92. Bond memorandum, "The Future Position of CNAC," Nov. 25, 1943, Young Papers.
93. Bond to the author, June 3, 1968.
94. Ibid.
95. Ibid.
96. Ibid.
97. "Brief of Pan American Airways," Feb. 17, 1947, PAA Records; Bond to the author, June 3, 1969.
98. Young to Bixby, Dec. 1, 1945, Young Papers.

CHAPTER 6

1. Bond to Bixby, Sept. 22, 1945, the Papers of Quentin Roosevelt, in the possession of Frances Roosevelt, Oyster Bay, N.Y.
2. Gordon B. Tweedy memorandum, "Civil Aviation in China," n.d. [c. Aug. 1947], copy supplied to the author by Mr. Tweedy; Foreign Air Transport Division, CAB, "China National Aviation Corporation," Jan. 31, 1946, PAA Records; Bond to the author, Sept. 25, 1970; Young memorandum, "Cost of Aviation in China," May 14, 1946, Young Papers.
3. Tweedy memorandum, "Civil Aviation in China," n.d. [c. Aug. 1947]; *China Weekly Review*, Oct. 11, 1947; Young memorandum, Aug. 3, 1947; Bond to Bixby, July 23, [1946], PAA Records.

4. Young memorandum, "Cost of Aviation in China," May 14, 1946, Young Papers.

5. For one proposal to rationalize China's postwar air service, see the folder, "Proposed China Air Transport Expansion Project," PAA Records.

6. Ministry of Information, *China Handbook, 1937–1945* (New York, 1947), pp. 236–38.

7. "Central Air Transport Corp. Grows Rapidly," *China Economist*, 2 (Aug. 1948), 203; *World Aviation Annual, 1948* (Washington, D.C., 1948), pp. 507–8.

8. On CAT, see my "Portrait of a Cold War Warrior: Whiting Willauer and Civil Air Transport," *Modern Asian Studies*, 5 (1971), 373–88.

9. McBride to the author, March 15, 1969; interview with J. R. Rossi, July 4, 1969.

10. Cedric Mah to the author, Sept. 30, 1968; Al Mah to the author, May 28, 1968.

11. Cedric Mah to the author, Sept. 30, 1968; Al Mah to the author, May 28, 1968.

12. John Robinson Beal, *Marshall in China* (New York, 1970), p. 12.

13. Ibid.; Bond to the author, June 3, 1969.

14. Bond to the author, June 28, 1969; interview with Bond, Aug. 24, 1967; Bond to Bixby, July 23, [1946], PAA Records.

15. Reynolds to his wife, Jan. 2, 1947, copy supplied to the author by Mr. Reynolds.

16. *New York Times*, Jan. 7, 27, 30, 1947.

17. *China Weekly Review*, Jan. 25, 1947.

18. Reynolds to his wife, Jan. 2, 1947.

19. Interview with Bond, Aug. 24, 1967; Roosevelt to Frances Roosevelt, Feb. 21, 1947, Roosevelt to Bixby, April 7, 1947, Tweedy to Roosevelt, April 30, 1947, Roosevelt Papers.

20. *Life*, 8 (Jan. 8, 1940), 30–37; *New York Times*, Dec. 22, 1948.

21. Department of State, *United States Relations with China, with Special Reference to the Period 1944–1949* (Washington, D.C., 1949), pp. 221, 361; Roosevelt to Frances Roosevelt, Feb. 21, 1947, and Roosevelt to Bixby, April 7, 1947, Roosevelt Papers.

22. Roosevelt to Bixby, April 7, 1947, Roosevelt Papers.

23. Ibid.

24. Bond to Roosevelt, n.d. [c. spring 1947], Roosevelt Papers.

25. Roosevelt to Frances Roosevelt, March 5, 1947, Roosevelt Papers.

26. *United States Relations with China*, pp. 317–18, 361.

27. Tweedy memorandum, "Civil Aviation in China," n.d. [c. Aug.

1947], and Tweedy to Colonel Liu, July 28, 1947, copies supplied to the author by Mr. Tweedy; Bixby to Trippe, Nov. 26, 1947, and Bixby to Bond, Nov. 28, 1947, Roosevelt Papers; Allison, "Operations Report, 1947," n.d. [c. Jan. 1948], Allison Papers; *China Handbook, 1950* (New York, 1950), pp. 626–28; *China Press*, Oct. 6, 1947.

28. *China Handbook, 1950*, pp. 629–31; Leary, "Portrait of a Cold War Warrior."

29. Roosevelt to Bixby, July 8, 1947, and Bixby to Trippe, Nov. 26, 1947, Roosevelt Papers.

30. Tweedy to Roosevelt, March 25, 1948, Roosevelt Papers.

31. Ibid.

32. Roosevelt to Bixby, Nov. 20, 1948, Roosevelt Papers.

33. Tweedy to Roosevelt, March 25, 1948, Roosevelt Papers.

34. Roosevelt to Frances Roosevelt, May 9, 1948, Roosevelt Papers.

35. Roosevelt to Bixby, June 15, 1948, Roosevelt Papers.

36. Roosevelt to Bixby, July 5 and 29, 1948, Roosevelt Papers; *New York Times*, July 18, 1948.

37. *United States Relations with China*, p. 400.

38. Stuart to Secretary of State Marshall, Aug. 23, 1948, ibid., p. 877.

39. Roosevelt to Bixby, Nov. 20, 1948, Roosevelt Papers.

40. Tweedy to Roosevelt, March 25, 1948, Roosevelt Papers.

41. Bixby to Trippe, April 22, 1948, Roosevelt Papers.

42. Roosevelt to Bixby, July 29, 1948, and Roosevelt to Daniel Longwell, July 20, 1948, Roosevelt Papers.

43. Roosevelt to Bixby, Aug. 3 and Sept. 7, 1948, Roosevelt Papers.

44. Bond to Harold E. Gray, Oct. 15, 1948, PAA Records.

45. Roosevelt to Bixby, Nov. 20, 1948, Roosevelt Papers; Ralph Mitchell to his family, Nov. 1, 1948, copy supplied to the author by Mr. Mitchell.

46. Leary, "Portrait of a Cold War Warrior."

47. Roosevelt to Bixby, Nov. 23, 1948, Roosevelt Papers.

48. Roosevelt to Bixby, Nov. 20, 1948, Roosevelt Papers.

49. Ibid.

50. Bixby to Roosevelt, Oct. 6, 1948, Roosevelt Papers.

51. Ralph Mitchell to his family, Dec. 26, 1948, copy supplied to the author by Mr. Mitchell.

52. Ibid.; Allison to the author, n.d. [c. Oct. 1, 1970]; *New York Times*, Dec. 22, 1948.

53. Allison to the author, n.d. [c. Oct. 1, 1970].

54. Ralph Mitchell to his family, Dec. 26, 1948.

55. Frances Roosevelt to her family, n.d. [c. Dec. 1948], Roosevelt Papers. Bond has written to the author, Sept. 25, 1970, that Frances

Roosevelt "was one of the bravest people I ever knew. She was doing a sketch of my wife when Quentin was killed. She finished it while arranging to go home. The tragedy that was in her heart she unknowingly put in my wife's eyes. It was a long time before we could hang it."

56. Bixby to Trippe et al., June 19, 1947, PAA Records.

57. Tang Tsou, *America's Failure in China* (Chicago, 1963), p. 497; F. F. Liu, *A Military History of Modern China, 1924–1949* (Princeton, 1956), pp. 264–70.

58. Bixby to Trippe et al., June 19, 1949, PAA Records.

59. Bixby to Vice President, J. T. Towers, Aug. 5, 1949, PAA Records.

60. Ibid.

61. Ibid.

62. Bixby to Trippe et al., June 19, 1949, PAA Records; *New York Times*, Aug. 13, 17, and 28, 1949.

63. Bond to K. L. Rankin, American Consul General, Hong Kong, Oct. 18, 1949, PAA Records.

64. Bond to Towers, Oct. 20, 1949, PAA Records.

65. Ibid.

66. Bond to Towers, Nov. 11, 1949, PAA Records.

67. Towers memorandum, "CNAC," Nov. 11–Dec. 30, 1949, and Bixby to Vice President Dean, Nov. 18, 1949, PAA Records; *South China Morning Post*, Nov. 12, 1949.

68. Bond to Towers, Nov. 17, 1949, PAA Records.

69. See my "Aircraft and Anti-Communists: CAT in Action, 1949–52," *China Quarterly*, 52 (1972), 654–69.

70. Bixby memorandum, Dec. 15, 1949, Towers to Bixby, Jan. 5, 1949 [1950], Merchant to Bixby, Jan. 6, 1950, PAA Records.

71. Towers to Bixby, Jan. 5, 1949 [1950], PAA Records.

72. Minutes of the Board of Directors' Meeting, CNAC, Dec. 31, 1949, and Minutes of the Shareholders' Meeting, CNAC, Dec. 31, 1949, Willauer Papers.

73. Leary, "Aircraft and Anti-Communists."

74. "Air Transport in the Chinese People's Republic," *Interavia* (Geneva), 11 (Jan. 1956), 46–47.

CONCLUSION

1. Telephone interview with Juan Trippe, Jan. 15, 1969; C. Y. W. Meng, "Foreign Enterprise in Postwar China," *Far Eastern Survey*, 12 (Nov. 3, 1943), 212–19.

2. C. C. Liang to Arthur N. Young, Feb. 20, 1969, original supplied to the author by Dr. Young; interview with Allison, Nov. 18, 1968.

BIBLIOGRAPHY

PRIMARY SOURCES

A. *Unpublished Papers, Letters, Diaries, and Archival Records*

Allison, Ernest M. Papers. In the possession of Mr. Allison, Arcadia, Cal.
Arnold, Julean. Papers. Hoover Institution, Stanford University.
Bixby, Harold M. "Top Side Ricksha," n.d. [*circa*. 1938]. In the possession of Mrs. Harold M. Bixby, Bolton Landing, N.Y.
Keys, Clement M. Papers. Firestone Library, Princeton University.
MacMurray, John Van Antwerp. Papers. Firestone Library, Princeton University.
McBride, Donald. Diary. In the possession of Mr. McBride, Orchard, Neb.
Mitchell, Hewitt F. Diary and Letters. In the possession of Ralph F. Mitchell, Los Altos, Cal.
Mitchell, Ralph F. Letters. In the possession of Mr. Mitchell, Los Altos, Cal.
Pan American Airways. Records. Pan Am Building, New York, N.Y.
Price, Ernest M. Papers. In the possession of the Price Family, Los Gatos, Cal.
Reynolds, Lincoln C. Papers. In the possession of Mr. Reynolds, San Mateo, Cal.
Roosevelt, Quentin. Papers. In the possession of Mrs. Quentin Roosevelt, Oyster Bay, N.Y.
United States Department of Commerce Archives. National Archives, Washington, D.C.
United States Department of State Archives. National Archives, Washington, D.C.

Westervelt, George Conrad. Papers. University of Virginia Library.
Willauer, Whiting. Papers. Firestone Library, Princeton University.
Young, Arthur N. Papers. Hoover Institution, Stanford University.

B. Published Documents

United States Civil Aeronautics Authority. *Decisions of the Civil Aeronautics Authority, February 1939 to July 1940.* Washington, D.C., 1941.

United States Civil Aeronautics Board, Foreign Air Transport Division. "China National Aviation Corporation," Jan. 31, 1946.

United States Department of Commerce, Bureau of Foreign and Domestic Commerce, Office of the Commercial Attaché, Shanghai. *China Monthly Trade Report.*

United States Department of State. *Papers Relating to the Foreign Relations of the United States.* Beginning in 1932, the title changed to *Foreign Relations of the United States: Diplomatic Papers.* All were printed in Washington, D.C. *1929* (3 vols. 1943–44), vol. 2; *1933* (5 vols. 1949–52), vol. 3; *1935* (4 vols. 1953), vol. 3; *1936* (5 vols. 1953–54), vol. 4; *1937* (5 vols. 1954), vol. 4; *1938* (5 vols. 1954–56), vol. 4; *1939* (5 vols. 1955–57), vol. 4; *1941* (7 vols. 1956–63), vol. 5; *1942, China* (1956); *1943, China* (1957); *Japan, 1931–1941* (2 vols. 1943), vol. 1.

———. *United States Relations With China, With Special Reference to the Period 1944–1949.* Washington, D.C., 1949.

United States Senate, Committee on the Judiciary. *Morgenthau Diary (China).* 2 vols. Washington, D.C., 1965.

C. Correspondence and Interviews

Ernest M. Allison, Ralph S. Barnaby, William L. Bond, Chang Kai-ngau, Hugh Chen, Ki Chun, Lauchlin Currie, James M. Dalby, James H. Doolittle, Rieta Westervelt du Manoir, Randall Gould, Doris Kent LeBlanc, Chin-chao Liang, Charles A. Lindbergh, Al

Mah, Cedric Mah, James R. McCleskey, Donald McBride, William C. McDonald, Ralph F. Mitchell, Walter Palmer, William D. Pawley, Robert W. Pottschmidt, Walter R. Quinn, Lincoln C. Reynolds, J. R. Rossi, George J. Schlenker, Charles L. Sharp, Jerry Sloniger, Zigmund Soldinsky, Juan T. Trippe, Gordon B. Tweedy, Charles S. Vaughn, Hugh L. Woods, Arthur N. Young, Clarence M. Young.

D. *Books, Newspapers, Periodicals, and other material contemporary to events discussed in the book*

Aeronautical Chamber of Commerce of America. *The Aircraft Year Book for 1934*. New York, 1934.
"Aeronautical Progress in China," *China Weekly Review*, April 27, 1929.
"Air Cargo Eclipses Burma Road's Record Set with 4,500 Trucks," *Air Transportation*, 4 (April 1944), 27–32.
"The Air Mail Problem in China," *Far Eastern Review*, 26 (Feb. 1930), 59–62.
"American Aircraft for the Orient," *Far Eastern Review*, 16 (July 1920), 343–48.
Arnold, Julean. "New Transportation for China," *Asia*, 34 (Nov. 1934), 664–70.
Burton, Wilbur. "The Airplane: Most Effective Weapon of State Ever Devised and Its Application in China," *China Weekly Review*, Oct. 20, 1934.
———. "'Mandate from Heaven,'" *Asia*, 35 (Aug. 1935), 458–65.
Campbell, K. Reid. "Aircraft Finance during 1929," *Aviation*, 28 (Feb. 1930), 315–17.
"Central Air Transport Corp. Grows Rapidly," *China Economist*, 2 (Aug. 1948), 203.
Chang Kai-ngau. "Development of Civil Aviation in China," *China Quarterly*, 4 (Autumn 1939), 601–13.
Chang, Walter K. S. "Aviation in China," *China Weekly Review*, Sept. 3, 1932.
Chennault, Claire Lee. *Way of a Fighter*. New York, 1949.
"The China National Aviation Corporation," *Far Eastern Review*, 21 (Feb. 1935), 77.

Ching, Theodore. "Commercial Aviation in China," *Far Eastern Review*, 24 (May 1928), 221, 224.
"Commercial Aviation in China," *China Weekly Review*, July 22, 1933.
"The Country's Aeronautic Project," *Chinese Economic Bulletin*, 14 (June 1929), 274-77.
"The Curtiss-Wright Corporation," *Aero Digest*, 24 (April 1934), 28-35, 60.
Dai Enki. "Aviation in China," *Far Eastern Review*, 33 (May 1937), 199-200, 205.
———. "The First Five Years of Commercial Aviation Activity in China," *China Weekly Review*, Dec. 22, 1934.
"The Dragon in Flight," *Aviation*, 32 (April 1933), 114-15.
Folson, Kenneth E. "The China National Aviation Corporation." Unpublished senior thesis, Princeton University, 1943.
Forman, Harrison. "China Spreads Her Wings," *Aviation*, 35 (May 1936), 11-14.
———. "Following the West," *Aviation*, 33 (May 1934), 148-49.
Friedman, Irving S. "Air Lines Preserve China's Outside Contacts," *Far Eastern Survey*, 8 (Dec. 1939), 284-86.
Gellhorn, Martha. "Flight Into Peril," *Collier's*, 105 (May 31, 1941), 21, 85-87.
Genovese, J. Gen. *We Flew Without Guns*. Philadelphia, 1945.
Gould, Randall. *China in the Sun*. New York, 1946.
———. "China Spreads Her Wings," *China Weekly Review*, Aug. 31, 1929.
Grooch, William Stephen. *Skyway to Asia*. New York, 1936.
———. *Winged Highway*. New York, 1938.
Hall, Russell E. "China's Domestic Transport System," *Far Eastern Survey*, 6 (Nov. 1937), 253-57.
———. "Expanding Airways in the Far East," *Far Eastern Survey*, 6 (April 1937), 95-101.
Hynes, Kenneth M. "U. S.-China Air Trade," *Air Transportation*, 11 (Oct. 1947), 10-17.
Ingles, Glenn. "Building the New China," *Far Eastern Survey*, 13 (June 1944), 116-20.

Johnsen, Birger. "War Birds of the Far East," *New York Herald Tribune Magazine*, Feb. 28, 1932.
Jones, Charles S. "Curtiss-Wright Corporation, 1931-1932," *Curtiss-Wright Review*, 3 (Jan. 1932), 1-2, 9.
Jouett, John H. "War Planes Over China," *Asia*, 37 (1937), 827-30.
Kennedy, Craig. "Asiatic Aviation," *Aero Digest*, 16 (Jan. 1930), 55ff.
Kent, Walter C. "Wings for China," *Atlantic Monthly*, 160 (Aug. 1937), 644-48.
Keys, Clement M., et al. "What Are the Prospects for 1930?" *Aviation*, 28 (Feb. 1930), 290-305.
Leonard, Royal. *I Flew for China*. New York, 1942.
Lewis, Cecil. *Sagittarius Rising*. London, 1936.
Lin, Yutang. "Flying Over the Hump," *Asia*, 44 (Dec. 1944), 555-57.
"Loening Cabin Amphibian," *Aviation*, 24 (April 1928), 888ff.
Loh, Han-chin. "Commercial Aviation," *The Chinese Year Book, 1937*. Shanghai, 1937.
"Memorandum on American Civil Aviation in the Pacific," *Far Eastern Survey*, May 1934, n.p.
Meng, C.Y.W. "Development of Airways in the 'Middle Kingdom,'" *China Weekly Review*, Aug. 6, 1932.
―――. "Foreign Enterprise in Postwar China," *Far Eastern Survey*, 12 (Nov. 1943), 212-19.
―――. "The Kweilin Tragedy and U. S. Policy," *China Weekly Review*, Sept. 17, 1938.
Murphy, Charles J. V. "Shanghai Reopened Under New Management," *Fortune*, 33 (Feb. 1946), 140-48, 206-23.
"Northern Aerial Link with Europe," *China at War*, 2 (June-July 1939), 50-52.
Olmstead, George. "Communications—China's Most Pressing Need," *China Weekly Review*, Dec. 15, 1945.
Osborn, Earl D. "The Industry's Progress During 1928," *Aviation*, 26 (Jan. 1929), 24-25, 64.
Payne, A. James. "Aviation Development in China," *Great Britian and the East*, 60 (Aug. 1943), 27, 29, 31.

Ray, J. Franklin. "Getting the Goods to China," *Far Eastern Survey*, 12 (March 1943), 51–54.
Reeves, Earl. "Why Aviation's Future is 'Strictly Business,'" *Forbes*, 23 (April 1929), 13, 48–51.
Rogers, Leighton W. "Competition in the World Market," *Aero Digest*, 16 (Jan. 1930), 51–53, 266.
Rosbert, C. J. "Only God Knew the Way," *Saturday Evening Post*, Feb. 12, 1944.
Snow, Edgar. "The 'Middle Kingdom' from the Clouds," *China Weekly Review*, Oct. 19, 1929.
Soo, Y. F. "Improvements Urged for China's Civil Aviation Operations," *China Weekly Review*, Jan. 25, 1947.
Stilwell, Joseph W. *The Stilwell Papers*. New York, 1948.
Swinehart, General D. E. "Aviation in North China," *Aviation*, 24 (March 1928), 636, 648.
T'ang Leang-Li (ed). *Reconstruction in China*. Shanghai, 1935.
Wang, George K. T. "Tibet and America to be Linked Up by Air," *China Weekly Review*, Feb. 24, 1934.
Weil, Kurt H. "Future of Air Transportation in Asia," 45 (Oct. 1945), 470–73.
White, Theodore H. "China's Last Lifeline," *Fortune*, 27 (May 1943), 105–10, 143ff.
———, and Jacoby, Annalee. *Thunder Out of China*. New York, 1946.
Woodhead, H. G. W. "Aviation," *The China Year Book, 1929–1930*. Shanghai, 1930.
———. "Aviation," *The China Year Book, 1931*. Shanghai, 1931.
———. "Aviation in China," *Oriental Affairs*, 1 (May 1934), 14–19.

SECONDARY SOURCES

Allen, G. C., and Donnithorne, Audrey G. *Western Enterprise in Far Eastern Economic Development: China and Japan*. London, 1954.
"Air Transport in the Chinese People's Republic," *Interavia* (Geneva), 11 (Jan. 1956), 46–47.

BIBLIOGRAPHY

Barnett, A. Doak. *China on the Eve of Communist Takeover*. London, 1963.
Beal, John Robinson. *Marshall in China*. New York, 1970.
Boorman, Harold L., and Howard, Richard C. (eds.). *Biographical Dictionary of Republican China*. 4 vols., New York, 1967-71.
Borg, Dorothy. *The United States and the Far Eastern Crisis of 1933-1938*. Cambridge, Mass., 1964.
Buhite, Russell D. *Nelson T. Johnson and American Policy Toward China, 1925-1941*. East Lansing, Mich., 1968.
Burden, William A. M. *The Struggle for Airways in Latin America*. New York, 1943.
Chang Kia-ngau. *China's Struggle for Railroad Development*. New York, 1943.
Cheng, Peng. "Civil Aviation in New China," *People's China*, April 16, 1954.
China National Aviation Association. *Wings Over Asia: A Brief History of China National Aviation Corporation*. 2 vols., privately published, 1971-72.
Cleveland, Reginald M. *Air Transport at War*. New York, 1946.
Craven, Wesley Frank, and Cate, James Lea (eds.). *The Army Air Forces in World War II*. 7 vols., Chicago, 1948-1958.
Davies, R. E. G. *A History of the World's Airlines*. London, 1964.
Dietrich, Ethel B. *Far Eastern Trade of the United States*. New York, 1940.
Feis, Herbert. *The China Tangle*. Princeton, 1953.
Freudenthal, Elsbeth E. *The Aviation Business*. New York, 1940.
Frillman, Paul, and Peck, Graham, *China—The Remembered Life*. Boston, 1968.
Hayashi, Saburo, and Coox, Alvin D. *Kōgun: The Japanese Army in the Pacific War*. Quantico, Va., 1959.
Hou, Chi-ming. *Foreign Investment and Economic Development in China, 1840-1937*. Cambridge, Mass., 1965.
Josephson, Matthew. *Empire of the Air*. New York, 1944.
Juptner, Joseph P. (ed.). *U. S. Civil Aircraft*. Los Angeles, 1962.
Knowlton, Hugh. *Air Transportation in the United States*. Chicago, 1941.

La Farge, Oliver. *The Eagle in the Egg*. Boston, 1949.
Leary, William M., Jr. "Air Transport for China: The Early Years," *Aerospace Historian*, 19 (1972), 32–37.
―――. "Aircraft and Anti-Communists: CAT in Action, 1949–52," *China Quarterly*, 52 (1972), 654–69.
―――. "Portrait of a Cold War Warrior: Whiting Willauer and Civil Air Transport," *Modern Asian Studies*, 5 (1971), 373–88.
―――. "Wings for China: The Jouett Mission, 1932–1935," *Pacific Historical Review*, 38 (1969), 447–62.
Lissitzyn, Oliver James. *International Air Transport and National Policy*. New York, 1942.
Liu, F. F. *A Military History of Modern China, 1924–1949*. Princeton, 1956.
Liu, Kwang-Ching. *Anglo-American Steamship Rivalry in China, 1862–1874*. Cambridge, Mass., 1962.
Loening, Grover. *Amphibian: The Story of the Loening Biplane*. Greenwich, Conn., 1973.
Mansfield, Harold. *Vision: A Saga of the Sky*. New York, 1956.
Miles, Milton E. *A Different Kind of War*. New York, 1967.
Morris, Lloyd, and Smith, Kendall. *Ceiling Unlimited*. New York, 1953.
Penrose, Harald. *British Aviation: The Great War and Armistice, 1915–1919*. London, 1969.
Rae, John B. *Climb to Greatness: The American Aircraft Industry, 1920–1960*. Cambridge, Mass., 1968.
Romanus, Charles F., and Sunderland, Riley, *Stilwell's Command Problems*. Washington, D.C., 1956.
―――. *Stilwell's Mission to China*. Washington, D.C., 1953.
Rosinger, Lawrence K. *China's Wartime Politics, 1937–1944*. Princeton, 1944.
Rowe, David Nelson. *China Among the Powers*. New York, 1945.
Smith, Henry Ladd. *Airways: A History of Commercial Aviation in the United States*. New York, 1942.
―――. *Airways Abroad*. Madison, Wisc., 1950.
Smith, Sydney Bernard. *Air Transport in the Pacific Area*. New York, 1941.
Snow, Edgar. *The Battle for Asia*. New York, 1941.

Starr, James F., and Mills, Samuel J. "The Chinese Air Post, 1920–1935," *Collectors Club Philatelist*, 15 (April 1936), 69–87, (July 1936), 153–72, (Oct. 1936), 243–68; 16 (Jan. 1937), 40–52, (April 1937), 110–21, (July 1937), 168–89.

Stettinius, Edward R., Jr. *Lend-Lease: Weapon for Victory*. New York, 1944.

Taylor, Frank J. *High Horizons*, New York, 1951.

Thorne, Bliss K. *The Hump*. Philadelphia, 1965.

Toynbee, Arnold J. *Survey of International Affairs*. London, annual volumes.

Tsang, Chih. *China's Postwar Markets*. New York, 1945.

Tsou, Tang. *America's Failure in China, 1941–50*. Chicago, 1963.

Tuchman, Barbara W. *Stilwell and the American Experience in China, 1911–1945*. New York, 1970.

Ware, Edith E. *Business and Politics in the Far East*. New Haven, 1932.

Wilbur, C. Martin. "Military Separatism and the Process of Reunification under the Nationalist Regime, 1922–1937." In Ping-ti Ho and Tang Tsou (eds.), *China in Crisis*, 1: 203–63. 3 vols., Chicago, 1968.

Willoughby, Westel W. *Foreign Rights and Interests in China*. 2 vols., Baltimore, 1927.

Young, Arthur N. *China and the Helping Hand, 1937–1945*. Cambridge, Mass., 1963.

———. *China's Economic and Financial Reconstruction*. New York, 1947.

———. *China's Nation-Building Effort, 1927–1937*. Stanford, 1971.

———. *China's Wartime Finance and Inflation, 1937–1945*. Cambridge, Mass., 1965.

INDEX

Aircraft accidents and losses, 41–42, 47, 53, 80–81, 82, 95, 102, 104, 118–20, 128–30, 141, 143, 147, 158, 163, 164, 172, 173, 175, 176, 177, 182, 201–3, 215–16
Aircraft in China (by type):
   Consolidated Commodore flying boat, 124, 126
   Curtiss C-46, 159, 160, 194, 196, 198, 202–3, 208, 212, 213
   Curtiss Condor, 126, 132–34, 143
   Curtiss Hawk, 66
   DeHaviland Dragon Rapide, 126
   Douglas DC-2 (C–39), 96–97, 100, 104, 106, 118–20, 122, 123, 126, 128–29, 130, 141, 143, 144, 181, 182
   Douglas DC-3 (C–47), 126, 129–30, 135, 141, 143, 144, 147–48, 151, 152–53, 157, 161–63, 181, 182, 194, 196, 201–2, 208
   Douglas DC-4 (C–54), 195, 198, 208, 215–16
   Douglas Dolphin, 83, 86, 103, 104
   Fleet trainer, 66
   Ford trimotor, 96, 100, 101–2, 104, 126, 129
   Handley Page 0/400, 2, 3
   Junkers Ju 53, 37
   Junkers W-34, 37, 196
   Lockheed Hudson, 196
   Loening Air Yacht, 18, 19, 21–22, 23, 35, 41–42, 46, 47, 52–53, 71, 75, 100, 103, 104
   Sikorsky S-38, 76–77, 78, 80–81, 82
   Sikorsky S-42, 115, 117
   Sikorsky S-43, 104
   Sommer biplane, 1
   Stinson Detroiter, 16, 22, 33, 51, 53, 71, 75, 88, 91, 92, 93, 95, 103, 104
   Vickers Vimy Commercial, 4
   Vultee trainer, 147

Air Transport Command (ATC), 157, 159–61, 166, 170–71, 194
Alexander, Edward H., 159–60, 161
Allison, Ernest M.: arrives in China, 18; commands first flight of China Airways, 23; on Baer, 41; and flight to Chungking, 45; and qualifications of Chinese pilots, 46, 226; on rebuilt aircraft, 47; as chief pilot of CNAC, 71, 75, 83, 88–91, 115–16; with Chinese government, 117, 123; Bond confides in, 129; and purchase of Condor aircraft, 132; appointed operations manager of CNAC, 204; Q. Roosevelt on, 206; and living allowance for CNAC personnel, 210; and Q. Roosevelt's crash, 216; his retirement, 222
Amau, Eiju, 67
American Volunteer Group (Flying Tigers), 148, 157, 166, 196–97
Anderson, George, 178
Angle, Robert S., 146
Army Air Corps Act of 1926, 6
Army Air Forces (U.S.), 151, 154–55, 156–57, 159–61
Arnold, H. H. 184, 185
Arnold, Julean, 57–58, 86, 93
Atcheson, George, 184
Atwater, Leo, 176
Aviation Exploration, Inc., 8, 13, 15, 16, 17, 19
Aviation industry (U.S.), 6–7

Baer, Paul F., 41–42, 47
Barnaby, Ralph S., 40
Barson, T. A., 2
Berle, Jr., Adolph E., 183
Bissell, Clayton L., 156
Bixby, Harold M.: his background, 73–74; arrives in China, 74–75; and

INDEX 273

transpacific service, 76–80, 82–86; and Chungking-Chengtu line, 87–90; and airport construction, 98–99; and fare reductions, 100–1; and Chungking-Kunming route, 101–2; and problems with Chinese, 105–7; on CNAC, 108; and Sino-Japanese war, 113–14, 116; and Hump air route, 136, 138; sends Q. Roosevelt to China, 204; and CNAC's management problems, 208; and CNAC's purchases, 212; on Bond, 215; recommends PAA liquidate interest in CNAC, 217–18; on relations with Communist government, 217–18; his discussions with State Department, 218–19, 221–22; his death, 222; mentioned, 146, 147, 190, 191, 200, 214
Blackmore, Jack, 203
Boeing, William, 39
Bond, William Langhorne: his background, 48–49; arrives in China, 50; and CNAC's problems, 50–51; Westervelt on, 53; and Shanghai Incident, 56; as CNAC operations manager, 67, 70, 75, 83; and flight to Canton, 77; at celebration for transpacific service, 86; and Chungking-Chengtu line, 88–90; and Chinese relations, 104–5, 106–7; and Sino-Japanese war, 114–17; and Hankow evacuation, 124–45; and Kent's death, 129, 131; his leadership, 131, 225; and advance of Japanese army, 132; on Condor aircraft, 133; on Nanshiung-Hong Kong service, 134; and Hong Kong evacuation, 143–47; and Hump air route, 135–42, 148–50, 154, 158–59, 161–64, 165; on AVG pilots, 157; on CNAC in 1942, 158; and wartime contract negotiations, 180–81; on expanded domestic service, 182; and Stilwell, 187; on CNAC's contract, 189–91; and CNAC's postwar service, 192, 193–95, 199–200, 204, 208; health problems of, 200; offers position to Q. Roosevelt, 206–7; Bixby on, 215; his discussions with State Department, 218; and sale of PAA's interest in CNAC, 219–22; his retirement, 222
Boyd, Casey, 173

Brereton, Lewis H., 51, 154–55
Brown, Homer, 94
Burma Road, 125–26, 132, 134, 138, 149, 174, 177

Capterton, A. L., 10
Caproni, Gianni, 49
Carlisle, Lady, 80, 81
Carlson, Ivan, 77, 82
Carroll, Glen, 175
Castle, William R., 58
Central Air Transport Corporation (CATC): establishment of, 196; postwar operations of, 199, 201, 203, 208, 210, 213, 220, 221, 225
Central Aviation School, 63–68, 111
Chang Ching-yu, 14–15
Chang Hseuh-liang, 38, 52
Chang, Loy, 144, 145
Chang, S. F., 80
Charles H. Babb Company, 132–33
Chen, C. L., 220
Chen, Hugh, 131, 146–47, 157
Chen, K. P., 144
Chen, W., 86
Chennault, Claire L.: and American Volunteer Group, 148, 157; and 14th Air Force, 171; and Civil Air Transport, 196–97, 208, 214; and acquisition of CNAC, 221, 222; mentioned, 166
Chiang Kai-shek: and political turbulence of 1920s, 6; his limited authority, 15; Hamilton on, 27; and political situation in 1930, 37–38; and Christmas Day Incident (1930), 42; and Manchurian Incident, 52, 54, 59; and development of military aviation, 64, 65, 66, 67; and Tangku truce, 70; and campaigns against Communists, 101; his kidnapping, 109; and reestablishment of air service, 117; and Hankow evacuation, 123; requests CNAC's aid, 153; his anger with British, 154; and Stilwell, 155, 180, 181; and battle of Hsuchow, 213; leaves mainland, 217; Bond on, 219–20; and sale of CNAC, 221; mentioned, 20, 91, 105, 125, 150, 184, 225
Chiang Kai-shek, Madame, 20, 116, 117, 123, 175
Chiao Bo-cheng, 4

274 INDEX

Chin, Ed, 157
Chin, Harold, 157
Chin, Moon, 124, 131, 145, 146, 152–53
China Airways: formation of, 19; establishes air service in China, 21–22; first flight of, 22–23; impact of Great Crash on, 23; its operation in 1929, 24; its need for subsidy, 30; absorbed into CNAC, 33, 34
China Defense Supplies Corporation (CDS), 138, 148, 152, 156, 172, 181
China National Aviation Corporation (old): formation of, 12–14; problems of, 15, 17, 22, 24; demise of, 33, 34
China National Aviation Corporation (CNAC): formation of, 32–35; in 1930, 38–39; and Peking service, 46–47, 51, 53–54, 71; financial problems of, 54–55; and Shanghai Incident, 55–56; seeks U.S. government support, 55–59; in 1932, 70; PAA purchases American interest in, 73; in 1933, 74–75; and Shanghai-Canton route, 76–83; and PAA's transpacific service, 84–86; PAA's attitude toward, 86–87; and Chengtu line, 87–90; and ground facilities and services, 90–100; in 1935, 100–1; and routes to Kunming and Hanoi, 101–4; during 1936–37, 104; and Sino-American relations, 104–7, 108, 225–26; and Chinese government, 109–10, 179–180; and Sino-Japanese war, 110–11, 113–16; and restoration of service, 117–18; Japanese attacks on, 118–21, 128–31; and Hankow evacuation, 121–25; and Chungking–Hong Kong service, 126–28; during 1938–40, 130–31; and freight service, 131–34; and Hump air route, 134–42; and Hong Kong evacuation, 143–47; wartime operations and economic problems of, 148–55, 157–58, 160, 161–70, 171–79, 187–89; and Stilwell, 155–56, 180–81, 187, 192; and aircraft for domestic service, 181–87; and contract with PAA, 189–91; during postwar years, 193–95, 198–204, 205, 209–12, 215–16; during civil war, 209, 212–14; and removal to Hong Kong, 214, 216–17; termination of, 217–22; Trippe on, 225
China Trade Act, 12, 19

Chinese government: and development of aviation after World War I, 1–5; and rise of Nationalists, 5–6; and proposal for establishment of air service, 8–9, 11–17; control of aviation within, 20–21, 22, 24–29; and formation of CNAC, 32–35; and formation of Eurasia, 36; its political position in 1930, 37–38; Westervelt on, 43–44, 55–56; its political problems in 1931, 52; and fall of Manchuria, 54; and Shanghai Incident, 55–56, 59; and military aviation, 60–68; its ties with northern region, 70–71; and Shanghai-Canton route, 76, 78, 79–80; and international air mail contract, 84–86; and airport construction, 98–99; and Tibet, 101; and campaigns against Communists, 101; and Hanoi air route, 102–14; and use of CNAC aircraft, 105–6; its attitude toward CNAC, 106–7; its political and economic progress during 1930s, 109–10; and war with Japan, 110–11; and reestablishment of service by CNAC, 116–17; isolation of, 124, 125, 126, 132; and U.S. assistance, 136, 148–50; attempts to place CNAC under military control, 179–80; and use of lend-lease aircraft, 180–81; and aircraft for domestic service, 183–84; and CNAC contract, 191; and military takeover of CNAC, 199–200; postwar economic problems of, 205, 207–8, 209, 210, 211–12; and civil war, 213–14, 217; Bond on, 217–20; and sale of CNAC, 221–22
Chinese National Relief and Rehabilitation Administration, 197
Chu Chia-hua, 80, 86, 106
Civil Air Transport (CAT), 196–98, 208, 213, 214, 221
Clark Kerr, Sir Archibald, 146
Cochrane, Sir Alexander, 135
Codrea, Don, 177
Commerce, Department of, 61–62
Cook, Captain, 173
Coolidge, Calvin, 9
Coulson, Captain, 177
Cunningham, Edwin S., 14, 58
Currie, Lauchlin, 126, 137–38, 140–41, 148
Curtiss-Wright: growth during 1920s,

INDEX

7–8, 17; and Great Crash, 23; in CNAC contract, 34; Westervelt joins, 40; engines produced by, 46–47, 52–53; and economic problems of CNAC, 54–55; and market for military aviation, 59, 68, 69; indifference toward CNAC, 70, 72, 90, 108; and sale of interest in CNAC to PAA, 73; summary of activities in China, 224, 225

Dai Enki, 104, 105, 107, 117
Daurat, Didier, 48–49, 51
Dean, Captain, 158
DeKantzow, Sidney, 163, 182
Dennys, Lancelot, 182
Dillon, Clarence, 8
Donald, W. H., 116, 117
Doolittle, James H., 152–53
Drysdale, Colonel, 92
Dzu, General, 93

Ehmer, William, 77, 78, 80
Eurasia Aviation Corporation, 36–37, 58, 71, 102, 126

Far Eastern Division. *See* State Department
Five-Year-Program Act (U.S. Navy), 6
Flying Tigers. *See* American Volunteer Group
Fox, A. Manuel, 144
Fox, James, 163
Frick, James, 82
Friendly, Henry J., 221

Gast, Robert, 77, 82
Gast, Mrs. Robert, 81
Gauss, Clarence E., 180, 182–83
Gelhorn, Martha, 126
George, Harold L., 161
Germany, 35
Giles, Barney M., 185–86
Glen Curtiss Company, 7–8
Gould, Randall, 93
Great Britain, 2–5, 29–30
Great Crash, 23
Greenwood, Captain, 201–2
Grew, Joseph C., 120–21
Groeger, Paul, 77, 81, 83
Grooch, William S., 77, 78, 81–82, 83
Grumman, Leroy, 18

Hall, Burton, 91

Hall, Les, 175
Hamilton, Maxwell G., 61–62
Hamilton, Minard, 26–27, 36, 38, 48, 51
Handley Page, 2, 3
Hardin, Thomas O., 161, 170
Hayward, R. O., 8, 12
Hemingway, Ernest, 126
Henderson, Paul, 9
Herrington, Arthur W., 153–54
Higgs, Frank, 131, 144, 146
Hill, James J., 8
Hinkel, Robert, 177
Ho Chi-wei, 55, 117
Hockswinder, Captain, 170
Holt, F. V., 2–5
Ho Mo-lin, 180
Hopkins, Harry L., 137, 150, 183–84, 185
Hornbeck, Stanley K.: on plan to establish airline, 9; opposes use of military personnel, 10; Keys writes to, 14; supports Bond and CNAC, 154, 155, 183
Howard, Edward P., 60–61, 62, 63, 64–65, 90–91
Howard, Roy, 92
Ho Ying-chin, 179
Hsu, Conrad, 80
Hsu Pei King, 65
Huang, George, 157
Huang, K. C., 104–5
Hull, Cordell, 120–21, 185
Hump air route: CNAC's plans for, 134–42, 148–51; Army Air Forces and, 151; Johnson-Herrington report on, 153–54; development of, 154–55; operated by AAF, 156–57; CNAC operations on, 157–58, 165, 171, 172, 225; ATC operations on, 159–61, 170–71; Stilwell on, 160; comparison of operations by ATC and CNAC on, 160; Bond describes flight over, 161–63; CNAC inaugurates night service on, 164; navigation of, 167–68; weather conditions on, 168; McBride describes operations on, 172–79
Hunsaker, Jerome C., 40
Hunt, William, 111, 112

Imperial Airways, 126, 128
Import-Export Bank, 137
India-China air route. *See* Hump air route

INDEX

Intercontinent Aviation Inc., 8, 19, 26
Italy, 65–66, 68

Japan: and fighting in Manchuria, 52, 54; and Shanghai Incident, 56, 59; and military assistance to China, 67; and military activity in northern China, 70–71; its attitude toward CNAC, 105, 114; and outbreak of war in China, 110–11; attacks CNAC aircraft, 118–21, 128–30; its military progress in China, 124, 125; and China's supply routes, 132; attacks Hong Kong, 143; its military operations during 1941–42, 148
Johnson, Birger, 18, 23
Johnson, Louis A., 152, 153–54, 155
Johnson, Nelson T., 58, 107
Jordan, Sir John, 2
Joubert de la Ferté, Sir Philip, 3–4
Jouett, John H., 61–68, 111
Just, Eric, 91, 123

Kaufman, S. T., 18
Keh Ching-on, 65
Kellogg, Frank B., 9
Kent, Walter C., 111–13, 128–29
Kessler, Paul W., 144–45, 146, 177
Keys, Clement M.: his background, 7–8; his philosophy toward aviation, 8, 19, 224; plans to establish air service, 9, 10–12, 14, 30; and problems in China, 16–17; selects Price to head China Airways, 19–20; and market crash, 23, 24–25; and Hamilton report, 26–27; financial problems of, 31; selects Polin to renegotiate contract, 32; sends Westervelt to China, 39; loses control of Curtiss-Wright, 69; mentioned, 28, 43, 50
Ki Chun, 101–2
King, Ernest J., 39
Kohler, Frederick L., 182
Kung, H. H., 65, 133, 175
Kung, Madame H. H., 20, 145, 175
Kurzman, Joseph, 178
Kweilin Incident, 118–21

Lampson, Sir Miles, 80
Langdon, William R., 185
Ledo Road, 171, 174, 178–79
Lem Wei-shing, 107, 113–14, 116
Leonard, Royal: joins CNAC, 117; and evacuation of Hankow, 122–23; describes Chungking–Hong Kong service, 127; mentioned, 128, 131
Leung, K. Y., 157
Liang, C. C., 225–26
Lignes Aérienne Latécoère, 48
Lindberg, Charles: impact of his transatlantic flight, 6, 49, 64; surveys transpacific route, 72; comments on Bixby, 74; mentioned, 18
Liu, C. Y., 204, 220
Liu Chung-chieh, 120
Liu Hsiang, 38, 44–45, 88, 89, 95–96
Liu Shu-fan, 16, 36
Liu Wen-wei, 89
Loening, Grover, 18
Loh, Joe, 162, 163
Loh, M. K., 157, 173
Loomis, Tom, 176–77
Lordi, General, 65
Lufthansa, 36
Lynch, Fenimore B., 182

McBride, Donald, 172–79
McClelland, Captain, 178
McCleskey, James R., 71, 91, 117
McDivitt, J. H., 204
McDonald, William C.: and Hong Kong evacuation, 144–45; as assistant to chief pilot, 166–67, 170; and postwar accidents, 201, 202–3; replaced as chief pilot, 204; mentioned, 131
McNear, Cyril, 32, 56
Mah, Al, 170
Mah, K. L., 177
Major, Miss, 170
Mantz, Paul, 91
Marchant, Richard, 176
Marshall, George C., 150
Meng, C. Y. W., 225
Merchant, Livingston, 218–19, 221–22
Mickelson, Einar, 173, 174, 175, 176, 177
Migeo, Marcel, 48–49
Mitchell, Hewitt F., 71, 90–97
Mitchell, William, 63
Morgan, Stokely, 114, 115
Morgan, Thomas, 73
Morgenthau, Henry, 134
Moss, Robert C., 176
Mussolini, Benito, 65, 66

Naiden, Earl L., 151, 154, 155

INDEX

Nelson, Floyd, 91–92, 93, 102
New York, Rio, and Buenos Aires Air Lines, 77
Nibson, C. S., 222

Odie, Tasker L., 58
O'Hara, Byron, 102
Olmstead, Ralph W., 197
Ott, Ray, 42, 123

Pan, K. F., 41
Pan American Airways (PAA): U.S. government subsidy to, 26; acquires American interest in CNAC, 69, 73; and transpacific route, 72, 76–86, 115; its relations with CNAC, 86–87, 98, 107, 208, 225; its relations with Chinese government, 110; and Sino-Japanese war, 114, 116–17; and Hump air route, 137, 149, 152; assists CNAC, 141; and Hong Kong evacuation, 143, 145; wartime ferry service of, 155; and contract with Chinese government, 189–91; its attitude toward Chinese Communist government, 217, 218; sells interest in CNAC, 219–22
Papajik, John, 203
Parrish, C. C., 212
Pawley, William D., 73
Peck, Willys R., 107
Petach, Jules, 178
Polin, Max S., 32–35, 36
Poole, Jesse, 95
Pottschmidt, Robert W., 117, 131, 167, 202
Pratt &Whitney, 18, 52–53
Prescott, Robert, 173
Preus, Rolf, 202–3
Price, Ernest B.: as first president of China Airways, 19–20; his plans for operations in China, 20–21; and problems with Chinese, 22, 23, 24–29; fired, 29, 69; his role in contract revision, 33
Priester, Andre, 77

Ralph, Fred S., 143
Reynolds, Lincoln C., 78, 80, 81, 200–4
Richards, Lewis J., 167
Rickenbacker, Edward V., 160, 161
Riggs, Roland R., 10, 13, 27
Robertson, G. A., 173

Robertson, William B., 10, 12–14, 19, 27, 32
Robertson, Mrs. William B., 10
Rogers, Leighton W., 61–62
Roosevelt, Franklin D.: and Jouett mission, 67; and supply route to China, 149, 150, 154, 160, 183, 192; sends Stratemeyer to China, 161; mentioned, 126, 137, 152
Roosevelt, Quentin: his background, 204–5; investigates CNAC, 205–6; his position with CNAC, 207, 208–9; and CNAC's operations in 1948, 209–15; death of, 215–16
Roosevelt, Mrs. Quentin, 216
Roosevelt, Jr., Mrs. Theodore, 111, 112
Rosbert, C. J., 163
Rummel, George, 77, 80, 81

Saint-Exupéry, Antoine de, 48
St. Louis, A. P., 19
Schafer, Charles, 145
Schaefer, K., 80
Schilling, Eriksen, 202
Schroeder, Captain, 164
Scoff, James, 170, 175, 176, 177
Scott, Emil, 182
Sellers, Cecil, 103
Shanghai-Chengtu Air Mail Line, 16, 22, 33, 46
Shanghai Incident (1932), 55–56
Sharkey, Charles J., 203
Sharp, Charles L.: employed by CNAC, 91; and Nanking accident, 102; flies military cargo, 113; returns to CNAC, 117; and Hankow evacuation, 122–23; his leadership, 131; and flight over Hump air route, 141; and Hong Kong evacuation, 145; Bond on, 146; his piloting skill, 147–48; replaced as operations manager, 200
Shaugnessy, M. X. Quinn, 152, 155
Shen, T. H., 204
Shute, Nevil, 82
Sinclair, Frank W., 149, 156
Sloniger, E. L., 10, 17
Smith, Cyrus R., 161
Smith, Harry G.: as first operations manager of China Airways, 17–19, 21, 23; surveys Hankow-Chungking route, 38; his discontent, 41, 50, 51, 69
Snow, Edgar, 22

Soldinsky, Zigmund, 77, 81
"Soong Dynasty," 20
Soong, T. V.: political influence of, 20; and problems of China Airways, 25-26, 28, 29; and development of military aviation, 60, 61, 62, 63; and Sino-Japanese war, 116; and Hump air route, 134, 136, 137, 138, 139, 149-51, 153; comments on Bond, 191; and sale of PAA's interest in CNAC, 221; mentioned, 107
Southwestern Aviation Corporation, 103-4
State, Department of: and plan to establish commercial air service, 9-10; opposes CNAC request for subsidy, 56-59; attitude toward development of military aviation, 61-62; opposes CNAC at outbreak of Sino-Japanese war, 113-14, 116; protests Japanese attack on CNAC aircraft, 120-21, 129; its wartime support of CNAC, 179-80, 183-86; and Communist proposal for air service, 218-19; and sale of PAA interest in CNAC, 221-22
Stilwell, Joseph W.: and need for air transport, 151, 152, 154, 155; and Hump air route, 160; his attitude toward CNAC, 155-56, 180, 181, 184, 187; his quarrel with Chinese government, 192
Stinson Aircraft Company, 16
Stratemeyer, George, 161
Stuart, John Leighton, 211
Sultan, Daniel, 179
Sundby, Charles, 215-16
Sun Fo: and establishment of air service, 8-9, 12, 32; as first president of China National Aviation Corporation (old), 13; his struggle over control of aviation, 14, 15, 16, 18, 20, 22, 24; and Price, 19; presses for expansion of air service, 23; resigns, 25; Hamilton on, 27
Sun Fo, Madame, 23
Sun Yat-sen, 20
Sun Yat-sen, Madame, 20
Sweet, Harold, 117, 126-27, 130, 144-45

Ting, Shih-yuan, 1-2, 3

Tinn King, 2
Thom, Joy, 129
Toynbee, Arnold, 38
Transcontinental Air Transport, 8
Trippe, Juan T.: as president of PAA, 72; and Curtiss-Wright, 73; and transpacific service, 83; and Sino-Japanese war, 114, 116-17; and Hump air route, 136, 137; and CNAC contract, 190-91; on CNAC, 225
Tunner, William H., 170
Tutwieler, Weldon, 175
Tweedy, Gordon, 201, 202, 208, 209-10, 212

United Aircraft Company, 7
United Aircraft Exports, 61
United Nations Relief and Rehabilitation Administration (UNRRA), 197, 208

Vallon, Monsieur, 1
Vaughn, Charles S.: and Christmas Day Incident of 1930, 42-43; on repair of aircraft, 47; Chinese seek to replace, 104-5; mentioned, 86, 117
Vickers Company, 2

Wang, C. F., 164-65, 180
Wang, C. H., 218
Wang, Fun-jao, 38, 45
Wang, M. H., 80
Wang Po-chun: and control of aviation, 15-16, 20; replaces Sun Fo, 25; opposes China Airways, 25-26, 27-28, 29; and contract revision, 32, 33; as first president of CNAC, 36
Wang Wen-san, 197-98
Watson, Captain, 202
Wei I-fu, 36
Welles, Sumner, 180
Welsh, Orin, 163
Westervelt, George Conrad: his background, 39-41; and CNAC's problems, 43-44, 54-55; and expansion of CNAC's routes, 44-45; and service to Peking, 46-47; selects Bond to head American interest in CNAC, 48; Bond and, 49-50; returns to China, 52; and Shanghai Incident, 55-56; proposes Manila-Amoy ser-

INDEX

vice, 57; and military aviation in China, 59, 60, 61; retires, 69, 70; mentioned, 51
Westervelt, Mrs. George Conrad, 40, 49
Whang Mo-sen, 94
Wheeler, Raymond A., 180, 181
White, Theodore, 126, 161
White, William Henry, 9
Wilke, Oscar, 19, 75
Willauer, Whiting: and China Defense Supplies, 156, 172; and Civil Air Transport, 196-97, 198, 208, 221, 222
Williams, Frank S., 14
Wilson, James, 10, 12, 27
Wong, Bernard, 129
Wong, Donald, 157
Wong, P. Y., 88, 117, 131
Wong Tsu, 39, 47, 51, 53
Wong Yu-mei, 120
Woo, C. H., 86
Woods, Hugh L.: arrives in China, 77; and Sino-Japanese war, 117; and *Kweilin* Incident, 118-20, 128-29; intercepted by Japanese fighters, 129-30; his professional skill, 131; and flight over Hump route, 135, 136; and air supply to Chinese troops, 153; and CNAC's postwar operations, 200-1, 204; mentioned, 170, 172
Wright, Al, 173
Wright, Burdett S., 9
Wu Te-chen, 99

Young Arthur N.: and contract with China Airways, 28; and development of military aviation, 60, 65-66; on economic progress of Chinese government, 109; recommends purchase of Condor aircraft, 133; and Hump air route, 136, 137, 138, 141, 151, 153; and CNAC's problems, 164-65, 188; on China's need for domestic air transport, 186-87; on aviation and foreign exchange, 195; mentioned, 87, 191
Young, Clarence M., 57
Yuan Shih-kai, 1
Yuemura, T., 82
Yü Fei-peng, 106